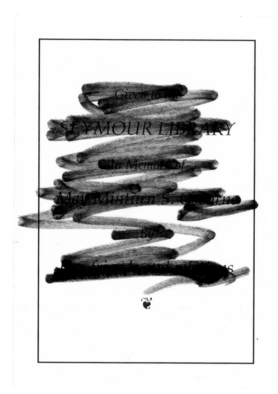

# VALUE-BASED
# FEES

# VALUE-BASED
# FEES

## How to Charge—and Get—
## WHAT YOU'RE WORTH

*A Guide for Consultants*

### Second Edition

## ALAN WEISS, PH.D.

Author of *The Ultimate Consultant*

**Pfeiffer**
A Wiley Imprint
www.pfeiffer.com

*The* ULTIMATE
CONSULTANT
*Series*

Published by Pfeiffer
An Imprint of Wiley
989 Market Street, San Francisco, CA 94103-1741
www.pfeiffer.com

For additional copies/bulk purchases of this book in the U.S. please contact 800-274-4434.

Pfeiffer books and products are available through most bookstores. To contact Pfeiffer directly call our Customer Care Department within the U.S. at 800-274-4434, outside the U.S. at 317-572-3985, fax 317-572-4002, or visit www.pfeiffer.com.

Pfeiffer also publishes its books in a variety of electronic formats. Some content that appears in print may not be available in electronic books.

**Library of Congress Cataloging-in-Publication Data**

Weiss, Alan, 1946–
    Value-based fees : how to charge—and get—what you're worth : a guide for consultants/
Alan Weiss.—2nd ed.
        p.    cm.—(The ultimate consultant series)
    Includes index.
    ISBN 978-0-470-27584-9 (cloth)
        1. Business consultants—Fees.   I. Title.
HD69.C6W466 2008
001—dc22
                                                                    2008014816

Acquiring Editor: Matthew Davis
Director of Development: Kathleen Dolan Davies
Senior Production Editor: Kelsey McGee
Editor: Bruce Emmer

Editorial Assistant: Lindsay Morton
Manufacturing Supervisor: Becky Morgan
Printed in the United States of America

HB Printing        10 9 8 7 6 5 4 3 2 1

*Dedicated to the heroic people
in our police and fire departments,
whose value will always exceed anything
any of us could ever afford to pay.*

# Other Works by Alan Weiss

*Books*

    *Best-Laid Plans*
    *Breaking Through Writer's Block*
    *Getting Started in Consulting*
    *Good Enough Isn't Enough*
    *The Great Big Book of Process Visuals*
    *Great Consulting Challenges*
    *How to Acquire Clients*
    *How to Establish a Unique Brand in the Consulting Profession*
    *How to Market, Brand, and Sell Professional Services*
    *How to Sell New Business and Expand Existing Business*
    *How to Write a Proposal That's Accepted Every Time*
    *The Innovation Formula* (with Mike Robert)
    *Life Balance*
    *Managing for Peak Performance*
    *Million Dollar Consulting*
    *Million Dollar Consulting® Toolkit*
    *Money Talks*
    *Organizational Consulting*
    *Our Emperors Have No Clothes*
    *Process Consulting*
    *The Second Great Big Book of Process Visuals*
    *The Ultimate Consultant*
    *The Unofficial Guide to Power Management*

*Booklets*

    *Doing Well by Doing Right*
    *How to Maximize Fees*
    *Leadership Every Day*
    *Raising the Bar*
    *Rejoicing in Diversity*

*Audiocassettes, CDs, Albums*

    *MBA* (Mentored by Alan), Vol. I
    *MBA,* Vol. II
    *MBA,* Vol. III
    *MBA,* Vol. IV
    *MBA,* Vol. V
    *Million Dollar Consulting® Skills*
    *Peak Performance*
    *The Consultant's Treasury*
    *The Odd Couple®* (with Patricia Fripp)
    *Winning the Race to the Market*

*Video*

    *Alan Weiss's Make-a-Million Marketing*

*Newsletter*

    *Balancing Act®*

# *About the Author*

Alan Weiss is one of those rare people who can say he is a consultant, speaker, and author and mean it. His consulting firm, Summit Consulting Group, Inc., has attracted clients such as Merck, Hewlett-Packard, GE, Mercedes-Benz, State Street Corporation, Times Mirror Group, the Federal Reserve, the New York Times Corporation, and more than five hundred other leading organizations. He serves on the board of directors of the Trinity Repertory Company, a Tony Award–winning New England regional theater; Festival Ballet; and is the chairman of the Newport International Film Festival.

His speaking typically includes thirty keynote addresses a year at major conferences, and he has been a visiting faculty member at Case Western Reserve University, Boston College, Tufts, Saint John's, the University of Illinois, the Institute of Management Studies, and the University of Georgia Graduate School of Business. He has held an appointment as adjunct professor in the Graduate School of Business at the University of Rhode Island, where he taught courses on advanced management and consulting skills. He holds the record for selling out the highest-priced workshop (on entrepreneurialism) in the twenty-one-year history of New York City's Learning Annex. His Ph.D. is in psychology, and he is a member of the American Psychological Society, the American Counseling

Association, Division 13 of the American Psychological Association, and the Society for Personality and Social Psychology. He serves on the board of governors of Harvard University's Center for Mental Illness and the Media. He has keynoted for the American Psychological Association on two occasions.

He is a 2006 inductee into the Professional Speaking Hall of Fame and the concurrent recipient of the National Speakers Association Council of Peers Award of Excellence, representing the top 1 percent of professional speakers in the world.

His prolific publishing includes more than five hundred articles and twenty-seven books, including his best-seller, *Million Dollar Consulting* (McGraw-Hill). His newest is *The Global Consultant* (Wiley). His books have been on the curriculum at Villanova, Temple University, and the Wharton School of Business and have been translated into German, Italian, Korean, Arabic, Spanish, Russian, and Chinese.

He is interviewed and quoted frequently in the media and is an active member of the American Federation of Television and Radio Artists. His career has taken him to fifty-six countries and forty-nine states (he is afraid to go to North Dakota). *Success Magazine* has cited him in an editorial devoted to his work as "a worldwide expert in executive education." The *New York Post* calls him "one of the most highly regarded independent consultants in America." He is the winner of the prestigious AXIEM Award for Excellence in Audio Presentation.

In 2006, he was presented with the Lifetime Achievement Award of the American Press Institute, the first ever for a nonjournalist and one of only seven awarded in the sixty-year history of the association.

He has coached the former and present Miss Rhode Island and Miss America candidates in interviewing skills. He once appeared on the popular American TV game show *Jeopardy,* where he lost badly in the first round to a dancing waiter from Iowa.

# Contents

*Introduction*                *xv*
*Preface to the Second Edition*      *xvii*
*Acknowledgments*          *xix*

CHAPTER 1

## The Concept of Fees    1
*Will People Actually Give Me Their*
*Money for My Advice?*

The Ethical Nature of Capitalism    2
The Mercedes-Benz Syndrome    5
The Importance of Buyer Commitment,
Not Compliance    9
Critical Steps for Buyer Commitment    11
The Buoyancy of Brands:
How Brands Help Fees    12
Creating Shared Success    15
Chapter ROI    18
*Interlude: A Case of Bottom-Line*
*Blindness*    *21*

CHAPTER 2

## The Lunacy of Time-and-Materials Models        23
*Who Wants to Be as Dumb as a Lawyer?*

Supply-and-Demand Illogic                         25
Ethical Conflicts of Interest and Other
Small Matters                                     28
Limiting Profits, or Why Not Just Forget
*Domani*?                                         32
Why Lawyers and CPAs Do So Poorly                 35
Educating the Buyer Incorrectly                   37
Chapter ROI                                       39

CHAPTER 3

## The Basics of Value-Based Fees        41
*It's Better to Be an Artist Than to Be an
Engineer*

Focusing on Outcomes, Not Inputs                  42
The Fallacy and Subversive Nature of
"Deliverables"                                    45
Quantitative and Qualitative Measures
and Criteria                                      49
Measuring the Unmeasurable                        52
Serving the Client's Self-Interest                54
The Subtle Transformation: Consultant
Past to Client Future                             56
Perpetual Motion, Perpetual Progress              58
Chapter ROI                                       60
*Interlude: The Case of the Annoying
Accountants*                                      61

CHAPTER 4

## How to Establish Value-Based Fees        63
*If You Read Only One Chapter . . .*

Conceptual Agreement: The Foundation
of Value                                          64

Establishing Your Unique Value                        68
Creating the "Good Deal" Dynamic                     72
The Incredibly Powerful "Choice of Yeses"        75
Some Formulas for the Faint of Heart                79
Chapter ROI                                                        82

CHAPTER 5

## How to Convert Existing Clients 85
*Correcting Your Own Mistakes*

Setting Priorities Among Existing Clients          86
Offering New Value                                             90
Finding New Buyers Within
Existing Clients                                                   94
Finding New Circumstances                              97
What If Clients Resist Conversion?                    99
Abandoning Business                                        101
Chapter ROI                                                      103
*Interlude: The Case of the*
*Loaded Loading Dock*                                     *105*

CHAPTER 6

## The Fine and High Art of Using Retainers 107
*It's Just the Smarts, Stupid*

Optimal Conditions for Retainer
Arrangements                                                    108
Choosing Time Frames and
Creating Realistic Expectations                        113
Organizing the Scope and Managing
Projects Within the Retainer                            116
Capitalizing on Retainer Relationships            119
Aggressively Marketing Retainer
Relationships                                                     121
Chapter ROI                                                      124
*Ethics and Fees, Fees and Ethics:*
*A Midbook Practicum*                                      *127*

CHAPTER 7    Seventy Ways to Raise Fees and/
or Increase Profits Immediately 141
*Act Today and Receive the*
*Bass-o-Matic Free of Charge!*
    Chapter ROI                                    159
*Interlude: The Case of the Rebounding*
*Retainer*                                         161

CHAPTER 8    How to Prevent and Rebut Fee
Objections                          163
*Since You've Heard Them All Before, How*
*Can You Not Know All the Answers?*
    The Four Fundamental Areas of
    Resistance                                     165
    Maintaining the Focus on Value                 170
    Boring In on the Subject                       173
    Offering Discounts                             176
    Using "Smack to the Head" Comparisons  177
    Ignoring the Competition                       179
    Chapter ROI                                    181
*Interlude: The Case of the Perverse*
*Purchasing Agent*                                 183

CHAPTER 9    Setting Fees for Nonconsulting
Opportunities                       185
*How to Make Money While You Sleep,*
*Eat, Play, and Make Money Elsewhere*
    Keynote Speaking: Don't Charge for Your
    Spoken Words                                   186
    Highly Leveraged Practices for Working
    with Bureaus                                   190
    Products                                       192

Exploring New Lucrative Fields   196
And Now for Some Perspective   202
Chapter ROI   204

CHAPTER 10

Fee Progression Strategies   205
*Why You Fall Behind When You
Stand Still*
Entry-Level Fees   206
Transition to a "Going Concern"   209
Transition to Word-of-Mouth   211
Transition to the Brand Phase   213
Transition to the Ultimate Consultant   217
The Book's ROI: Alan's Axioms for the
"Good Deal"   219
*Interlude: The Case of the Fee Feng Shui*   225

CHAPTER 11

Technology and Fees   227
*Greater Wealth in the Brave New World*
The Service Enhancement   227
The Publishing Prerogative   230
The Remote Consultant   233
Passive Income   236
The Bottom Line   238
Chapter ROI   240

APPENDIX A:

Questions for Qualifying the
Economic Buyer   241

APPENDIX B:

Questions for Establishing
Business Objectives   243

APPENDIX **C:** Questions for Establishing
Measures of Success            245

APPENDIX **D:** Questions for Establishing
Value                          247

APPENDIX **E:** Questions for Assessing Personal
Value Contribution             249

APPENDIX **F:** The Difference Between
Inputs and Business Outputs    251

*Index*                        *253*

# Introduction

The Ultimate Consultant series is intended for successful practitioners who are seeking to scale still loftier heights. I'm happy to be among them.

This book is probably on the topic most eagerly anticipated of any I've written about in consulting. For the first time, I've recorded everything I know about the techniques that have worked best for me in raising fees, obtaining fees from unlikely sources, and supporting continuing fees. Yet this is by no means a mercenary book.

I believe in two aspects of consulting very strongly. First, you can't help others until you help yourself. Consequently, unless you're at least comfortable and secure financially, it's difficult to engage in pro bono work, to contribute to charities, and to help others to achieve their goals. Second, the basis for any successful client relationship is a win-win dynamic, the "good deal" you'll read about throughout this book. Therefore, you have to be treated well financially, and the client has to appreciate your value.

And when you come right down to it, there's a third aspect: clients truly believe that they get what they pay for. No buyer ever bragged about being successful in capturing the cheapest consultant available, someone sitting by the phone with no business who took on the assignment in return for food.

No, buyers—and their egos—revel in telling people that they snagged a consultant impossible to obtain, had to pay dearly, and expect everyone to listen closely.

After I worked on a project for a total of about six hours, the CEO asked his top officers what they would have charged had they been I. They guessed about $2,000 or less, having multiplied and divided by the $150 or $200 hourly rate that they charged.

"Well," said the CEO, "he's charging us $18,000, so listen up!"

Dizzy Dean said once, "If you can do it, it ain't braggin'." As you read on, you might want to listen up.

Alan Weiss, Ph.D.
*East Greenwich, Rhode Island*
*March 2008*

# *Preface to the Second Edition*

This book has proved to be the most popular of the Ultimate Consultant series. Small wonder. Consultants endure great risk and plow through tough work to create a successful practice, much less a thriving brand. Yet they all too often undermine themselves by overdelivering and undercharging.

Today more than ever, in an age of increased ethical focus and corporate scrutiny, I believe that hourly and per diem billing are unethical and antithetical to clients' best interests. I'm proud to have pioneered the concept of value-based billing in the late 1980s for solo practitioners, and I'm delighted to be furthering that cause today. You'll find herein my latest techniques and approaches, which embrace the new technology, globalization, competition, and societal changes affecting our world today.

The client is best served by rapid resolutions and improvements in a changing world. The consultant is best served for the contribution made to the client's success. That's as perfect an equation as there is in nature, and it is what made me the Million Dollar Consulting® expert. Please read along and join the club.

Alan Weiss, Ph.D.
*East Greenwich, Rhode Island*
*March 2008*

# *Acknowledgments*

My thanks go to the people who have made the fees possible, the wonderful clients with whom I've had the good fortune to work over the past two decades. I immodestly think that they're better off, and I know that I am. They are wonderful people.

Who says that nice guys finish last?

Here's to the most enduring clients: Dr. William Winter, Keith Darcy, George Rizk, Art Strohmer, Jarvis Coffin, Marilyn Martiny, Wayne Cooper, Lowell Anderson, Roseann Strichnoth, and Jerry Arbarbanal.

Deep appreciation goes to the wonderful editors at Jossey-Bass/Pfeiffer, headed by Kathleen Dolan Davies, the only human who speaks even faster than I do. It has been a joy to work with them all.

My thanks also go to Matt Davis for suggesting and assisting in this new edition.

Once again to L.T. Weiss, my love and affection—I know you hear me.

A.W.

# VALUE-BASED
# FEES

## CHAPTER 1

# The Concept of Fees

*Will People Actually Give Me Their Money for My Advice?*

A fee is remuneration provided in return for perceived value received. I'm now tempted to write, "End of Chapter One."

The concept of providing a fee for services rendered is a very old one that probably began in earnest with the end of subsistence farming. Once people had the knowledge and the primitive technology to grow more food than they could personally consume, they created the first medium for a fee: surplus goods of perceived value (food, of course, being of immense value to people who are hungry). The farmer could now acquire goods and services that could not be produced personally due to lack of time, lack of knowledge, and lack of tools.

Consequently, a class of people arose who could not or chose not to farm but could earn their food by providing such goods and services. Some people provided things directly relevant to farming: tools, seeds, animals. But others provided for more personal needs: furniture, clothing, medicines. Still others, however, provided for the more conceptual needs: education, amusement, art.

It was only a matter of time before consultants were offering advice in return for food. You don't believe me? Every early potentate and satrap had court advisers, ranging from astrologers to fortune-tellers, from high priests to military experts. Some day archaeologists will unearth the pyramid that housed the thousands of consultants who guided that entire construction project. Their fees just might have been immortality.

My point is that people have been receiving fees in return for advice in one way, shape, or form for millennia, so we shouldn't be tentative or hesitant about the process here in the twenty-first century.

## THE ETHICAL NATURE OF CAPITALISM

We live in a capitalistic society. It is apparently a creaky system that happens to work far better than others, since in our lifetimes we've seen it grow to be the dominant economic configuration in the world. The exchange of goods and services for some form of remuneration, with a minimum of government interference or arbitrary regulation, is the system within which we live.[1]

Capitalism is based on a highly ethical set of premises: You agree to deliver a product or service of an agreed-on quality at a certain time and in a certain condition; in return, I agree to provide certain remuneration in a specified amount on a particular date. That sounds simple, but it's actually the basis for all of our transactions involving the exchange of value for compensation.

Russia has failed at capitalism not because of an underlying or lingering communist belief system and not because of a lack of resources (it has oil and natural gas wealth, which could finally enable it to dictate terms to

---

[1]Of course, capitalism is far better for generating wealth than for distributing wealth, which is why communism, socialism, and other mechanisms of state control have been popular (or at least tolerated) at various times. But they wind up creating an even worse class system, a fact to which any communist state, from the old Soviet Union to the lingering Cuba, can attest.

western Europe) or an unwilling populace. It has failed because the ethical basis required for the system to work is not firmly in place. There is still too much of an attitude of "Can I get away with this?" and "How can I take advantage of the other party?" We can also see this situationally in some professions, in certain industries, and in some organizations.

> Fees are actually dependent on only two things: is there perceived value for the services provided that justifies the fee, and do both parties possess the intent of acting ethically?

For a consultant, the questions are about value, not fees. Fees are dependent on value provided in the perception of the buyer and on the intent of the buyer and the consultant to do the right thing—to act ethically. The consultant, who provides what is often nothing more than advice—whispers in the buyer's ear—must be diligent to ensure that the buyer perceives the value of the advice and will act properly upon receiving it (pay the bill, preferably promptly).

The mistakes consultants make about fees at the conceptual, strategic, and 50,000-foot level are these:

- Failing to understand that perceived value is the basis of the fee and consequently attempting to manage (lower) the fee rather than manage (raise) the value.
- Failing to translate the importance of their advice into long-term gains for the client in the client's perception and therefore believing that they must base their value on deliverables, time, and materials, which are actually low-value commodities.
- Failing to create a relationship with a legitimate, economic buyer,[2] meaning that the client may not do the right thing ethically (delay payment, argue about your value, arbitrarily change objectives).

---

[2]See my *Million-Dollar Consulting, Getting Started in Consulting,* and *The Ultimate Consultant* for more discussion of identifying and reaching economic buyers.

- Failing to have the courage and belief system that support the high value delivered to the client, thereby reducing fees to a level commensurate with the consultant's own low self-esteem. That's right, consultants, not clients, are the main cause of low consulting fees.
- Failing to listen to modern consulting business advice and immersing themselves amid the old guard, who foolishly believe that you take your annual income need, divide it by hours available, and thereby establish an hourly fee. Even the atavistic legal profession, which recently introduced $1,000-per-hour fees, seems to recognize that this is a good tactic to drive clients to a project-billing system.
- Failing to "push back" at the client and explain that it doesn't matter that every prior consultant charged by the hour (or day or parsec), but that value-based fees are more ethical and productive for the client.

One of the main causes for failing to create a perception of value is that the consultant doesn't appreciate that value. Since there are no "consulting schools" (with the immodest exception of my own Million Dollar Consulting® Colleges and Graduate Schools) and not even an objective certification or licensing process for consultants, there is also no canon of consulting performance or behavior. Over 80 percent of the consultants I've met[3] fail to obtain a statement of value from the buyer relative to the success of the project. In other words, consultants are focused on the input side of the equation, trying to determine numbers of billable hours and just what that hourly rate can be, rather than focused on the output side: What will the project accomplish in terms of business goals? What is my contribution to that lasting benefit? and What is the proper fee to be paid in exchange for that large contribution, which the buyer has already stipulated?

The absence of conceptual agreement with an economic buyer on the value of the project to the organization is the primary cause of an inability to calculate return on investment (ROI), thereby forcing the buyer to look at cost and not results.

---

[3]I've conducted a formal mentoring program for consultants around the world for more than a dozen years, so my experience base here is rather comprehensive. I've also consulted with some of the largest consulting firms in the world and scores of boutique firms, especially in Europe.

I suspect that in the old days, the farmer would say to the teacher, "If you tutor my children once a week, I'll give you a chicken and a bag of grain." Even today, the government says to the teacher, "Teach the community's children, and here's what we'll pay you" (not really much more than a chicken and a bag of grain, taking into account inflation over several thousand years). But a consultant—the ultimate business teacher—should be saying to the client, "Here's the value we will create together, and here's your share, and here's my share." The problem is that too many consultants are still working for chicken feed.

> Establishing value with the client is key. If the focus is on fees and not on value, the client has taken control of the discussion, and the client's focus will never be on maximizing your fees.

Ethically, the transaction should be based on fair remuneration for fair value delivered. That early teacher wasn't providing a morning a week of teaching but rather the opportunity for the farmer's children to escape the daylong drudgery of farming and the limited life it afforded (especially after technology made the need for children on the farm less vital and transient workers provided extra labor in exchange for food). What is the value of one's children escaping their parents' lowly lot, avoiding an impoverished life, and building a better future (and perhaps taking care of their parents with their future fortunes)? It's got to be worth at least two chickens and maybe a pig.

## THE MERCEDES-BENZ SYNDROME

People believe they get what they pay for. Moreover, emotion makes them act, while logic only makes them think. Put those two immutable theorems together, and you have what I've termed the Mercedes-Benz syndrome (MBS).

When people enter an auto showroom today, no matter at what economic stratum, the salespeople don't launch into intricate pitches about the electronic fuel injection or the wonders of rack-and-pinion steering. They encourage the potential buyer to sit in the car and then mention, with a straight face,

"You really look cool in that car!" Yes, and the more expensive the model, the cooler we tend to look.

No one needs a Mercedes-Benz for transportation. Not at that price level, they don't. But a car purchase is, after all, a lifestyle statement, and a Mercedes can begin to look quite reasonable in that light. When women try on a new frock, the sales help always say, "That was made for you; it brings out your eyes!" Despite the fact that I've never understood why a woman wants her eyes brought out, this ploy is always effective, even though it's repeated 26,000 times every day in the same department. When a man orders wine at dinner, the captain always says in response, "Excellent choice!" as the guy preens in that complimentary glow. (Never mind that he ordered Wild Coyote Road Kill or that May wasn't such a good month.)

Fees are based on perceived value. That perceived value is in the eyes and the cerebellum of the buyer. Consequently, the buyer's perception of value is the first point of attack for a consultant who wishes to maximize income.

> Psychologically, people believe they get what they pay for. Consequently, there is tremendous power in helping the buyer stipulate his or her perceived value from the project and then working to maximize that perception.

Consultants are almost always remiss when it comes to obtaining some agreement from the buyer on the value of the results of the project. Sometimes the consultant is too anxious to attempt to close the sale; sometimes the relationship isn't yet strong enough to do it; many times the consultant feels inferior and not enough of a peer to suggest it; sometimes the skills are missing; and often it's plain sloth.

Here are some basic questions to use to help the buyer arrive at some measure of value for any given project. You don't need to ask these interrogation-style, but it is a good idea to have them written somewhere and work them conversationally into the discussion until you're comfortable that you've obtained a clear expression of value.

*Thirteen Questions for Establishing Value with the Buyer*[4]

1. What will be the difference in your organization at the conclusion of this project?
2. What if you did nothing?
3. What if this project failed (or have these attempts failed in the past)?
4. What will you be able to do that you can't do now?
5. What will be the effect on revenues (sales, profits, market share, and so on)?
6. What will be the difference for your reputation (image, standing, stature, and so on)?
7. What are the three greatest impacts of the result of this project's success? (People love to think in threes.)
8. What will your boss's reaction be to this success? (Even economic buyers have a boss; sometimes it's the board.)
9. What will this mean to you personally?
10. What peripheral and secondary value do you see accruing to this project?
11. What will you be proudest of at the conclusion of the project?
12. What will be the legacy of this project?
13. What will it mean to be on the leading edge, the thought leader in the field?

You can create another bunch of questions if you like. My point is that you have to be prepared to discuss value with the buyer very early, prior to discussing methodology, options, timing, or, heaven forfend, fees.

Another fascinating aspect of MBS is that buyers have egos, which can greatly affect the buying process if you allow them to (and you want to allow them to, believe me). No buyer in my experience has ever said, "OK, we've managed to secure the cheapest consultant we can find for our sales development. He was sitting at home with nothing to do, waiting to go to his

---

[4]I'm tired of "top ten" lists, so here's an extra 33 percent of value from me to you. Also note that these questions are useless unless applied with the economic buyer—the person capable of writing the check.

normal day job, but I've persuaded him to work with us for $250 a day. We can afford that much, so let's use him as best we can."

Buyers are much more apt to say this to the troops: "Listen up. I've hired the finest consultant in the country on sales development. She graciously agreed to postpone a vacation to be with us. She's very expensive but worth every cent if we use her right. Now pay close attention, and plan to work with her closely."

When a CEO is in trouble, that person will call either someone who has clearly helped in the past or, if no one comes to mind, a "name" or a "brand" such as McKinsey or Andersen. No CEO wants to appear before the board and introduce a consulting firm without a track record or without a recognizable name. The executive ego will not permit it ("This person is taking advice from someone I've never heard of?"). The same holds true for every buyer. People believe they get what they pay for—and with their careers and businesses, they want the best.

Consequently, does your image fit the MBS? Do your materials bespeak a successful consultant? Are you proud of your Web site? Is your appearance professional and that of a peer to the buyer's? Intellectually, are you able to interact and even "push back" to demonstrate value in the earliest meetings? Are you building a brand and cementing your position as an expert? You can't start this too early, and you can never stop doing it.

---

Value is often a function of *not* agreeing, *not* being supportive, and *not* being a "yes person." How willing are you to disagree, question basic premises, and refuse impossible expectations?

---

Finally, the MBS creates rising expectations, which means that the buyer is prone to improve his or her condition through perceived high-value assistance. Why purchase a less expensive model when the (perceived) better one is only a few hundred dollars more per month on the lease payment? Why take a basic consulting approach when a more sophisticated one is available?

That presupposes that a more sophisticated one is available, meaning that higher fees will always depend on the buyer's seeing a set of options.

The ultimate consultant always provides options for the client's review so that the buyer can determine just how much value is available in terms of differing investments.

Offering options—a choices of yeses—moves the buyer psychologically from "Should I do this?" to "*How* should I do this?" You've just increased your odds of a high-fee sale by at least 50 percent.

A consultant once asked me, "Aren't we ethically compelled to provide every possible assistance to meet the client's objectives?" Unequivocally no. We must meet the client's objectives. But if the client's objective is, say, "increasing sales closing rates," then conducting industrywide benchmarking studies or longitudinal analyses for two years or 360-degree feedback on four levels of management represents value above and beyond merely meeting the objective of "increasing sales closing rates," for example.

Offer a client various "value packages" that help the buyer ascend the MBS ladder. Over the course of my career, buyers have chosen my least expensive option less than 10 percent of the time and my most expensive option over 35 percent of the time.

How much money are you leaving on the table? If it's $50,000 a year, in ten years that's *half a million dollars that can never be recovered.* If it's $100,000 annually, just $10,000 on ten projects a year, you are going to lose millions.

## THE IMPORTANCE OF BUYER COMMITMENT, NOT COMPLIANCE

I can prove anything on a double-axis chart,[5] but the matrix in Figure 1.1. happens to hold true. As you can see in the figure, the ideal relationship occurs when buyer commitment to the project (and to you) is high and your fee is high. If buyer commitment is high and your fee is low, you are wasting an opportunity. If buyer commitment is low and your fee is low, you will, at best, create an indifferent sale. And when fees are high but commitment is low, you will be shown the door.

---

[5]In fact, my *Great Big Book of Process Visuals* bears the subtitle *Give Me a Double-Axis Chart and I Can Rule the World.*

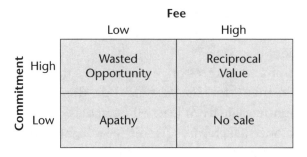

**Figure 1.1**  The Relationships Between Fees and Buyer Commitment.

My estimate is that most consultants' approaches (whether or not they actually get the business) are in the bottom left quadrant about 25 percent of the time, in the bottom right quadrant about 10 percent of the time, in the upper left quadrant about 60 percent of the time, and in the upper right quadrant only about 5 percent of the time!

That's right: most consultants, including most of you reading this, habitually undercharge for your services and deliver far more than you are receiving in remuneration, considering your contribution to success. You are undercharging and overdelivering, and lest you consider that an exalted position, consider trying to pay your mortgage or IRA contribution with that combination.

Most buyers *comply*. That is, they are willing to go along with the "expert," even if it's sometimes against their better judgment. Or they will delegate you to someone they believe has the technical ability to evaluate your proposition, typically in the human resource department, finance, or legal. (Put these together, and they are an anagram for "no business here.") Buyers who merely comply may be seen at first blush as easy to work with, but they are actually land mines waiting for some weight to trigger them. That's because they hold the consultant responsible for everything. They believe that you are doing something to them or for them or at them, but certainly not *with* them.

Compliance is dangerous because the buyer usually takes no inherent responsibility for the project but rather abdicates to the consultant. I've never found a project that a consultant can unilaterally implement successfully, since consultants have responsibility but no real authority. (When that dynamic is reversed, it's the sign of a very poor implementation scheme.)

Consulting projects should be true partnerships between the consultant and the economic buyer. This begins prior to the proposal's being signed and is an integral aspect of obtaining high fees. A merely compliant buyer will grudgingly or apathetically go along with the implementation but will do so at the lowest possible fee. The head is involved but not the gut (logic makes people think, but emotion makes them act). Large fees are dependent on emotional buy-in, and that must be achieved in the relationship aspect of the consulting sequence, well prior to the actual closing of business.

This is why patience in formulating the right relationship is more important than attempting to make a "fast sale." The former is a partnership where fees are academic; the latter is a unilateral benefit where fees are often the main point of contention.

> The buyer's commitment to outcomes and to his or her role in the partnership being formed to reach those outcomes is the key determinant of high fees. Buyers who are too willing to go along with your recommendations are as potentially fatal as those who dig in their heels after you've said hello.

## CRITICAL STEPS FOR BUYER COMMITMENT

It's worth repeating here briefly the sequence of events in the consulting business acquisition process that engenders the highest-quality commitment, the first three shown in the graphic in Figure 1.2.

- *Shared Values:* Those common business beliefs that will allow you to work effectively with the prospect—for example, a mutual antipathy for downsizing or a common belief in the importance of ongoing employee feedback
- *Relationship:* That level of a trusting interaction in which you and the buyer are comfortable with each other, can be honest (even in disagreeing), and share insights and assistance with each other on a mutual basis

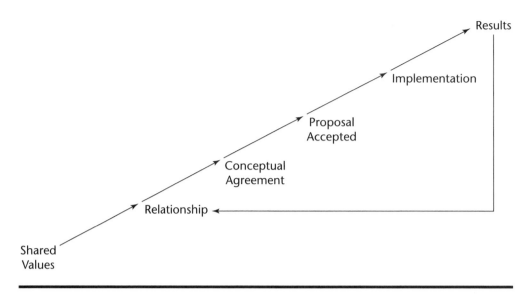

**Figure 1.2**  Consulting Business Acquisition Sequence.

- *Conceptual Agreement:* Agreement between you and the buyer on the *objectives for the project,* expressed as *business outcomes; metrics,* measures of progress toward those objectives; and *value,* the buyer's stipulation of how he or she and the organization will be better off as a result of those objectives being met

These three critical steps, each dependent on the prior step being success-fully in place and addressed in detail in Chapters Three and Four, will garner buyer commitment. The absence of conceptual agreement will result in either a lost sale or a lousy sale (and the latter is often more damaging than the former).

Fees are dependent on buyer commitment well before a proposal is ever tendered. Note that fees are not even on my chart.

## THE BUOYANCY OF BRANDS: HOW BRANDS HELP FEES

The second book in this series was dedicated to branding for consultants. One of the key reasons for effective branding is to enhance fees.

Fees are (or should be) based on value. That value is always in the eye of the beholder—in our case, the economic buyer. Hence the more value conveyed to that buyer by the most powerful means, the less downward pressure on fees. Effective branding actually creates a fee "buoyancy."

> There is actually one thing better than a buyer impressed by you and respecting you on sight, and that is the buyer impressed by you and respecting you before ever laying eyes on you.

No CEO ever said, "Get McKinsey in here," when strategy work was needed, then followed up by saying, "I think they're too expensive." As they say in the Ferrari showroom when someone asks about gas mileage or insurance costs, "If that's your concern, you really shouldn't be here."

Ferrari is a brand that evokes certain immediate understandings on the part of the potential individual buyer:

- High cost
- Top status
- High maintenance
- High insurance
- High repair costs
- Unique image
- Personal ego needs met

You know those things going in, and they are not points for discussion when dealing with a salesperson.

Similarly, McKinsey is a brand that evokes certain immediate understandings on the part of the potential corporate buyer:

- High cost (fees will not be negotiable)
- Top status (no one can say we're giving this short shrift)

- High maintenance (a lot of junior partners will appear)
- High insurance (the board can't complain about quality of the help)
- High repair costs (they will recommend tough interventions)
- Unique image (the cachet alone will raise expectations)
- Personal ego needs met (only the best for the best)

You get my point. The mere power of a brand is sufficient to overcome any resistance to fees and in fact often elevates fees merely by dint of association with such brand images as quality, reputation, client history, and media attention.

There is no brand as powerful as your name, although strong company brands can also serve quite well. When a potential client says, "Get me Jane Jones" or "Get me the Teambuilder," that client is articulating a clear imperative: don't go shopping, don't compare prices, and don't issue a request for proposals; just get me that person I've heard so much about. (That is *far* superior to the buyer saying, "Get me a great leadership consultant" and your name is one of several in the hat.)

As noted in our discussion of the Mercedes-Benz syndrome, brands create an upward expectation of both quality and commensurate fees. No one expects an outstanding person to come cheap. In the MBS, you usually have to convince the buyer of that quality through careful relationship building. But a strong brand shortcuts that process considerably. The relationship building still needs to be done (for reasons of commitment, as noted earlier), but the time required is significantly reduced. The buyer wants to be a partner, wants to follow your suggestions, and wants to participate *because your credibility has preceded you.*

---

Brands are accelerators of credibility and therefore of relationships. They immediately justify higher fees in the mind of the buyer, and that is the only mind that counts on that matter. Brands are expressions of uniform quality. The ultimate brand for most solo consultants is their name, as in: "Get me Joan James."

---

It's not the intent of this book to explore how to create a brand.[6] However, it is vital to understand brand importance in the fee-setting process. Like bank loans being hard to acquire when you need them and easy to obtain when you no longer need them, high fees are most difficult when no one has ever heard of you and you desperately need the income and easiest when you're well known and business is rolling in.

The crime here is that many successful consultants either don't bother to use their past success to create effective brands or have created brands that they don't properly leverage for higher fees. Tom Clancy has never written a book nearly as good as his original, *The Hunt for Red October,* but he's certainly been paid far more for every subsequent work than for that first effort. He has been a smart marketer and a hugely successful "brand" (to the extent that he hasn't even written some work but simply inserts "Tom Clancy" on the cover and it's sufficient, with due writing credit to another author).

Brands create higher fees. And higher fees enable you to solidify the credibility of your brand. That's a great cycle.

## CREATING SHARED SUCCESS

Many consultants take the position (out of arrogance or ignorance) of "Let me show you how I'm going to improve things around here." The success is the consultant's, a sort of largesse provided for the lucky client. There is a certain power in being "the expert" without whom all goes to hell, but there is a huge risk, although not the one that might be apparent.

The apparent risk is that the client might not benefit as desired or, heaven forbid, might actually suffer a reversal of fortune. Remember the physician's sage credo, "First, do no harm." It's no accident that large consulting firms are being sued right and left in this litigious society. They have not "delivered" the desired results.

However, the greater risk is that even with demonstrable success, the buyer feels alienated, disenfranchised, and apart from it. The fee in this case,

---

[6]But do feel free to read the prior book in this series, *How to Establish a Unique Brand in the Consulting Profession.*

despite success, will be paid grudgingly. For one thing, the client is now fearful of long-term dependence and doesn't want to incur huge costs each time the consultant's "expertise" is required to solve another problem. For another, the buyer does not feel the intrinsic ownership and sense of well-being that would emotionally overwhelm any reservations about costs. Third, from an ego perspective, the buyer will feel the need to insert some leverage into the relationship to retain the perceived upper hand and emphasize that the consultant serves at the buyer's pleasure (especially if the results are so visible that others in the organization are talking about them).

> True partners never begrudge each other their proper due. In fact, there's an implicit trust that neither partner will take advantage of the other and that terms, conditions, and time frames are innately fair.

Fee pressure decreases with a sense of shared investment, shared accountabilities, and shared success. Figure 1.3 shows the difference between a focus on a buyer and seller (top) who are locked into a battle over costs with only vague benefits established and two partners (bottom) who have agreed on tangible results where the fee is simply an intelligent and economical investment.

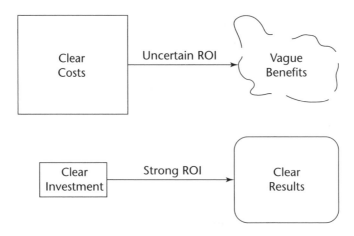

**Figure 1.3**  Costs from the Expert Versus Investment from the Partner.

When the buyer simply views the consultant as another vendor providing certain expertise, the cost of acquisition becomes the key focus, because this is a commodity purchase (Who can provide the cheapest computer monitors per our specifications?). However, when the buyer's self-image and role are as a partner in the consulting process, the decision becomes one of return on investment, and the clearer the outcomes (under the conceptual agreement discussed earlier) and the more dramatic, the higher the investment that is justified.

This is particularly true when that investment includes the buyer and key organization people in the partnership. Some of the most successful consulting projects I've landed—and the ones most impervious to fee pressure— are those in which a "virtual consulting team" was formed comprising key client resources and myself. No educated buyer will want to underfund or hedge on that investment.

These are some of the key factors in shared success:

- A "we" mentality from the first contact with the prospect
- Literature, Web sites, and promotional materials that talk about partnering and shared responsibilities
- A formal description of "joint accountabilities" in the proposal itself[7]
- A strong focus on outcomes and business results, not on tasks or deliverables
- Ample opportunity for the buyer and other key people to take credit and to bask in the success
- Candor in tackling inevitable problems and setbacks
- The consultant's being seen as an object of interest and center of expertise in the field

---

Err on the side of the client and buyer receiving more accolades for success than you. But also err on the side of higher fees and faster payment of those fees. That's the quid pro quo.

---

[7]See my *How to Write a Proposal That's Accepted Every Time.*

It really doesn't matter what the organization believes. What matters is what the current and future buyers believe. The danger of consultants trying to "do it alone" is that the client runs through this sequence:

1. Who's John Adams?
2. Get me that guy John Adams.
3. Get John Adams.
4. Get John Adams if you can.
5. Get someone close to John Adams.
6. Get me a young John Adams.
7. Who's John Adams?

In a true partnership that focuses on shared success, however, no buyer will try to eliminate one half of the successful combination.

## CHAPTER ROI

- One has to develop a philosophy about fees. They are not a "necessary evil" or a "dirty part of the job" but rather a wonderful and appropriate exchange for the superb value you are delivering to the client. That exchange has a long tradition and represents the highest ethical canon of modern capitalism: agreed payment for agreed value.
- Buyers tend to believe that they get what they pay for, and higher fees actually convey higher quality for most buyers. Higher fees also guarantee a higher level of buyer commitment, and commitment, not compliance, is key to producing a return-on-investment mentality rather than a cost-reducing mentality.
- Brands tend to raise buyers' perception of quality still higher, which is why strategic marketing is an essential aspect of the consultant's repertoire.
- The consultant must anticipate and plan to overcome objections about how other, less enlightened consultants have charged, are charging, or will charge. That is, literally, neither here nor there.
- Leaving money on the table is the equivalent of burning money—you will never, ever recover it, and we are talking millions of dollars over one's career.

- Finally, shared success—understood from the outset and achieved at the conclusion—is vital to the belief in consultant worth as part of a partnership with the buyer.

*The One Percent Solution®: Believe in your own value, and build your perceived value in demonstrable ways every day. That is the fuel for the acceleration of fees.*[8]

---

[8]I've come up with what I call The 1% Solution®: improve by 1 percent a day, and in just seventy days, you're twice as good.

# A Case of Bottom-Line Blindness

I was mentoring an individual, Roy, who was getting started in the consulting business as a second career. He was a quick learner and willing student.

He provided a proposal to a client, using my proposal templates and methods, with an option at $72,000 and another at $86,000. He offered a 10 percent discount for payment at acceptance for either option.

The client replied that he clearly needed the $86,000 option but had only $70,000 he could free up. Roy came to me proudly and said, "I'm sticking to my guns. It's the full amount or no deal. But I thought I should just test that with you." Mind you, this would be Roy's largest client do date, just nine months after launching his business.

"What if you asked for the full $70,000 up front?" I responded. "That sounds like a win-win to me."

"But that's giving him option two at option one fees," protested Roy.

Well, let's do the math. We would be offering a $16,000 discount on an $86,000 fee, which is 18.6 percent. "That's way too much," said Roy. "A 10 percent discount would come to $77,400."

"Right," I acknowledged, but you get seventy grand in hand, no expenses that aren't reimbursed by the client, and your biggest sale to date. You'll have a prestige client on your list, testimonials, referrals, and a chance to hone your consulting skills.

"Wow, I nearly blew this," said Roy.

Yes, he did. I advocate maximizing fees but not mercenary madness. I've always said that if you sell something for $100,000 but could have gladly done it for $85,000 or happily accepted $115,000, it doesn't matter. In my system, it's *all profit*. If a client makes a reasonable request and there's a quid pro quo (here, payment in advance), then don't stand rigidly by. Consider the gestalt of the sale and the margin.

*Moral: It doesn't make sense to stick to your guns if they are too stuck to be used.*

## CHAPTER 2

# The Lunacy of Time-and-Materials Models

## *Who Wants to Be as Dumb as a Lawyer?*

Historically, consultants have billed for their services on the basis of time units, usually hourly rates or per diem assessments. There is no logical reason for doing so, but the underlying reasons seem to have included the following:

- Other professionals had set a precedent, most notably lawyers and accountants, both of whom preceded consultants on the business stage.[1] (Architects, designers, and other professionals also charge in this manner.) Recently, some New York attorneys made headlines by moving rates to $1,000 per hour, which they readily conceded they didn't expect anyone to pay.

- Most of the conventional working trades—plumbers, electricians, carpenters, and the like—have placed a premium on their time.
- Time is the universal objective, in that the client and the consultant can agree on the length of an hour or a day. (Of course, how much of that duration is spent on qualitative work is another matter entirely.)
- Consultants have had a ready-made lever for increasing their business by merely increasing their time investment.
- One's consulting worth was usually perceived as the same as one's physical presence, thereby attaching worth to "showing up." It was easy to attach a fee to that presumed worth: "If I'm here, I must be helping, so I ought to be paid."
- The uncertainty of the work required that the consultant "protect" future time by charging for all time spent, since there was no firm way of predicting how much time would be required, what new and unforeseen developments might affect the project, or what increasing demands the client might come up with. The belief was that time spent on one client was irretrievably lost and was therefore denied another client (and another client's potential fee).

Seeing that consultants offer advice for long-term enrichment, why charge for short-term visits? My recommendations are worth far more than my company.

---

[1]The first management consultant was probably Frederick Winslow Taylor, the founder of time and motion studies and the author of *Principles of Scientific Management* (which wasn't so scientific at all). He worked in the early part of the twentieth century, his oeuvre being published in 1911. The first management conference was held in 1882 by the German Post Office. No one showed up.

Finally, there seems to be a widespread belief, unaccountably held to most dearly by the larger consulting firms, that the only consulting items of value are either time or materials (deliverables) and that clients wouldn't pay for anything as ephemeral as pure advice. Of course, stated that way, this proposition is true. The point, however, is that clients will pay a great deal for the outcomes, results, and long-term value of that advice.

And that value has nothing whatsoever to do with time.

## SUPPLY-AND-DEMAND ILLOGIC

One of the worst pieces of advice I ever heard was from a professional speaker who pontificated to the audience that speakers should "raise fees when demand exceeds supply." That might work for soybeans or cement, but it's simply goofy when applied to professional services.

Demand *never* exceeds supply. Not only do I know of no consultants who are booked every day of the year, but I can't imagine one who would want to be. The idea, I always thought, was to work a minimal amount of time while earning a maximum amount of money. (My ideal client is one who pays me $5 million to work for twenty minutes a year. My wife points out that if I can work for twenty minutes, I can certainly manage forty minutes.)

Moreover, supply and demand rest on the trembling foundation that a single client at a single time usurps all attention. It is possible to do something for multiple clients at any given time: research, joint meetings, newsletters, focus groups, interviews, and a plethora of other activities can benefit numerous clients in unique ways. (The lawyers achieve this by billing different clients for an aggregate of hours that only slightly exceeds by a factor of four the total number in any one day.)

> The idea is to meet demand with a minimal supply of labor and, in fact, meet growing demand by an increasingly diminishing investment of time. This is called working smart, not hard.

There are actually formulas that advise that consultants take the following steps:

1. Determine the amount of money they need to support their total lifestyle.
2. Calculate the total number of hours available to consult during a year, eliminating holidays, personal needs, and so on.
3. Determine an approximate usage rate for the remaining time (for example, what percentage of time will the consultant probably be booked, given the marketplace and focus?).
4. Divide the result of the usage rate applied to the net available hours by the lifestyle needs total. This gives the hourly rate needed to meet financial goals within the given time constraints.

Now, there are only about seventy or eighty things wrong with this, but I'll concentrate only on the relative few needed to thoroughly debunk this point of view.

First, it's absolutely nuts to use your current lifestyle (or even an intended lifestyle) as the basis for income needs. What about unanticipated expenses (illnesses, extended family needs, unexpected opportunities to invest, and so on)? Especially for younger consultants (or for anyone without fully funded, totally comfortable retirement savings), why delimit yourself during your highest potential earning years?

Second, how do you intelligently arrive at a number of hours you think are available? The number will always go down from that estimate, never up, meaning that your hourly rates will be inadequate and you'll either have to raise them or take more hours from "private time." Time is always usurped by the unforeseen, which, by definition one would think, can't be forecast. (This is the currently fashionable "black swan" phenomenon.)

Third, approximations of usage rates are absurd because high rates aren't necessarily good. It's simply not smart to be booked 80 percent or more of the time, because your flexibility is eliminated (just as any good medical consultant will tell a medical practice not to book all available hours every week but to set aside time for emergencies and other exigencies). Wouldn't we all rather work less for fascinating clients who pay us well rather than more for dull clients who pay us poorly?

Fourth and finally, the resultant hourly rate in the equation has no bearing on the market, the client need, the unique conditions, or the value of the help delivered. It reduces the consultant to an arbitrary commodity, to be compared to other hourly rates and other commodities, like fish or movie tickets. When you deliberately remove market uniqueness and differentiation, you also remove the basis for high fees.

> The last thing a good consultant wants to happen is for a client to make comparisons based not on the value of the contribution but rather on the charge per hour. Our value is simply not conveyed by merely showing up (thank goodness).

So the very basis for a "supply and demand" dynamic is fallacious. We do not have a limited supply of expertise, nor do we seek higher and higher demand (not if we want to maintain a life). What we should want to accomplish is an ideal relationship of interesting, growth-oriented work and fees based on our contribution to the client's results.

The "Big Four" (or whatever it is at this reading, having come down from the "Big Eight") consultancies are the stepchildren of accounting and audit firms. Consequently, they have been fixated on billing rates that are based on hours, fit nicely into boxes on a spreadsheet, and can be conveyed in a no-thinking-required fee schedule. These are, after all, descendants of the primeval bean counter. Their dilemma, facing the tremendous overhead of multiple offices, advertising, and huge recruiting costs, has been addressed by creating an army of inexpensive technicians who descend on the client with an hourly billing rate that is somehow digestible but significant enough to generate profit when multiplied by the legion of consultants assigned to the account. This model has been adopted by smaller firms and independent practitioners who, frankly, should know better.

Supply and demand tends to get way out of whack when the consulting firm can produce a prodigal supply of low-level people, irrespective of the actual client demand. And this tactic has, understandably, driven clients to ask: "Can you do this with fewer people?" "Can you do this in fewer days?" "Can you do this with cheaper people?"

These are not the questions we want a client to be asking. I'd rather hear a client ask: "How can we maximize the results?" "Will you work with me on this as a partner for as long as it takes?" "Will you assure me access to you personally?"

These latter questions represent the value of a long-term relationship, not an attempt to get me out before I run up too much of a bill.

Leave supply and demand to the economists or the people raising ostriches. It has nothing to do with good consulting, and it should never be used as a basis for fees.

## ETHICAL CONFLICTS OF INTEREST AND OTHER SMALL MATTERS

Whenever a consultant accepts work on the basis of being paid for time spent on the project, an immediate conflict of interest arises. There is no way around this, the problem is always present, and it is caused by the following.

### The Basis for Profit

First of all, the consultant only makes money when physically present or able to demonstrate that time is being expended somehow, somewhere for the client. This tends to compel the consultant to do the following:

- Maximize, not minimize, the number of physical activities (focus groups, interviews, observations, meetings, and so on)
- Accept peripheral assignments that may not be integral—or even important—to the actual project
- Encourage and not discourage scope creep, since there is no penalty for blurring the project boundaries
- Recommend nonessential tasks that don't contribute to results but do contribute to billable hours[2]

---

[2]I know there are many of you saying, "Yes, but honorable people wouldn't do that." Maybe, but honorable people regularly cheat on their taxes, cross the street against the light, and rip off the phone company simply because an opportunity presents itself and the incorrect action is only a brief rationalization away (what's the government done for me lately, there's

> Value-based fees are far better for the client because they remove the ethical compromises that attend hourly or daily billing. You want the client to make a single return-on-investment decision at the time of the proposal, not a new ROI decision every day (or hour).

## The Client Need Quandary

The client has to make an investment decision, in effect, every time the consultant may be able to offer some help. Hence a normal helping relationship is reduced to ROI concerns on even the most minor occasions:

- The client may decide that a $10,000 issue isn't worth $2,500 of consulting help, ignoring the fact that the consultant's expertise could help unearth the $400,000 issue underlying it.
- Subordinates are loath to use the consultant because approval is required from superiors for the additional fees, and the subordinates may not want to admit so readily that help is needed so frequently.
- Clients may forgo legitimate additional extensions of the project purely out of cost considerations, even though work in those areas would add immeasurably to the client's betterment.

## Conflicts with Client Purchasing Policies

Most organizations have policies for dealing with "vendors," and once you quote time-based fees, you will become no less a vendor than the plumber or the computer repair guy.

- In putting yourself in the same category as other hourly vendors, you are asking the client to treat you differently by not requiring a limit on

---

no traffic that I can see or can't outrun). We need to eliminate temptations that lead to unethical behavior, not expect that everyone will act honorably.

hours or by not adhering to company hourly billing policies. ("We never pay trainers more than $2,500 a day." "But I'm not a trainer." "You're in the same category.")

- A good purchasing manager or vendor coordinator is paid to extract the best possible rates from vendors. Consequently, they will always try to minimize your time rates, and you will be in danger of pitting your corporate buyer against his or her own purchasing function.
- If the company accepts billing for hourly units, how do you conscientiously bill for portion of hours or quick phone responses? Do you emulate the legal practice of making everything a fifteen-minute minimum, even if the call takes two minutes? Do you aggregate them and somehow justify them on a time sheet? This is not all that far from fudging the numbers. (If you're doing research that benefits two clients, do you charge them each for the same half-day, or do you prorate it?)

## Preserving Client Budgetary Limits

Almost any client will reasonably ask for some estimate of investment so that a proper budget can be allocated. Even with the most exacting formula, these are always only estimates, and the client's budget is actually endangered constantly.

- If, at a critical point in the project investigation, you and the client find an unforeseen critical need, how can the client appropriately budget more funds or preserve those already in place? Must you lower your hourly rate, demand additional funds, or ignore the urgency?
- The client is too often forced into a Hobson's choice: some priorities can be met but not others as the hours and days build and the meter constantly ticks away at the fixed budget.
- If there is more than one budget involved among multiple buyers, how are the funds correctly allocated? If the actions of one department demand remedial work in another, which should be properly assessed, and by how much? Not everyone is going to be happy with the decision.

As projects unfold, something has to give: either the client will have to come up with additional funds to pay for more hours, or the consultant will have to leave work undone (or work free of charge). Why on earth get into that position?

There's one final ethical issue I want to discuss, which often doesn't arise as an ethical problem but actually is one: downward pressure on consulting fees when they are based on time and materials.

The client's natural compulsion will be to reduce one or both of the only two variables representing the buyer's costs: amount of time or amount of money per time unit. The consultant will be compelled to try to do the exact opposite. However, since the client is the only one who can say yes or no, the buyer's determination will prevail. Three bad things immediately transpire:

1. The buyer and consultant are in an adversarial position, despite working together, presumably as partners, on the same goals. One is trying to minimize involvement, and the other is trying to maximize it. Yet the point should be active collaboration toward goals, not concern about the methodology or involvement to reach the goals.
2. The buyer will want to minimize time, requiring the consultant to use fewer resources, make fewer visits, or narrow the scope. All of this may be highly detrimental to the quality of the investigation.
3. The buyer will want to minimize hourly rates, which often forces the consultant to make concessions. This, in turn, has two consequences: it endangers the "magic formula" based on the consultant's earnings needs calculations, and it tells the buyer that the consultant has padded the fees and prompts even the most benign of buyers to wonder, "How low can this guy go?" (I can name that tune in two notes.)

For legitimate ethical interests, for the client and the consultant, time-and-materials billing is problematic and compromising. Not *usually* compromising. *Always* compromising.

## LIMITING PROFITS, OR WHY NOT JUST FORGET *DOMANI?*

The very worst aspect of billing based on time is the limitation it places on profitability. I've never believed in business plans, for myself or for my clients, because the danger with a plan is that you might achieve it.[3]

Consultants—and this applies particularly aptly to solo practitioners—take extraordinary business risks. Why shouldn't they reap the commensurate rewards? The only intelligent business proposition is to attempt to maximize profitability. Note that I'm not saying "maximize business," because that might lead to harder work, longer hours, and an infringement on one's life balance. But I am saying "maximize profits" because we wouldn't be very good businesspeople or consultants if we didn't.

Therefore, why create a straw man of an artificial business plan that delimits growth? (Have you ever really seen managers in October still managing against a plan created the prior June?) The mantra-like focus on "increasing business by 20 percent" or "gaining five new coaching clients" or "gaining 5 percent in the Canadian marketplace" is rather pointless if, in fact, the conditions were such that you should have increased by 40 percent, gained twelve new coaching clients, or become one of the major players in the Canadian market.

An hourly fee is a similar delimiting factor. You will always be at the mercy of the "cap" in your marketplace. (The best New York attorneys, senior partners, working for the best clients, are hard-pressed to go much above $650 an hour—despite the $1,000-per-hour ego trips—and they represent a small fraction of all attorneys, whose average income is about $88,000 in the United States.) And the larger firms with junior help will always be able to undercut you with junior rates.

If I estimate that I can work forty weeks a year and that I'll be "billable" an astonishing 80 percent of the time, that provides me with 1,280 hours (80 percent times 40 equals 32 times 40 hours in a workweek). At a New York

---

[3]Of course, major organizations need business plans to show the shareholders that management is fiscally responsible, but they also put out beautiful annual reports that have nothing whatsoever to do with the actual business. No one should manage against a business plan for fear of hitting it and missing untold opportunities.

lawyer's healthy fee of $500 an hour, that comes to $640,000—not a bad year's work (although not anywhere close to the best solo practitioner consultants). However, a more reasonable rate is probably half that, resulting in $320,000, and a more reasonable billing percentage might be 60 percent, not 80 percent, resulting in $240,000. Now that's still not exactly shabby, but is that the number that will support your lifestyle through marriage, children, tuition, retirement, care for elderly parents, vacations, investments, unexpected emergencies, and the pure joie de vivre of it all?

I think not. I tell my mentorees all the time that $100,000 ain't what it used to be.

It is absolutely crazy to adapt any billing scheme that can place a cap on your income. Time unit billing does just that. The only good reason for deliberately making less money is the urge to work less, and even there, I have a hard time believing that you must also make less money if you're smart.

Architects are famous for their hourly billing, and they are probably the only profession that had a decrease in net income over the boom years of the mid- to late 1990s.[4] They were done in by a number of factors, all within their own means to control, but particularly these:

- Hourly billing, which declined as hours declined due to competition from general contractors, engineers, and others who freely "poached" on architects' turf
- Fierce competition and resultant pressure on prices caused by a plethora of architects, not unlike today's burgeoning number of consultants (In Duluth, Minnesota, no less, a focus group told me, "Stop any three

---

[4]The American Institute of Architects was a client of mine for several years, and this was perhaps the major concern of the association and the membership.

people on the street, and two of them are architects." I immediately termed this the "Duluth architect syndrome.")

- An absence of negotiation skills with educated buyers, meaning that the only variable the architects would manipulate was their own hourly fees, and the direction was always downward
- Blindness to the real profit margins caused by love of the profession (Every architect wants to build a cathedral and keeps waiting for that contract, even though architects are overwhelmingly engaged in house extensions and garage additions. Consequently, they are always too willing to take on unprofitable projects to keep them busy "until the real thing comes along," and they tell you that they'll make up the shortfall "on volume.")[5]

Consultants have been little better. The focus on "billable time" has driven both independents and large consulting operations to focus on work, use, and task, on the assumption that something is better than nothing—we can't let all those billable hours be spent sitting here at a desk, after all. This mentality severely limits profits because, as happened with the architects, it forces one to do work that shouldn't be undertaken at rates that can't be countenanced. Something is *not* better than nothing. Some things are worse than nothing because they cost you money.

Billable hours, and the formulas on which the more methodical base them, are pernicious and insidious dampeners of profit. Moreover, the need to be competitive on such a commodity ultimately forces downward pressure on all time unit rates. So in the tactical application—fees based on time for the project—the consultant will suffer from continuing downward pressure when played off on others offering the same commodity pricing, and in the strategic sense—using time units to create a year's living expenses—there will never be enough hours or a high enough rate to dramatically improve income.

Aside from their tactical and strategic failures, time-based fees are great.

---

[5]One of the funniest skits I've ever seen was a pseudocommercial on the NBC show *Saturday Night Live* in which Phil Hartman was a pitchman for a bank that only made change, nothing else—no loans, no mortgages, no investments, only change. "I know what you're wondering," he would deadpan into the camera. "How can we do it? The secret is one word: volume."

# WHY LAWYERS AND CPAs DO SO POORLY

The problem with professions that use time-and-materials charges is that the practitioners have no real appreciation for their own value and hence cannot adequately (or dramatically) convey their value to the client. Let's look at some cases in point.

## Attorneys

Lawyers have finally understood that their ultimate worth is not in their activity but in their results. Therefore, contingency fees have begun to proliferate. It's not uncommon for a law firm to take 30 percent or 40 percent (or even more in some conditions) of the total client settlement.

The problem is that the attorneys often take this, as they say at the craps tables in Las Vegas, as "betting on the come." This means that if they lose the case, they not only fail to collect any fee but are also out their legitimate legal expenses. This is high-stakes gambling, and it leads to at least four ethical quandaries:

1. Pushing the case beyond the plaintiff's patience or commitment, because, in for a dime in for a dollar, it's cheaper to invest more on the hope of a possible victory than to simply abandon all prior investment
2. Avoiding early settlements in the hope of hitting the jackpot of a huge jury decision or a more favorable last-minute settlement in the face of a damaging trial
3. Taking on cases of questionable legal merit or suing parties not really at fault but who have deep pockets and wealthy insurers
4. Desperate legal tactics to try to save a case at the last minute

---

There isn't one profession using time units or percentages as billing bases that can match the potential fees of consultant using value-based frees. Not one.

---

Attorneys are locked into a terrible billing system that does not represent their true value to their clients (which is why they wind up billing $8.40 for duplicating and postage, so desperate are they to recoup costs).

Even on a more modest basis, effective and legally tight wills, estates, divorces, house closings, partnership agreements, and the myriad of other business aspects that lawyers undertake are worth a great deal to the beneficiary of such expertise. How much? Well, far more than a couple of hundred dollars an hour, that's for sure.

In one class-action lawsuit against a Fortune 500 company for some kind of minor technical charges, the lawyers collected millions in fees, and each member of the class action suit received $2.85.

## CPAs

Since these folks are fixated on neat boxes and clear rates as a professional pathology, it's not surprising that they cheat themselves out of their fair remuneration.

These are people who balance books, save tax dollars, highlight areas of enhanced profitability, set up effective retirement plans, provide investment advice, and generally help you exhaust every legal nook and cranny to keep your money where it belongs—in your own pocket. For the glory of providing this value, they charge $150 or so an hour.

CPAs don't get it (although more and more financial planners are beginning to). They see their value as tasks performed, which are tightly tied to and choreographed by time involved. They even have fee schedules for their various tasks, on the assumption that they can pretty accurately forecast the amount of hours needed for each task. And they probably can, which is neither here nor there.

I love the guy who does my taxes and financial planning, who may have saved me hundreds of thousands over the years (and kept me out of jail in the bargain). But I'm glad he doesn't read my books—because if he did and decided to change his billing basis, I'd have no choice but to go along.

I'd have to pay him more. I have no fear about printing this here. I'm sure he will never read it!

## Search Firms

I include these folks because they think they're smart and believe they've devised a billing basis that overcomes time units: a percentage of first-year compensation. (And some of these firms are contingency firms, not retainer firms, meaning they don't get paid unless they produce.)

I ask you to simply consider this: a search firm placed Lou Gerstner at IBM when that company was severely suffering. During his tenure, CEO Gerstner increased the stock price, improved the value of the company, gained market share, boosted both revenues and profitability, found new sources of lucrative business (for example, IBM consulting services), and provided a host of other important improvements. His net contribution to IBM's well-being is in the billions of dollars.

And how was the foxy search firm paid that placed him at IBM? It received about a third of his first-year total compensation. Let's say that was as much as $500,000, which I doubt. Even so, is a half-million fair compensation for a consulting firm that produced billions of dollars in improvement? I wouldn't accept it. It seems to me that $100 million or so is reasonable and cheap at twice the price.

> Taking a percentage of some arbitrary figure is no better than time unit billing. Why not be paid for the true value you bring? If you don't believe that, the client won't either.

Professions that focus on commodity billing—be they legal, financial, architectural, search, consulting, or any other—are those that don't believe their own value proposition in terms of client outcome and therefore can't adequately make a case for it.

## EDUCATING THE BUYER INCORRECTLY

An inherent problem in the lunacy of time-and-materials billing is that we educate the client incorrectly from the first meeting. Buyers are willing to believe that we operate in certain ways—just as the client does—and that those methods of operating will somehow have to be accommodated.

Yet we often show up as supplicants and fawners, obsequious in our determination to get the business. We position ourselves as vendors and "salespeople" from the outset, not as credible peers of the buyer with our own valuable trove of expertise.

Hear this: in true client-consultant partnerships, neither party wants to put the other at a disadvantage. Partners simply don't do that to each other. But in superior-subordinate relationships, the superior usually doesn't care, either out of callousness, noblesse oblige, or indifference.

Our job is to educate prospects from the outset about how we operate. That means that certain steps are important to take and others important to avoid. Use the following as a checklist to assess your own effectiveness in educating buyers.

### Prospect Education Checklist

1. Never quote a fee before project objectives and their value to the client are stipulated (see Chapter Four).
2. Don't quote any time unit basis at all.
3. Explain to the client, if pressed, that single, value-based fees are in the client's best interests.
4. Resist comparison to other consultants by pointing out that your potential client probably also operates differently in many respects from his or her own competitors.
5. Never commit to arbitrary amounts of time for the accomplishment of objectives.
6. Focus on results, not tasks.
7. Never accept a prospect's conclusion—stated or implied—that you will constantly be onsite or that you're available "on call."
8. Emphasize results, not deliverables; in fact, minimize deliverables.
9. Don't accept contingency fees or "pay for performance"; you're not a trained animal act. Variables are often outside your control, and besides, you're being paid for your best advice. It's up to the client to implement it effectively.
10. Provide value immediately. Shift the focus to how much value you provide, not how much work there is to be done.

I've found that in most cases, consultants create their own quicksand by undermining any possibility of establishing value-based fees at initial meetings by ignoring or acting contrary to the rules just stated.

> If you explain to the client that you're a performing horse, the client will understandably ask you to jump over hurdles and stand on your hind legs. If you explain that you're a partner interested in helping generate results, the client will understandably ask, "How do we do that best?"

Two parties are concerned about maximizing results—you and the client. But only one of you is concerned about maximizing your fees. If you emphasize the former, the latter will occur. But if you treat these as two separate considerations with the buyer, that person will try to maximize the former and minimize the latter every time.

Wouldn't you?

## CHAPTER ROI

- Supply and demand is for commodities, not consultants. Your supply will always exceed demand, and that tells you something about the inherent stupidity of this bromide.
- There are legitimate and obvious ethical reasons not to use time units for billing bases.
- Profitability should not be arbitrarily delimited by finite measures of time, materials, deliverables, or costs.
- Other professions do it incorrectly. Why would you want to emulate them?
- The buyer is educable, and you are the teacher. Don't abdicate that huge responsibility.

*The average attorney's income is under $100,000 annually. Successful people drive cars that cost more than that. What model are you using as your income paradigm, and what model car are you driving?*

## CHAPTER 3

# The Basics of Value-Based Fees

## It's Better to Be an Artist Than to Be an Engineer

Clients are traditionally somewhat stunned by and resistant to fees based on anything other than time and materials. That's because we, as consultants, have educated them all wrong. In fact, most consultants are somewhat stunned and resistant to fees based on value, so it's not surprising that the client assumes the same position!

Before we examine the components of the approach that reverses this mentality, let's examine a requisite philosophy: the goal of a consulting intervention is to improve the client's condition by meeting or exceeding mutually established project goals that are expressed as business outcomes. If those goals and outcomes are thus met or bettered, the resultant improvements will justify any reasonable investment required to achieve that particular return.

Whether quantitatively or qualitatively, whether analytically or viscerally, whether long-term or short-term, whether deep-water or blue-sky, we are seeking improvements that dwarf the costs of the consultant (see Figure 1.3 in Chapter One). This is both art and science. Part of the art is that the resultant picture has to be enjoyable for the client. Some paintings are very lifelike, some are Cubist, some are abstract. But the point is that the client likes the resulting work. (If the client longs for landscapes, a picture of a soup can won't do.)

If the client is delighted, it doesn't matter whether your fee could have been $15,000 higher or lower so long as the client is happy and you believe you've been paid fairly and well. Consequently, the point of value-based fees is that both the client and the consultant feel well treated and are happy with the finished picture. Engineers seek perfection of angles, lines, and support. Artists seek happiness.

Here is some phrasing that I'm usually asked to repeat three times in my speeches. You may reread it as many times as necessary or place a Post-it Note here so you can find it:

**Q:** How can any buyer whom you have established as a peer and with whom you have a trusting relationship possibly object to this description of your fee basis?

**A:** My fees are based on my contribution to the value of the outcomes of this project and represent a dramatic return on investment for you and equitable compensation for me.

## FOCUSING ON OUTCOMES, NOT INPUTS

The very worst failing in relation to fees on the part of consultants has nothing to do with fees and everything to do with outcomes. If you accept the fact that the results of a project—the client's improved condition—will determine the acceptable range of investment for that return, then the outcomes for the client are the key determinant in fees.

That's right: it's the outcome, not the tasks, that matter.

If you don't believe me, then please accept this challenge. Visit the Web sites or review the printed literature of any five consultants at random.

> Most consultants place their value proposition at the wrong end
> of the equation: they focus on their ability to do rather than on the
> client's ability to improve.

(Or at an event, engage them in conversation and ask them the reasons for their success.) You will find that the following applies to four out of the five, at a minimum:

- *Too many words.* The promotional literature will have far too much text, using a thousand words in place of every possible picture.
- *An obsession with the obvious.* "We believe in the highest level of ethics and integrity." (Really? I was looking specifically for an unethical consultant. Too bad.")
- *Self-aggrandizing.* The material will overwhelmingly focus on what the consultant does and how it is done.
- *Smothered in technology or methodology.* There will be detailed discussions of the consulting approaches, including analogies, graphs, steps, and jargon.
- *Programmatic orientation.* There will be client "options" in terms of workshops, interventions, materials, and even fee ranges.
- *Value secrecy.* There will be precious little of value to the reader or the listener in terms of immediate improvement.

I can make money by betting on the outcome of this test every time. The problem is that consultants focus on task—what they do—and not on result—what the client gets.

Not only is this a rather unappealing sales proposition (it's nothing more than the "billboard on a highway" approach), but it establishes improper criteria from the very earliest prospect interactions. If that prospect becomes a client, he or she has been inculcated—by us—to appreciate our value based on what we do and how often we do it. In other words, it's the brushstrokes, the framing, and the colors used in creating the painting, rather than the overall aesthetic power of the finished picture.

Every intervention and activity you propose to the client must be cast as an outcome, a result. The intrinsic value of actions is minor. Tasks are basically commodities that can be compared and contrasted. The intrinsic value of outcomes is enormous because they meet client emotional and visceral needs and can't be compared to anything else. Thus the sole difference in the client's perception of task (commodity) versus result (outcome) is within your power to influence. Yet most of us have abdicated that responsibility.

In the following table, the statement on the left is a task; the one on the right represents a possible outcome.

| Task | Possible Outcome |
|---|---|
| Conduct focus groups throughout the sales division | Determine the causes for turnover among top sales talent |
| Coach the senior vice president of finance | Enable the CFO to become a full partner in the executive team during a time of acquisitions and mergers in this company |
| Clarify understanding of strategy during a retreat and gain senior management consensus on direction | Establish a new and aggressive strategy for the next two years, which will fulfill the board's desire for double-digit revenue growth and 10 percent gain in market share |
| Analyze the feasibility of purchasing the competitor's Acme Division | Maximize the return on the prospective $2 billion Acme acquisition or protect the company from making a bad investment |

> Most of us think in terms of what we do, not in terms of how the client will prosper. It's absurd to base fees on things that are important to us instead of on what's important to the client.

This slight change of emphasis from our help to the client's outcome is simple to accomplish, yet is the main ingredient in preparing the client for value-based pricing. Our job is to establish the client's improvement, not to harp on the efficacy of our approaches (which aren't really efficacious anyway unless this particular client sees improvement). I love the consultants who claim, "My recommendations were excellent, based on outstanding focus group work. Your managers just aren't using the findings to gain the needed changes." I've got news for you: if the changes aren't forthcoming, the project has failed, irrespective of the focus groups and the recommendations.

Move the prospect from what you do to how the prospect benefits as early as possible in your contacts or discussions. Ultimately, your fees will be based on those early moments.

Anything that is not a desirable result for the client—problem solved, new level achieved, plan implemented—is an input that can be judged as a commodity against someone else's similar input. Once you change the focus to the client's outcome, the commodity mentality tends to disappear ("You can do that? How much?" becomes "I can achieve that? How soon?").

## THE FALLACY AND SUBVERSIVE NATURE OF "DELIVERABLES"

Because consultants tend to place little value on their advice and counsel (which is a low-self-esteem issue), they have to find some device or technique in which to vest their value. That alternative is usually the dreaded D-word: deliverables.

I've seen proposals that feature deliverables as the key aspect of the entire consulting engagement.[1] Imagine this: a report, manual, class, set of recommendations, or presentation to management becomes the signal aspect of the consultant's contribution to results. There's a reason why a schoolteacher makes $40,000 for a year's work and General Colin Powell makes $100,000 for a forty-five-minute keynote speech. Teachers are not evaluated on results (student admission to college, acquisition of good jobs, scores on standardized tests, and so on) and in fact have fought against just that. Former Defense Secretary Powell was evaluated on the results of his appearance at the event for employees, customers, management, leadership, morale, and so on. As long as both are positioned as they are, both deserve what they get. (No one

---

[1]A deliverable is a means to an end. It is a progress point or stop along the way to client results. But deliverables themselves are not client results, and they should never be emphasized or confused in that regard.

would pay $100,000 for forty-five minutes of speaking, and no one would pay only $40,000 for his or her child's future. This is why so few of us stand out in a crowd.)

> There is no reason on earth that a consulting project can't be sold, implemented successfully, and concluded brilliantly without a single mention of "deliverables"—unless, of course, that's what the consultant is selling, implementing, and concluding.

The key in avoiding deliverables is not to talk about them but to talk about value and outcomes instead. Don't underestimate the importance of the self-esteem factor, because other consultants have probably educated the buyer incorrectly, and the buyer might be using deliverables as a favorite criterion to assess consulting proposals.

It's fair to give your prospect a notion of the type of methodology you'll be using. For example, focus groups require active client participation, whereas telephone interviews with clients require practically none. Classroom training requires scheduling; job performance aids do not. Observation of the client environment and conditions creates a Hawthorne effect (changes in the behavior of the people being observed merely by dint of being observed); sending "mystery shoppers" to the customer's business does not. However, providing numbers of programs, exact participation, reports stipulated at given junctures, and appearances at meetings is more than the client needs to know.

You are the consulting expert. You've been contacted, presumably, because the client needs help that is not available internally and hasn't thus far been secured externally. If the client were adept at consulting—or even at improving the desired condition—you wouldn't be involved in the conversation. The prospect needs help not currently accessible.

Don't sacrifice that potential power base by acceding to client demands that are arbitrary, anxiety-driven, and often amateurish. The answer to "How many reports will you provide and how often?" is not "How many do you want and how frequently?" or "About twice a month." The answer is

"The reports aren't the point. Improvement in your retention rate is the point, and we'll all know that when we see it."

---

I was contacted by Mercedes-Benz North America, which has an incredibly stringent method of choosing consultants. First, Mercedes sent a delegation to hear me speak at a client event. Second, they invited me in to meet with another level of evaluators. Third, they placed the few of us who survived in front of the buyer.

The buyer, a tough authoritarian figure from the German parent company, told me how the consulting project would be conducted, asked me how I would conform to those specifications, and wanted a precise schedule of deliverables. He also demanded to know the precise depth of my auto expertise and what I intended to do prior to the engagement to strengthen it.

I told him that I didn't operate that way and that it wouldn't help him even if I did.

He was aghast. (His subordinates ducked for cover.) I told him, as I gestured around the room, that he was surrounded by auto experts, and the last thing he needed was another one from the outside. Mercedes knew how to make cars. I wasn't going to tell the experts how to improve the cars' fuel injection or brake linings. But I knew how to consult, and I wasn't about to let Mercedes tell me how to gather data or validate my findings. The partnership had to be based on what each of us was good at, or else there could be no synergy and hence no partnership.

I got the job, and the fee was never discussed until my proposal was signed. The buyer, since retired, told me much later on that he wished his subordinates had the courage to speak to him the way I had.

---

The Basics of Value-Based Fees

In fact, we may decide, as the consulting experts, to change, add, or delete deliverables as the project progresses, so it's folly to base our value on the types and volume of such things. If I brief a client by phone, a written report may no longer be necessary. If five focus groups turn up an absolutely valid pattern, then the other five may be dispensed with (and if all ten are inconclusive, you might have to do another ten). I've seen "deliverables" from consultants that were superfluous, redundant, simplistic, and superficial.[2] But they were "delivered" nonetheless, because the consultant and client both believed that they were what the client was paying for.

A final word on deliverables, to intentionally belabor the obvious. The absolute worst deliverable to suggest, commit to, and base fees on is your *time*. When your value is based on showing up, you tend to show up whether you're needed or not. When the client expects to see you, the client looks for you whether it makes sense for you to be there or not. I've seen proposals that quoted as a deliverable "fourteen days onsite over two months" or "visits to every site twice a month" or "participation in every weekly executive committee meeting."

> If your fees are based on deliverables and your primary deliverable
> is your time, you might as well become a plumber or an electrician.
> They are booked more often than you, have clear and finite projects,
> and seldom require a plane trip to fix a sink or repair an outlet.

If you employ value-based fees, the need to spend additional time on the project—at the client's behest or of your own volition—is harmless. Your margins are so big that the additional time investment is of no import—and let's face it, you were only going to be using the extra time watching reruns of *Seinfeld* anyway.

---

[2]Heaven protect us from the "needs assessments," which aren't accurate assessments and seldom elucidate needs. This is one of the greatest examples of pointless work that I know of in the consulting field.

I've conducted projects for Hewlett-Packard, one of the greatest and smartest organizations on the planet, during which I never showed up once. That's right; everything took place by phone, fax, e-mail, research, teleconference, and other remote means. The company has been ecstatic with the results. I've been ecstatic with the fees. No one has asked why they haven't seen me lately. Part of the key is that HP is truly a global company, with key people at every level of management located all over the world. They don't expect to see each other, and they don't expect to see me. ("I'm just trying to fit in," I told one startled exception in management, who couldn't believe I wouldn't be spending time onsite.)

You need to get into an "HP frame of mind."

## QUANTITATIVE AND QUALITATIVE MEASURES AND CRITERIA

Fees that are based on true outcomes and client results require that some metrics be established for those results so that you and the client can relate the improved client condition to your involvement and not the fate or actions of others. (One thing about deliverables is that the client knows when you've delivered them, but that's hardly justification for basing fees on them.)

There are two kinds of metrics to assign to the desired client outcomes: quantitative (improvement by an objective yardstick) and qualitative (improvement by an agreed-upon subjective reference point).

### Quantitative or Objective Criteria

The objective measures of client improvement are clear and obvious. They include areas such as market share, revenues, profits, response time, customer ratings, employee ratings, return on investment, return on sales, return on equity, return on assets, retention of clients, retention of employees, numbers of new sales, margin per sale, product to market time, and installed systems—the list could go on and on. However, there are several critical aspects to even such clear and objective measures.

First, the nature of the measurement device must be agreed on. Will it be the monthly sales reports, the sales call sheets, the finance department's weekly profit report, or the six-month review of retained business? In many cases, clients will think they are measuring objective data, but they are really relying on anecdotal reports from subjective sources. (Sales managers are notorious for this.) It's up to the consultant to evaluate the metric and help the client establish a sound one if none exists or if the current one is inadequate. By assisting in the evaluation and possible development of metrics, you are immediately adding value to the project, which should be reflected in your fee. (That's right: establishing the criteria for your own project's success justifies a higher fee. This is an often overlooked aspect of providing value and basing fees on value—helping the client recognize success.)

> The direction of the result is far better—and safer—than the specification of the exact result. There are too many variables involved for you to rely on the attainment of a "magic number."

Second, you cannot base your contribution on what I call a "magic number." Even though a 6 percent increase in sales might be highly desirable and even, in your opinion, very achievable, it's never a good idea to peg your success to that magic number. The reason is that there are far too many variables that can affect that number adversely for you to take that risk. For example, if three top salespeople are recruited away by a competitor's unmatchable offer or a new technology undermines the client's older technology or three key client customers suffer setbacks affecting the client's business, you can hardly be held accountable.

It's better to state that you will assist in maximizing the sales increase or drive attrition down to industry averages or increase profit per sale or decrease costs of acquisition. But tying yourself to a magic number is fraught with danger.

If you feel pressured to agree to some number by a client who is not comfortable with ambiguity, ask what a *conservative* improvement or achievement would represent. Once the client arrives at it, *cut that number in half.* This will ensure an unequivocal ROI ratio. Even better, ask for a range, and take the low end of the range and cut that in half.

I know what you're thinking: what if the outcomes are far in excess of an agreed-on number? Can't I take a piece of that greater result? If it's just "progress toward," then I'm cheating myself.

This is contingency fee theory, and the lawyers love it. But I'd warn you about this: first, excessive results are probably not going to be attributed to you anyway, since the client will tend to say, "We're doing so well, we probably didn't need you after all." Second, the client will tend to be resentful at paying you more and more as results climb and climb. Third, this dynamic means that you'll have to reduce your fee if you fail to hit the magic mark (fair is fair). Finally, your own consulting judgment will be clouded by the conflict of true long-term progress versus short-term growth and your mercenary stake in it.

You're better off taking a single flat fee with a very high margin and counting on future business if the client is hugely successful. You're almost guaranteed to get it under such circumstances. Consultants who provide dramatic success, in excess of expected improvements, *always* have their calls returned by the buyer.

## Qualitative or Subjective Criteria

In some of my most successful projects, the criteria for success were subjective, although of very high quality nonetheless. By "high quality," I mean that different outcomes represent very different levels of satisfaction. The beauty of a building, the public reputation of a firm, and the comfort of office furniture are all examples of rather subjective yet high-quality outcomes. An unaesthetic building, a lousy reputation, and uncomfortable seating are all major problems, despite the subjectivity of one's measure.

The key, of course, is, do we agree on who is doing the measuring and what standards are being applied?

I don't get involved in aesthetics or furniture comfort, but I do take on image, reputation, stress, teamwork, communications, and a host of related issues that aren't very conducive to quantitative measures. (The "experts" who claim that "if you can't measure it, it isn't important" are simply spouting another bromide and are almost always academics or human resource people.) Years ago, an organization no less august than the Harvard School of Law undertook a major project with McKinsey & Co. to create a better feeling about the school among its graduates after surveys disclosed that students felt their education was excellent but that the Harvard Law experience was rather dreadful. Firms such as Andersen were also in on the bidding, which ran to very significant numbers.

> Qualitative measures can be among the most powerful and create the highest fees *if* a significant buyer is doing the measuring.

"I'll know it when I see it" may be a sufficient criterion for some members of the Supreme Court to evaluate pornography, but it is insufficient for a consulting project. In fact, here are the parameters for creating a successful, anecdotal series of measures for a project:

- The buyer will personally judge the result.
- Determination of effectiveness will rely on observed behavior and factual evidence.
- There will be gradations of success, not success or failure (a rheostat, not an on-or-off switch).
- Reasonable time limits must be in place.
- Employees remark favorably about their perceptions of results.
- Customers remark favorably about their perceptions of results.

People will change behavior for the long term—that is, with commitment and not just compliance—only if their rational self-interest is met. Motivation is intrinsic, and people can motivate only themselves to change.

## MEASURING THE UNMEASURABLE

The CEO of a $600 million operation told me that his objective was to create better teamwork among his direct reports. His own total compensation package was about $2 million a year. I asked him why (the value) he wanted to do this, and he told me that improved teamwork would achieve the following goals:

- Free him up from petty turf issues
- Allow him to focus on the board's requirements for expansion
- Evaluate which subordinates were possible successors
- Speed cross-functional collaboration (since subordinates erected the turf boundaries that their bosses designed)
- Reduce the high frequency and long duration of meetings that were necessary to sort out all the conflict

This was obviously a high-value project. But how would we know that we had achieved something? "I'll know it when I see it, believe me," he said, but I didn't believe him. "How would you prove this to the board," I asked, "or to a newspaper reporter doing a story on how much you and I have improved teamwork?"

We arrived at the following measures, which he and I would agree were present, or not, through observation and participation, which would improve by degrees and would require about six months for complete effect:

- Meetings would reduce in frequency and duration, and agenda items would contain fewer and fewer issues to be resolved among departments.
- Customers would cease complaining that they were receiving conflicting advice, duplicate bills, and too many sales calls from different people.
- Talent would be transferred across departmental lines for succession planning and career development without human resources demanding that impasses be broken by the CEO.
- Cross-functional collaboration and knowledge sharing would decline from the top spot in the annual employee survey of "most needed" improvements.
- The CEO would receive fewer and fewer phone calls and private visits from direct reports demanding that he intercede with their peers.

We applied these measures at our own semimonthly meetings, judged our progress, and made plans for next steps. The project was a great success. The keys for all of us, when dealing with subjective and anecdotal measures, is to agree on the specific behaviors and evidence with the buyer and to compare notes on relative progress frequently.

Qualitative and subjective measures are often the most valuable that a buyer wants to pursue, so don't demand that they be somehow metamorphosed into quantitative metrics and numbers.

## SERVING THE CLIENT'S SELF-INTEREST

Value-based fees are most directly related to the client's self-interest being served. That self-interest may be organizational: higher sales, better retention, improved image—or personal: less stress, better time use, improved effectiveness. In either case, it's the buyer who counts.

---

People will only change behavior for the long term—that is, with commitment and not just compliance—if their rational self-interest is met. Motivation is intrinsic, and people can only motivate themselves to change.

---

Prospects will often tell you what they want, but they won't often articulate what they really need. That's because they often don't know. They will want an obvious solution or alternative because they haven't been in a position or had the advice to view the situation more dispassionately and objectively or haven't had the frame of reference or innovative ability to create a better response.

Don't forget that most clients are at worst reacting to some alarm and at best are opportunistic, trying to seize higher ground at the moment. Very few of them have the means and inclination to take longer-term perspectives.

That's why they need you or me. It's the height of folly to sacrifice that need by dutifully and mindlessly (and valuelessly) complying with the buyer's stated "wants." After all the work and intelligence required to reach a true buyer, it's worse than negligent to simply reply to that person's desires without examining them for deeper and more important needs.

The key question at this juncture is a simple one: "Why?" Why does the buyer want a sales training program? If more sales are required to compensate for client turnover, maybe the real need is better customer service. If the buyer wants coaching to improve delegation skills, maybe the real need is to change a culture that is authoritarian and rejects empowerment and delegation. If the client wants a mentoring program to improve retention of new employees, maybe the selection process is using incorrect criteria or the competition uses better nonfinancial incentives to lure people away.

All clients know what they want. Few know what they need. It's imperative to explore this early and tap into the buyer's self-interest, which is always going to be to find the best organizational or personal improvement. If that improvement is more than they had envisioned, all the better, and your method for obtaining it and compensation for your method are small potatoes indeed.

Many consultants attempt to enlarge sales (especially those based on a time-and-materials billing system) by "enlarging" them to include more areas, more people, or longer durations. This is madness, since it also increases the labor intensity of the project, which is arithmetic growth at best.

The key to geometric growth is to find that rich vein of true need and mine it assiduously. When the buyer says, "We've never looked at it that way before" or "Why, that's counterintuitive" or "I've never considered that, and I can't imagine why not," you've achieved a wonderful sale, which you can louse up only if you don't understand where you are.

This is why promoting how good you are, touting your methodology, demonstrating your patents and copyrights and trademarks, and attempting to dazzle the prospect with the beauty of your intricate approaches are all so silly. None of that is in the prospect's self-interest. But I can sit down without one sheet of paper (and without, thank the fates, any reference at all to PowerPoint) and demonstrate exactly how the buyer will be better off as a result of our partnership, including in those areas where the buyer hadn't even been aware of the opportunities.

That beats a slide show any day.

Figure 3.1 shows graphically what I call "value distance," which I define as the distance created from the mere "want" toward the true "need." The greater the distance, the greater your value.

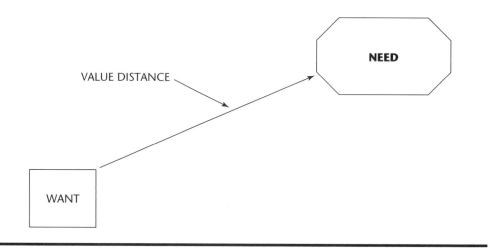

**Figure 3.1** Value Distance.

The ability to use a selected variety of interventions to interpret our past for the client's improved future is a rare dynamic, one shared, perhaps, with doctors and lawyers. But the doctors seldom have our range of possible work, and the lawyers have no idea how to charge for their value. That leaves the field to us.

No one cares, really, about how good you are. Clients care about how good they are going to be when you're done with them.

## THE SUBTLE TRANSFORMATION: CONSULTANT PAST TO CLIENT FUTURE

The final major consideration to think about—or perhaps internalize—is that we, as consultants, are engaged in a rather grand venture. We are not worth our on-site visits, we are not worth our technology, and we are not worth our tactical advice. Of course, you can charge for all that, but your fees will be delimited by the very nature of the limitations of those components.

Value-Based Fees

| Consultant's Past | Current Intervention | Client's Future |
|---|---|---|
| • experiences | • coaching | • higher productivity |
| • education | • survey | • lower attrition |
| • accomplishments | • redesign | • higher morale |
| • development | • workshop | • improved image |
| • travels | • retreat | • better performance |
| • work history | • etc. | • greater market share |
| • beliefs | | • greater profit |
| • victories/defeats | | • more growth |
| • risks/adversity | | • more innovation |
| • experimentation | | • problems solved |
| | | • happier customers |
| | | • superior service |

**Process Flow**

⟶

**Figure 3.2**  Transforming Consultant Past to Client Future.

We are actually worth the transformation that we achieve in turning our history into the client's future. Figure 3.2 shows the actual process flow that all of us should bear in mind with every project.

Each of us possesses a unique background that we should accentuate, not blend into a homogeneous "consultant hash." The longer we work and the more diverse our projects, the richer that background. (This is also why I preach that academic degrees are only a small part of one's armamentarium.) We transfer that past to the client through a series of interventions, which might include major interactive devices (training, focus groups), personalized interaction (coaching, interviews), proprietary approaches (books, models), and individual work (observations, advice).

The mistake is to attach a value and a fee to either of the first two columns in the figure. The only column that matters is the third column: the client results, which, of course, constitute the client's future.

Yet even the best of consultants, while acknowledging project objectives and outcomes, retrogress and assess their fees based on the number of retreats or the size of a survey or their history in that industry or how many sites they'll have to visit. The worst consultants never visit the third column at all.

When I tell people to provide client options, which you'll find discussed in other parts of this book, they often simply increase numbers of deliverables (!)

and point out that another option is to have twice as much training or three times as many coaching contacts. That's crazy.

I invite you to use Figure 3.2 as a template.[3] The left column's generic headings should be replaced by your own unique past, and that column should grow continually. (If it's not growing after every single engagement, then you're taking on projects you can do blindfolded and, hence, you're not growing and not increasing your potential value.) The middle column should be your particular interventions, and they might be stable or grow (or even decline). For example, you may add "expert witness" to that column. I, for one, have deleted "training" from that column, which I choose not to do anymore. Generally, since we have a limited range of competencies and tend to focus on what we do best, this column will be relatively shorter than the others.

The third column we should generate for each particular client. It should be as long as possible and be created with the buyer's active collaboration and contributions (thus stipulating to the value we're providing). Yet overwhelmingly, our approaches, promotional material, conversations, and even ideas about self-worth tend to focus on the first two columns and not the third. As Marshal Ney said when told of the assassination of a rival ordered by Napoleon, "It's worse than a crime. It's a blunder."

Here's a hint: constantly survey your past clients to determine your full breadth and scope in that third column. We are often ignorant of what the client feels has been the true impact of our partnership. Clients will often say, "What surprised me is that we were able to do this in addition to what we discussed. That was a great fringe benefit." Fringe benefits to one party are primary benefits to another. Record and codify such things.

## PERPETUAL MOTION, PERPETUAL PROGRESS

There is nothing magic or even new about my models. Substitute them for others of your own design if you like. But the point not to be lost is that you must have a conscious model for determining your value to the client, and your

---

[3]The form in Figure 3.2 first appeared in the first book of this series, *The Ultimate Consultant,* which I hope you'll read if you haven't already.

models, whatever they are, must start with your own acceptance and buy-in. The first sale is always to yourself.

Most consultants are unaware of their own business model.

Never view the client as a fixed position moving to another fixed position. I'm told that the best airplane pilots are able to immediately visualize movements in three dimensions, since an airplane, even when taking off, is not moving merely forward or up but in several directions at once whenever airborne. Similarly, a client doesn't merely move from position A to position B but rather moves dynamically, somewhat to the left or right, a little up or down. Client success is a moving target, which should always be a goal, not a destination.

Therefore, our ability to influence the client's future is an ongoing need and a continual value. If we're really good, the collaboration isn't just about reaching point B; it's about continually describing and preparing for new futures and the requisite journeys.

And as you accompany the client on that journey, you are constantly learning and increasing the fuel in the first column, enabling the third column to continually be enriched. That's right, the very work you do with a client should make you more valuable to that client as time progresses. One of the bromides in this business is that a consultant comes to study a problem and remains to become part of it. I don't doubt that many do just that. But the flip side of the value coin is that once you're working in partnership with the buyer to enrich the future, and you're constantly learning during the process—thereby further increasing your value—why would a client want you to leave?

Don't misunderstand. I'm not advocating clients for life or some kind of viral approach where the client is never free of you. But I am maintaining that we come and go too quickly, in general, and that we underestimate the improving value we provide simply by dint of successfully working with the client and reaching our mutual goals in real time. We leave too early because we disengage too early, and we disengage too early because we don't think it's right to market while we deliver.

This is crazy. It's perfectly fine to continue to improve our own value while providing the client with increasing value as a result. I worked with Merck for twelve years in a row; with Calgon for five; with Hewlett-Packard for over fifteen; and with the American Press Institute for over twenty. There were and are some very smart people in all these organizations. I'd like to think they recognized a good thing—a high value—when they saw it.

This is the "good deal" to which I periodically refer. When a buyer says, "He was a bargain," and I say, "I was well paid," that's the basis for continued high value and ongoing high profits—for both parties.

> The opportunity to turn our past into the client's future is very existential. Our past improves as our work with the client progresses. As that value grows, so should our client relationship and the duration of our partnership.

## CHAPTER ROI

- Value-based fees should reflect client results, not consultant tasks. We tend to focus on the wrong side of that equation.
- "Deliverables" are a consultant-invented shibboleth that is easy to describe and produce but of very little ultimate value.
- Measures of success can be quantitative and qualitative, and the latter—with the subjective assessment of the buyer—can be more valuable than the former.
- Buyer self-interest—either organizational or individual—is the key. Consultant self-interest is merely a function of the buyer's needs.
- What a buyer wants and what a buyer needs are two different things in most cases, and it's up to the consultant to demonstrate the difference and the greater value of that difference.
- We transform our unique past into the client's unique future. When stated (and believed) in that framework, it's difficult to place a high enough fee on that tremendous value.
- Discretionary time for a buyer constitutes tremendous wealth. Don't merely focus on the monetary or on the business.

*Consulting is art and science. The danger is that we become excellent technicians and lose our aesthetic sense. We need to paint visions of the future—for our clients and for ourselves.*

# The Case of the Annoying Accountants

I had been hired to help a major consulting firm transition just one of its practices to value-based fees. This practice was considered unusually appropriate in its subject area and was led by a partner who fully backed the conversion. It was hoped that the "pilot" would help countervail the ossified culture of billing by the hour ingrained in the rest of the company.

We worked to select those people who would be most amenable within the practice and who had accounts or prospects most likely to be converted by a value-based approach and its benefits to the client, such as no meter running, no investment decisions needed daily, and so forth.

In short, we maximized our chances of success, and it worked.

Fairly soon we had two clients converted and all new prospects discussing solely value-based fees. New proposals talked only of value-based fees. Then an unexpected monkey wrench was tossed into the works.

In the largest such project, about $460,000 in revenue, the accounting department said they would not accept the business as earned income or distribute the credit unless the monies were accounted for in terms of hours applied and within the limits of hourly rates of partners, associates, and so forth. In other words, since there were neither enough billable hours nor sufficient leeway on charges by the hour, the project couldn't be accounted for!

The practice leader was at his wits' end, but the head of accounting refused to budge, citing "a terrible precedent." Since my retirement plan wasn't vested in my client and *I had already been paid a value-based fee up front,* it was agreed that I was the best weapon.

So I send a note to the head of the division and asked which he preferred in terms of his bonus plan that year: a $460,000 project that accounting would have to find new ways to allocate or a $220,000 project, which was the maximum we could justify using allocated hours and hourly rates.

Not long after, accounting found some mysterious way to accept and credit the revenue, though they never revealed how.

You would be surprised at how many companies are driven by their internal bookkeeping functions. Don't allow that mentality to enter your office.

*Moral: No airline pilot ever shouted over the public address system, "Is there an accountant on board??!!"*

## CHAPTER 4

# How to Establish Value-Based Fees

---

*If You Read Only One Chapter . . .*

**E**ver since I began promoting value-based pricing for consultants (and the variety of other occupations and professions that have sought to heed the call), I've been asked one question consistently by a minority of the acolytes: "What formula should I use?"

That, of course, is the million-dollar question. Fee setting is art and science, and mostly the former. Consequently, the engineers, architects, and other highly structured among us have had to be revived when told that there is no magic formula. However, that's not to say that there aren't excellent ways to create fees based on value, if you're willing to be flexible, confident, and diagnostic.

So if you haven't rushed to get your money back after the first two paragraphs, I can be of considerable help. In fact, for the first time, I'm going to be very explicit in writing about the creation of value-based fees. But please keep these precepts in mind:

- The idea is to create high margins, not merely high fees. That way, you can afford to be less precise about fees, since the margins will allow for plenty of flexibility.
- Value is in the eye of the beholder. There is no law, nor any ethical imperative, that says that you must charge two clients the exact same amount for the same services. First, the services are rarely identical. Second, the value to those respective clients will always be different.
- The fact that you could do something for less money or that you could do more for the same amount of money is irrelevant. The only relevant facts are: Are you meeting the client's objectives, improving the client's condition, and delighting your buyer? To answer that, you virtually never have to provide details of every single service, every scintilla of information, or every day of your life to do that.

I also want to emphasize that fees are means to more important ends. Wealth, to me, is about discretionary time. You can always make more money, but you can never make more time. Those daily twenty-four hours are all you have.

Some of you can create wealth with less money than others. It depends on your lifestyle, age, career trajectory, personal values, family size, and many other factors. But never lose sight of the fact that fees are a means to create wealth, and wealth is a function of your freedom to allocate time to important personal objectives and needs.

## CONCEPTUAL AGREEMENT: THE FOUNDATION OF VALUE

Consulting is a relationship business. Trust is essential to relationships. When a buyer trusts you and you trust the buyer, you are in a position to acquire the three essential building blocks for a value-based project:

1. The business objectives to be met
2. The metrics or measures of success to assess progress
3. The value to the client of meeting those objectives

A relationship with an economic buyer is *always* the first step in a value-based project. You don't need anyone else, but you can't make the sale with anyone else either. It's that simple.

That's it. That's all you need from the client to set a fee based on value. And you can only obtain that from the economic buyer. The sequence here is simple and straightforward, but also ineffable (see Figure 4.1).

As you can see in the figure, our marketing efforts create leads, which we pursue and qualify to find the true (economic) buyer—the person who can write a check for our services. We then establish a relationship with that buyer so that we can gain conceptual agreement about the three criteria above. Without the economic buyer, the discussion is irrelevant; without a trusting relationship, the important information is unlikely to be shared; and without conceptual agreement, we are unable to establish the value as perceived by the client, which is the key input to determining our own fees.

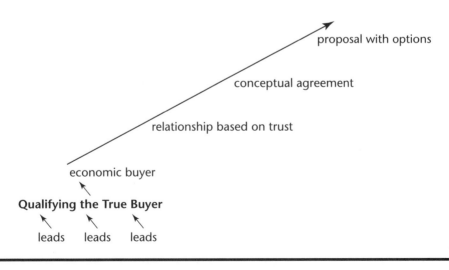

**Figure 4.1**  The Value-Based Fees Sequence.

One last time, then:

- *Objectives:* Business outcomes (for example, higher sales, better team-work, faster time to market) that are essential for the project to deliver for the client
- *Measures:* Objective or subjective (anecdotal) criteria that will indicate progress and, eventually, completion for client and consultant
- *Value:* The demonstrable organizational or personal benefit stipulated by the client as representing the actual improvement in the client's condition

> Setting value-based fees is both an art and science. But a key criterion is simply this: what fee range is likely to prompt the client to say, "That was a terrific return on my investment, and I'd like to work with that person again," and you to say, "I was paid very well for my contribution, and the margin was excellent"?

I'll provide some "formulas" for this at the end of this chapter, but it's imperative that you understand the underlying rationale first. The economic buyer must agree to outcomes, measures, and value of the improvements in collaboration with you prior to setting fees. If you accomplish this, your proposals will be accepted more than 80 percent of the time (although you'll probably submit fewer proposals than you do now). If you ignore this, your chances of having value-based proposals accepted are less than 5 percent.

Here's an example for our purposes:

### Project
- Improve retention of new employees in a zero-unemployment, highly competitive environment

### Objectives
- Current rate of new employee turnover (32 percent) lowered toward the industry average (22 percent) over one year's time

- Hiring process improved so that fewer poor candidates survive to the third round of interviews
- Causes for high turnover understood and patterns traced to relevant sources: interviews, orientation, training, mentor, supervisor, and so on

*Measures*
- Monthly retention report and turnover statistics
- Exit interview analysis
- Survey (to be created) for new hires to accept and reject company offer letter
- Six-, twelve-, and eighteen-month survivor rates

*Value*
- Current turnover costing $545,000 annually in actual salary, benefits, and related expenses
- Estimated cost of lost work, poor productivity, overtime, and related costs until vacated jobs are ultimately filled by qualified and trained replacements: $2.6 million annually
- Estimated cost of "failure work" in senior management interviewing candidates who should have been eliminated at lower levels: $350,000 annually

In my basic example, this client is spending about $3.5 million on an inadequate and ineffective hiring process. And that's every year. We'll return to this example once we've establish a few more basics. But note that the economic buyer has provided these numbers in discussions with the consultant.[1]

Here's a second example:

*Project*
- Coaching the president of a $450 million division

---

[1]See Appendixes A through F for examples of the questions that can be used with the economic buyer to establish objectives, measures, value, and so on.

*Objectives*

- Masters the ability to influence and impress the press and outside directors
- Creates a positive, nonthreatening environment for subordinates' ideas
- Establishes a succession plan for officers with three-deep bench strength

*Measures*

- Outside directors comment favorably at meetings on communications
- Positive press stories appear monthly; negatives decline
- Regular meetings are established for purely innovation and creative thinking
- New services and product development expand at a greater rate
- Plan are in place with candidates, and there are empty slots for outside recruiting

*Value*

- More investors, stock price is higher, board approves more funding
- Growth initiatives, funded properly, provide a competitive edge
- New ideas boost market share and publicity in the media
- Decreased recruiting costs, higher retention of top people

Even with a "simple" coaching project, you can create true value-based projects with no reliance on how many days you spend or how much access there is to you. The results and commensurate value are the keys.

## ESTABLISHING YOUR UNIQUE VALUE

The examples show how to establish value in terms of buyer needs. A second major component of value, however, can be ascertained without the buyer's involvement, and that's your uniqueness and personal contribution.

There are three questions that you should answer in every single engagement, prior to establishing fees:

1. Why me?
2. Why now?
3. Why in this manner?

## Why Me?

If there are hundreds of consultants who can do the work in question and provide the value the client requests, you are less valuable to the success of the project. But if the number of consultants who can do the work is limited, your value increases. This is basic supply and demand mentality, but in this limited instance, it works.

Here are some components of this question that can help you determine whether you are uniquely valuable or simply another fish in the school:

- Is the buyer talking to other consultants? If so, to a limited range or a great many?
- Do you possess some unique expertise or history (you "wrote the book," you once worked in the industry, you worked for the buyer in the past, or the like)?
- Have you been referred to the buyer by a trusted source?
- Are you known within the industry, or do you have a unique reputation?
- Are you at the right place at the right time (you're local, you're available to start immediately, and so on)?

Ask yourself whether you bring some inherent value that others can't, whether by design (a book you've written) or by accident (you're the only one who can begin next week). Sometimes it's as important to be lucky as it is to be good at what you do.

---

It's easy to assess your own unique value, but most consultants don't bother. If you don't do it, no one else is going to do it for you.

---

## Why Now?

Is there some special value about this juncture that needs to be factored in? After all, there is often a reason why the discussion is being undertaken today and not six months ago or six months from now, and that reason is often desperation!

Here are some component questions:

- What if the client were to do nothing? Would the situation be stable or deteriorate still further?
- Is there a limited window of opportunity during which gains must be made or they will be lost?
- Has something occurred that has increased the urgency significantly (for example, the CEO has said, "Get it done!")?
- Are certain conditions in place that need to be capitalized on or they will be lost (for example, a competitor's temporary misfortune)?
- Is there funding available that will disappear if not used (often the case at the conclusion of a fiscal year)?

When a prospect contacts you, there is always an implied urgency. The key is to determine just how great it is or to increase it through your relationship with the buyer.

## Why in This Manner?

Hiring a consultant is hardly a default position, much as we all wish it were. There must be compelling reasons in favor of such a hire if the buyer is bothering to talk to you (irrespective of whether the buyer reached out to you or you to the buyer).[2]

Here are some additional questions:

- Why aren't they doing this internally?
- Have they tried this in the past and failed?
- Have they used other consultants in the past, and if so, with what result?

---

[2]I want to emphasize that my remarks pertain to true buyers. Gatekeepers, trainers, human resource people, purchasing agents, and others will often reach out simply to "shop" and compare prices. These approaches are not designed for such contacts. The only thing to do with those contacts is to use them to reach an economic buyer.

- Why is this buyer the one sponsoring this project?
- Who else is involved in this project and why?

By determining special circumstances, you'll be in a position to establish your ability to contribute to those special needs.

In establishing your own unique value, you have another important input to your fee determination. (Note that many of the questions in these three areas may be answered in your relationship building with the buyer. Keep them in mind—even written in your notes—as your discussion progresses.)

> Whenever a client contacts you, there is the strong possibility that the urgency and need for a resolution are greater than initially indicated. This is why effective marketing is so important: prospects who contact you are much more inherently valuable than prospects you contact. The value proposition is entirely different in the two situations.

Here is a simple test that might scare you into value-based fees. Draw three columns. Label the first one "Strengths," the second one "Transfer Mechanism," and the third one "Results." Now, in column one, write down your five greatest strengths (good listener, M.B.A., international experience, outstanding writer, and so on). In the second column, write down the main transfer mechanisms you use to convey these strengths to the client (workshop, coaching, consulting, writing, facilitating, and so on). Finally, in the third column, write down five typical results your clients derive from working with you (higher profit, less attrition, reduced stress, better image, and so on).

Now step back and take a look. You are probably charging for the first two columns (your credentials or your time and materials) but not for the client results. It's time to change your focus. You are overdelivering and undercharging.

At this point, you have two excellent sources or indicators of the contribution you are providing to the client's improvement:

1. The stipulated value that the successful completion of the project will deliver to the client
2. The unique qualities that you, personally, bring to the equation to ensure that those results are met and exceeded

It's now time to appreciate the extent of this mutual "good deal."

## CREATING THE "GOOD DEAL" DYNAMIC

Customers buy cheap pens and expensive cars for the same reason: the purchase makes sense in terms of what they care to invest at that moment. The pen may be easily lost on the job and is used only for internal sign-offs on inventory, so the quality doesn't matter as long as the loss isn't too great when the pen inevitably disappears. In that case, 19 cents makes sense.

The car may cost $75,000, but there are few like it, you feel good in it, and you've always wanted one. You can now afford it. The emotional gratification more than compensates for the difference in the basic cost of transportation that could be saved with a less expensive vehicle.

In either case, it's a "good deal" for the customer. You have to make a "good deal" for the buyer. Note that this is more than merely a return on investment. That's because good deals are based on visceral and subjective needs as much as on analytical and objective needs (which is why you always want to stay away from the obsessively detailed denizens of the purchasing department). Focus on these "good deal" factors while building your relationship and establishing conceptual agreement (and find out which are most crucial to your buyer):

- Responsiveness (a plus for solo practitioners)
- Referral source (the transferred trust from the person referring you)
- Speed of completion

- Transfer of skills so that the client can replicate
- Using an "authority" or acknowledged "expert"
- Documentation
- Involvement of client personnel
- Confidentiality, nondisclosure, noncompete restrictions
- Use or transfer of proprietary material
- Guarantees and assurances
- Industry knowledge or experience[3]
- Accountability for tough decisions (you are the "black hat")
- Ability to travel and visit sites
- Technological compatibility
- Safety (malpractice insurance, liability insurance, and so on)[4]

Not all of these issues will apply. But you won't know unless you check for them. Also, you'll note that "fees" or "costs" are never mentioned as part of the "good deal" evaluation. That's because the good deal is based on value and not on fees. At no point are we attempting to establish a good deal on the basis of lower price, because a good deal must benefit both parties, and lower fees do not benefit the consultant. Consequently, fees should not be a part of this list.

---

Assess all the emotional and psychological factors that may prompt a buyer to perceive that he or she is getting a really good deal. That same process will enable you to raise fees, provided that the "good deal" is not about lowering fees!

---

[3]Although I'm not an advocate of industry specialization, if you just happen to have worked in the field, you probably have an advantage if you position it correctly.

[4]For example, a consultant cannot work for Hewlett-Packard without providing evidence of an in-force malpractice insurance policy.

The "good deal" equation for the buyer can include any or all of these variables:

- *Duration:* The benefits of the project are annualized and forever, while the fee is one time and fixed.
- *Skills Transfer:* The client's people will be able to do this themselves in the future, not only solving the immediate problem but also creating an internal capability for future problems.
- *Leading Edge:* The client will be assuming a leading-edge position in the industry, marketplace, community, or other environment; above and beyond the issue, the perception and image impact are substantial.
- *Control of One's Destiny:* Just by dint of doing something—hiring you—the client has extricated the organization from the morass; almost any action can have a positive effect,[5] even if results aren't immediately appreciated.

Ultimately, the equation might look like Figure 4.2.

$$\frac{\text{Tangible Outcomes} \times \text{Expected Duration of Outcomes} + \text{Intangible Outcomes} \times \text{Emotional Impact of Intangibles} + \text{Peripheral Benefits} + \text{Variables Positively Affected}}{\text{Fixed Investment Required}} = \text{Client's "Good Deal"}$$

**Figure 4.2** The "Good Deal" Equation.

---

VIGNETTE

An attorney at one of the largest consulting firms in the world told me that he was an advocate of value-based fees. His problem was that his accounting department insisted that all fees be expressed on an hourly

---

[5]The classic case being the near-legendary Hawthorne studies, which showed that raising the lighting positively affected performance, but so did lowering the lighting. It was the *attention*, not the actual light setting, that mattered in terms of productivity.

basis, and the result—in this case, $2,500 per hour—was impossible for even the most liberal and understanding client to swallow.

So even though a client company initially didn't mind paying $60,000 for the value of the attorney's consulting, it balked when the attorney's firm, which would bill only on the basis of actual time spent and not value delivered to the client, expressed it as a huge amount per hour.

The attorney asked my advice for how to handle the client. I told him not to handle the client but to handle his own operation. He had to go to his own CEO and explain that either he could reduce the fees he generated for the consulting firm by 80 percent or the CEO could pressure accounting into changing its procedures for recording and billing revenues. Would the CEO prefer to stick to the current outdated bookkeeping and $250,000 of revenue or a value-based system and over $1 million for the same work?

Not surprisingly, accounting soon found another way to record income.

There's no excuse for sticking to old ways that undercut profitability, either in large, bureaucratic firms or, especially, in small firms or solo practices.

The key is this: don't seek to lower the divisor by lowering fees; seek to increase the dividend (the benefits and peripherals) so that the quotient—the good deal—is maximized.

## THE INCREDIBLY POWERFUL "CHOICE OF YESES"

No client should ever have to make a "go or no-go" decision, yet that is exactly the narrow box that most consultants force on their buyers.

The psychological shift from "Should I use Alan?" to "How should I use Alan?" is enormous. The buyer, in the latter instance, actually enters into a collaboration with you to determine how best to apply your talents and use your contribution. The former, a binary choice, is a sales proposition; the latter, a pluralistic choice, is a partnership proposition.

> By simply providing options, you move the sale to an assumptive close and the fees to a "migratory range" that is ever upward. Every buyer wants to lower fees, but not one wants to lower value.

Another powerful effect of options is that they relentlessly drive fees upward. When confronted with three options, each one promising higher value for the client, the buyer will tend to move at least to the second and often to the third. This can't happen with a "take it or leave it" proposal. Buyers may seek to lower fees, but they also seek to maximize value.

Here is a brief example of options used in a project involving gathering employee feedback on desirable benefits to retain talent.

*Option 1:* We will conduct focus groups throughout the company, representing about 15 percent of the population. The value of these includes "self-sanctioning" groups, which will separate a "one-off" opinion from the prevailing opinions and also allow for follow-up and causal questions.

*Option 2:* We will also provide one-on-one interviews with about 5 percent of the population. This provides the opportunity to bolster the focus groups with confidential opinions, drawn at random, without exposing the individual to a larger group. People are often more candid in this situation, particularly those who are relatively unassertive in groups.

*Option 3:* We will provide a paper-and-pencil or Internet survey for all members of the population. This will bolster the other options, providing every employee the opportunity to provide feedback on a confidential and anonymous basis. Note that similar patterns that emerge from the three diverse avenues will be highly valid and most reliable.

*Option 4:* We will compare the results of whatever options you choose to benchmark studies we have conducted for other organizations, which will also give you a relative insight into your employees' desires and complaints compared to a wider general population.

*Option 5:* We will provide a series of workshops for your key managers on how to deal with, react to, discuss, and take action on the results of the studies just described. It's imperative that you have a plan in place to respond rapidly and accurately, without committing yourself to inappropriate solutions.

In this example, the first option (based on the overall value of the project to employee retention) might be priced at $45,000; the second (which includes the first) at $65,000; the third (which includes the first and second) at $95,000; and the fourth at an additional $35,000, regardless of which of the first three options are chosen. The fifth might be an additional $45,000. The buyer is in a position to determine whether to take the "risk" of a single avenue of feedback (which, if only one, you determine is best as a focus group) or whether to minimize that risk with other options, including preparing the management team for how to deal with that feedback (option 5). The decision as to whether to provide for management team training to accompany, say, option 2, is a far cry from deciding whether to proceed or not.

Such is the power of options. They can be used at any point in the sale (for example, "We can have a conference call this afternoon, I can call you alone tomorrow, or I can visit you on Monday—which do you prefer?") but are especially key in the proposal when providing for a basis for fees.

Once you've established a general fee range for your contribution based on the value generated (all the factors discussed previously in this chapter), you can then spread them across a "choice of yeses" to engage the buyer in the best outcome for the client.

---

Never place a buyer in a "go or no-go" dynamic, and never be constrained by a stated budget. If you really believe it's about value, then any budget can be adjusted by a buyer who perceives greater value than expected.

---

Here's a terrific hint for getting a fee even above the buyer's stated budget. When you provide the options, cite two that are within the budget and one—with even greater and perhaps irresistible value—above the budget. A client who can "find" $175,000 for a project can "find" another $50,000, if warranted. You never know until you ask. No client will ever say, "Be sure to quote me something above my budget." But with the "choice of yeses" approach, you can justifiably do that by providing options within the budget and an additional one that happens to be over the budget but also provides far greater value.

If you don't believe that this approach will work, consider how many times you've bought extras for your car, computer, phone, garden equipment, pool, or other possessions that you scarcely wanted at the time but then realized you couldn't live without. If the manufacturer or catalogue or store clerk hadn't brought them to your attention, you still wouldn't own them.

Here are ten guidelines for options, or the "choice of yeses":

1. It's OK to discuss possible options during conceptual agreement, but never assign any fees to them, ever. Simply impress on the buyer that he or she will have choices to make with varying degrees of value and protection against risk.
2. Don't "bundle." You're better off "unbundling." Most consultants don't have options because they place every single thing they are able to deliver in their "go or no-go" proposal, as if that's the only way to justify their value.
3. Keep a good distance between options. You don't want a mere $5,000 of separation. Each one must represent significantly more income to you.
4. Commensurately with option 3 in the example, make sure that each option clearly provides additional unquestioned value to the buyer. Simply promising more of something or greater frequency does not add value; it merely adds time and materials. For instance, in the sample list of options, there is no option for additional focus groups or interviews. Each option is clearly distinct.
5. Some options may include prior, lower-value ones, and others may stand alone no matter which prior option is chosen. In the example, options 1, 2, and 3 are mutually exclusive, each higher one containing the former; but options 4 and 5 can be combined with any of the first three.

6. Cite your options formally in your proposal, under a heading such as "Methodology and Options."[6]

7. Don't attach fees to the options. Cite the fees separately in the proposal under a heading such as "Terms and Conditions." This is because you want the buyer to focus solely on the value of each option and not immediately connect it with investment. Let the buyer make a mental choice prior to introducing the fee.

8. If a buyer says, "I like option 3, but I only have the budget for option 2," reply, "Fine, then option 2 it is." This is not a negotiation.

9. If a buyer asks for a slightly lower fee associated with a particular option, reply, "Fine, but what value would you like me to remove?" *Never* decrease a fee without decreasing perceived value.

10. Keep your options relatively simple. This is not rocket science. And be prepared to show the differences in value (or the decrease in project risk) as you work your way up the choices.

---

Don't use a fixed-fee formula. But do have some guidelines that you can apply until you're comfortable moving away from the "science" and toward the "art."

---

## SOME FORMULAS FOR THE FAINT OF HEART

I'm always being asked, "Well, you must really estimate days, right?" Wrong. I only estimate client value and my contribution to it.

I'm aware, however, that many of you will prefer help in the form of analytical science until the more intuitive art kicks in. (Don't forget that there is nothing wrong or unethical about the art form of value-based fees so long as the client believes that the resultant value more than justifies the investment in your help in gaining it.)

---

[6]For a formal template and illustrations, see my book *How to Write a Proposal That's Accepted Every Time.*

So for the first time anywhere, here are a formula and some other criteria for establishing value-based fees. While the engineers in the audience won't be pleased ("What's after the fourth decimal place?") and the lawyers will be discomfited ("What, exactly, do you mean by a 'fee'?"), I think the rest of you will at least be happy with the framework.

### The Step-by-Step Choice of Yeses

*Step 1:* Establish the value with the economic buyer in the conceptual agreement phase, after ascertaining objectives to be achieved and the measures of progress. (Questions to ask for the conceptual agreement components appear in the appendixes.)

*Step 2:* Establish your own value based on your uniqueness (why you, why now, why in this manner).

*Step 3:* Create your options, clearly delineated by increasing value. They may be cumulative or mutually exclusive.

*Step 4:* Given the value of the project, estimate a profound and significant return on the investment, working backward. In other words, if the buyer has stipulated a $2 million savings annualized, then a return of 20 to 1 on the first year alone would be represented by a $100,000 investment.

*Step 5:* Create your "choice of yeses" using that conservative 20-to-1 return rate as your least expensive option. Increase your other options by a factor of a minimum of 20 percent. In this case, option 2 would be $120,000, and option 3 would be $144,000 (20 percent above option 2).

*Step 6:* Now go back to step 2. If your own unique value is high on the why me, why now, why in this manner scale, add another 20 percent to each option. If your uniqueness is moderate, add 10 percent. If your uniqueness is low, don't add anything above the step 4 calculations.

*Step 7:* Look at the project objectives and value to the organization in their entirety, and then review your fees resulting from the first six steps. Ask yourself, "Is this a good deal—a bargain—for the client in view of the value, and is it a good deal for me in terms of large margins? If not, adjust up or down, but by no more than 15 percent. Then submit it.

*Step 8:* Stop worrying. You'll close about 60 to 80 percent of these deals, which is better than your prior rate (don't lie) and at higher profitability.

> The "formula" is simple, but the toughest part of this sale is to yourself, not the buyer.

If you must use a formula, fix it at 20 to 1 or better—in other words, 10 to 1 is just fine. Bolster your case with these beliefs (mainly for yourself):

- The client is probably spending more on warranties for copy machines and ruined postage than for your project.
- The value to the organization, if anything, is probably understated and conservative.
- Your fees are highly conservative (actually, a 5-to-1 return would be a great investment).
- You've probably underestimated your own uniqueness for this client.
- The value is based on first-year returns. The annualized basis would probably represent a return of 100 to 1.
- It doesn't matter whether you could have done it for $20,000 less or the client would have paid $20,000 more. The margins are still terrific for you, and the benefits still terrific for the buyer. That is all that matters.

If it appears that the toughest sell is to yourself, you've read between the lines quite accurately.

The key to even this formulaic approach is to work backward from the ultimate client value through your unique contribution to the current fee schedule spread over options. Do not work forward, trying to calculate the amount of time, number of days, volume of deliverables, or variety of tasks. They are commodities and, no matter what margin you add to these activities and commodities, it will be minuscule compared to your margin for a truly value-based approach.

The most conservative and even timid value-based approach will be far more lucrative to you, while highly attractive to the buyer, than the most aggressive time-and-materials calculation. Stop selling yourself short.

The formula presented here is meant as a "halfway house"—enough science to get you through until you've mastered the art form and it becomes second nature.

Finally, here is a strategic and conceptual "formula" for those who are really enthused by the idea of value-based fees and ready to try them:

$$\frac{\substack{\text{Tangible Outcomes} \times \text{Expected Duration of Outcomes} + \\ \text{Intangible Outcomes} \times \text{Emotional Impact of Intangibles} + \\ \text{Peripheral Benefits} + \text{Variables Positively Affected}}}{\text{Fixed Investment Required}} = \text{VALUE}$$

The tangible outcome and its annualized duration; plus the intangible benefits and the worth of those, emotionally, to the buyer; plus the peripheral benefits (such as being seen as thought leaders) times the number of people who will appreciate them—all of this divided by the investment—equals the value. How can you *not* demonstrate a huge ROI?

## CHAPTER ROI

- Conceptual agreement is at the heart of the value-based billing process. Any time invested in gaining conceptual agreement, based on a trusting relationship with a true economic buyer, will actually speed the sale at higher margins.
- Your own uniqueness is an essential component that only you can calculate. But it's as much based on self-esteem and self-belief as it is on any pragmatic background or history.
- The reciprocity of the "good deal" creates the win-win dynamic. The client deserves a good deal, but so do you. One is incomplete without the other.
- The "choice of yeses"—options—is the key tactic in moving a buyer to a consideration of value-based fees, and the propensity will be to move upward through increasing value. Never submit a proposal without options of distinctly different value propositions.
- You have an internal assessment about your own worth that you can calculate.

*Use the fee formula until you get comfortable, then let the art overtake the science. Remember that you never have to justify your fee basis to a client, and only low-level people will usually make such a demand. You only have to demonstrate the value of the outcomes. Fee setting is a time to be aggressive, not defensive.*

*If you can't articulate your own value, you can't very well suggest value-based fees. Look in the mirror, and practice on the toughest buyer of all. The first sale is to yourself.*

## CHAPTER 5

# How to Convert Existing Clients

## *Correcting Your Own Mistakes*

The most popular question I receive after "How do I create value-based fees?" is "How do I move existing clients from hourly billing to value-based fees?"

The answer is, "Very carefully."

You've spent a considerable amount of time educating those clients incorrectly—and you've been very effective at it. You've also consistently enabled their behavior by replying to their demands for hourly or daily rates, reductions in rates, reductions in time, and perhaps reduction in numbers of people. They've become quite comfortable using your services in the manner maximally beneficial to them and minimally beneficial to you.

Furthermore, you're highly credible! After all, your advice has been well received, your suggestions well taken, and your plans well thought through. Why shouldn't your billing scheme be as adept and effective as your consulting expertise?

Fortunately, that's the extent of the bad news. (I know, that's sufficient!) You've also developed a solid relationship with a buyer who would probably be very loath to see you leave, no matter how vigorous the protests against your fees and rates in the past. You also have a client base that permits you to set some criteria for which clients may be most suitable for "transfer" to a new billing arrangement. Finally, you're successful enough so that you might want to "fire" some clients rather than keep working with them on a basis that is unfair to you.

Nothing raises fees like your willingness to walk away from business. But remember, the first sale is always to yourself. While you don't want to take bread off the table, you also don't want your time so entangled with low-profit clients that you can't work for more and tastier bread in the future. We'll deal with that contingency in this chapter as well.

## SETTING PRIORITIES AMONG EXISTING CLIENTS

The first order of business is to establish the decision criteria to determine which clients even to approach. A general "triage" system works best:

1. High-potential clients for change to value-based projects
2. Clients who could go either way but require more work
3. Clients who will not change short of having their legs broken

To establish who's who on your list,[1] I've created the test in Exhibit 5.1.

---

[1]Since this series is aimed at highly successful consultants, my assumption is that your firm has a dozen to two dozen active clients and another dozen to two dozen periodic clients. But even if you have fewer than that, the criteria will still apply, and you should use them to differentiate among your buyers.

**Exhibit 5.1** Test to Determine the Potential to Shift a Client to Value-Based Fees.

Complete this form for those clients you might wish to convert to value-based fees. Use the following scale: 3 = yes, 2 = maybe, 1 = doubtful.

1. Does this client represent significant long-term business potential? _____

2. Has this client generally accepted your prior fee schedule with little protest? _____

3. Has this client provided you with a very senior or high-level buyer? _____

4. Does this client have multiple buyers you have sold to or can sell to? _____

5. Is this a client you would hate to lose? _____

6. Has this client generated a substantial return on your consulting work? _____

7. Has this client paid you promptly and never debated charges or fees? _____

8. Has this client ever said or implied, "Just do it and send us the bill"? _____

9. Does this client have a buyer with whom you are especially close? _____

10. Does this client serve as a reference or exemplar for other clients? _____

Add up your score.  Total score: _____

Here is the scoring key:

23 to 30: Client has high potential and deserves a change strategy.
14 to 22: Client has moderate potential; approach after first priorities.
0 to 21: Don't waste your time trying to convert this client.

Depending on your client base, you might have as few as three or four candidates or as many as a dozen or so. The key is to approach each one with a clear and customized strategy (which we'll talk about in the following sections). But the good news is that you've been able to establish some parameters for your efforts. In essence, the top priorities can't be lost, so while the goal is to move them to a value-based system, the essential is not to drive them away.

It's almost impossible to convert all current clients to value-based billing, but it's always possible to convert a few if you carefully establish your targets.

Conversely, the bottom-tier companies aren't worth your time anyway. (One of my tenets is to deliberately abandon the bottom 15 percent of your business at least every two years, and these are your candidates. See my book *Million Dollar Consulting* for the details.) You could, theoretically, simply announce the change in your billing to them and allow the majority to disappear. (They may well be one-time clients in any case.) Those in the middle will require individual decisions, but their potential isn't high enough to demand that kind of attention at the moment. You might as well continue to collect hourly rates until you're ready to deal with them.

Let's be clear: you don't want to lose significant clients; that's the bottom line. You would like to transfer as many of them as possible to value-based fees. That's the goal. Ignore low-potential clients, and focus on increasing perceived value to high-potential clients.

Once you've identified the top priorities with which to attempt conversion, you can build those plans into your normal visits. In other words, you can lay the groundwork during your regular interactions with the buyer, rather than spring the "new approach" on the buyer in one fell swoop.

Your best businesses are those that you don't want to lose at any cost but also those that you most want to convert to a true value-based approach. Don't abandon the latter need just because of the former fact.

That groundwork can be laid with the following dialogue, observations, and reminders with the buyer:

- "Your people indicate they'd like to call on me more often, but they're justifiably sensitive to 'running up a bill' every time they need me, despite the fact that I can provide immediate help."
- "Neither one of us can estimate how much time your request is going to require. I think we need to 'stop the meter' so that we can both invest whatever is necessary."
- "I've begun a new relationship with new clients, and I'd be remiss if I didn't offer it to my best clients. Could we put some time aside to discuss it on my next visit?"
- "I know you've been somewhat unhappy about a 'meter running' and uncapped costs. I'd like to suggest a way to change that dynamic that will help both of us."
- "I'd like to automatically be able to provide you with updates to my intellectual property whenever they develop."
- "I think we'd both feel better if I were able to perform audits on the progress every ninety days for at least a year."
- "You often have board meetings on Monday or early mornings during the week. It may be valuable for me to be available on some weekends or late nights for you."

Before we turn to the actual strategies, please keep these four critical factors in mind:

1. *Every* piece of new and potential business should be treated exclusively as a value-based prospect. Never offer any other kind of arrangement to new clients. Educate them correctly from the beginning.
2. The first sale is always to yourself. You must convince yourself first of the advantages to the buyer before you can effectively employ this change strategy.
3. Although the idea is to retain the client at all costs, you can't be fearful. Enthusiasm, assurance, and absolute belief carry the day. Hesitancy, tentativeness, and uncertainty will waste everyone's time.
4. You must provide additional value as perceived by your buyer.

## OFFERING NEW VALUE

The most important and most effective method for converting existing clients to a value-based fee system is to offer new value. There is no reason in the world for a client to move from your hourly or daily rate to a fixed fee for the exact same value the buyer is now receiving. Think about it: if people change only in accordance with their own self-interests ("What's in it for me?"), why abandon a clear, reasonable (that is, cheap), and long-standing billing arrangement?

Well, you abandon it if a new system provides more value and better appeals to their self-interest. I'm going to say that again: Clients will abandon an old system if a new system provides more value and better appeals to their self-interest.

If you focus on nothing else, focus on that. What new value can you offer the buyer in the next phase of the project, in a new project, or in the negotiation of a new agreement that will encourage consideration of switching to a value-based system? Remember our graphic from Chapter One, repeated in Figure 5.1. We have to create a dynamic in which the buyer appreciates the greater value inherent in a new, clear set of benefits so that the investment seems extraordinarily reasonable.

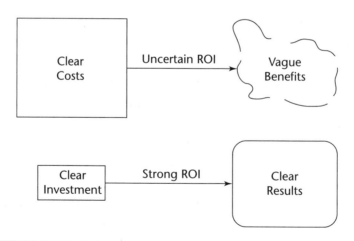

**Figure 5.1**  Revisiting ROI.

Here are some examples:

- I would pay more for postage if the postal service picked up at my door or delivered in the early morning.
- I would pay more for groceries if they were delivered (as they are in some major cities).
- I would pay more for copy services that also sent my work automatically to chosen destinations (which Kinko's will do).
- I would pay more for more leg room on an aircraft.
- I would pay more for technical assistance available twenty-four hours a day by phone.

You would pay more for your own set of high-value needs. Ergo, you must determine what your client would pay more for, since value-based pricing must provide more income than hourly or daily work.

---

You can't change your billing basis without creating a different value basis for the buyer. So focus on the latter in order to create the former.

---

Here are some generic methods to provide increased value with existing clients (whether on new projects, which are easier, or existing projects up for expansion or renewal). You can further modify and strengthen these with specific details for each unique client relationship.

## Unlimited Access

Provide "unlimited access" to you. That's not as severe as it sounds. At the moment, the client must make an investment decision every time you're needed ("Is this problem and Alan's help worth $4,500?"). That's a terrible position for the buyer to be in. Offer access at any time, subject to mutually convenient schedules, by phone, fax, e-mail, or in person, if needed.

No client will abuse this privilege (just as no executive was ever prohibited from performing by too many people walking through an "open door"). However, it does provide the immediate perception of far more extensive interaction for a fixed fee.

## New Services

Let's say you've been doing executive coaching. Introduce a 360-degree feedback intervention, and tell the buyer that you'd like to combine, in the buyer's best interests, the existing coaching work and the new instrument into a single fee for management coaching services. If you're helping with strategy formulation, offer a planning process that bridges to implementation. If you're doing diversity audits, offer a training package for managers to use the feedback properly.

New services, which might seem prohibitive on a per diem, cumulative basis, will seem like a bargain when combined with ongoing services under a single fee for a finite time frame.

## Wider Access

Demonstrate that the results you've been generating for the financial area can be readily duplicated in other support areas: human resources, MIS, legal, and so forth. But show that the current hourly basis will be unnecessarily severe, since a great deal of the work is repetitive.

Offer to combine as many other operations as requested under a single fee (even if various budgets contribute to it).

## Combined Buyers

If your projects typically involve several buyers who each contribute to the budget, then suggest that by operating under a single fee, their respective contributions are capped, they no longer have to battle about who should pay for which aspect, and you can be responsive to all of them without additional investment.

Value-based fees can be strong compromises for the client who is unsure which budgets should be used, how to charge back time, and how often to take advantage of the consultant as a resource.

> You are capable of offering much more value than you are currently providing. You're probably in a rut no better than your client in terms of your utilization. Make sure you know the total value of offerings you can provide before approaching the client.

## New Access Points

Perhaps you can provide a special set of Web pages to that client only, using a password; or you can create a newsletter oriented toward the client's employees; or you can arrange a special toll-free number; or you can place the client's logo in books that are ordered from you. As part of a value-based proposition, find new and unique access points so that the client feels a more comprehensive relationship.

Don't be afraid to ask the buyer what he or she would find most desirable in terms of a more comprehensive, sustained, and interactive partnership. You may be able to provide the desired service at virtually no cost but use it as the basis for a higher, value-based fee.

Finally, discipline yourself to unbundle the potential value propositions that you can deliver to a client. Use an easel sheet or a spreadsheet or have a colleague help you determine the full array of services you can deliver. I guarantee you that (1) it's far more than you think or (2) it's all combined into a single, grand alternative that you deliver each time.

## "Membership" in Perceived Benefit

This can include an "insider" Web site or newsletter, automatic provision of "best practices" regularly from around the globe, discounts from other professional service providers, and joint bylines on articles contributed to by the client.

Use the strength of your own community to include excellent clients in interactions (breakfasts, teleconferences, chat rooms, and so on) only available to your elite buyers.

## FINDING NEW BUYERS WITHIN EXISTING CLIENTS

If you operate in the small-business, closely held market (for my examples, under $50 million in revenues), there is probably a single buyer who is the owner or CEO. But in larger markets, there are scores or even hundreds of buyers. The problem is that we don't reach out laterally while we're effectively delivering our consulting help.

A new buyer within an existing business does not necessarily have to undertake a project with you on the same basis as others have. The important strategy is to refrain from educating the new buyers incorrectly, as you have the existing buyers!

The advantages of new buyers within existing businesses include the following:

- There are no marketing or acquisition costs.
- The buyers have heard of you or can readily become familiar with your work elsewhere within that client system.
- They respect and know the people who have hired you in the past.

- They are probably not familiar with your prior billing policy.
- It's easy to see them and to accommodate their schedules, since you're onsite frequently.
- Results you've generated elsewhere can be made relevant for them.

> Most consultants refrain from reaching out to new buyers because of self-imposed limitations. As long as you're doing a good job for the current client, why should anyone object?

Remember that buyers are seldom perched solely at the very peak of the organizational hierarchy. They need to meet only two criteria:

1. Does your value proposition enhance their goals (their self-interests) professionally or personally?
2. Can they write a check (or cause the computer to disgorge one) to acquire that value?

I've seen consultants virtually wade through groups of potential buyers while hurriedly on their way to the cafeteria. That's a lost opportunity. You have to be willing to do a little marketing while you're on the client site.

How do you do that gracefully? Well, if you believe that new buyers within the client organization represent new sales that can be placed on a value basis, then they deserve quite a bit of effort. Here are seven tactics to reach them efficiently and effectively:

1. Ask your current buyer for recommendations. This is anathema to many consultants, but a pleased buyer should have no hesitation about sharing your value in the company so long as that buyer is not shortchanged. (In fact, in terms of self-interest, the buyer can often claim credit for "discovering" you.) The salient point here is to ask and even to seek an introduction. This is the single most overlooked avenue of expanded business and potential conversion business (to a value basis).

2. Seek out meetings at which to present your reports and suggest that "interested others" and support groups attend. I've presented results at any number of management meetings where people have come up to me and asked, "Can you do that same thing for a support organization?" or "Is it possible to do that overseas?" Guess what? It always is.

3. Listen for key names of power brokers, and when you find yourself with them for any reason at all, introduce yourself. After a second or third encounter, ask them for some time to discuss the ramifications of your work in their area.

4. Publish in the organization's house organ or, even better, allow them to interview you and discuss the results of your work. I once received a six-page, color spread in Merck's in-house magazine on my ethics audits, which brought inquiries from managers I had never even heard of. This is a very effective, objective way to reach out to other buyers.

5. Offer to brief support units, internal customers, internal suppliers, and any other even remotely interested parties. Explain to your client that a synopsis of your work might help others help your client and that sharing the work will certainly earn admiration in any case. One-on-one or small group briefings are usually the best, since you want to focus only on potential decision makers.

6. Volunteer within the company. I've donated to company-sponsored charities, attended award ceremonies, participated in picnics and recreational opportunities, and tried to become a "part of the crowd." You never know who you'll wind up meeting in comfortable, social, and convivial circumstances.

7. Monitor personal changes, promotions, transfers, and other internal events. You never know when someone with whom you've had positive interactions moves into a buying position. It helps to read the house organ, bulletin boards, and other in-house media and to use things like Google Alerts to receive any press releases sent out by your client.

Finding new buyers within existing clients is essential for any highly successful consultant but absolutely critical for the consultant who wants to convert existing, high-potential hourly clients into long-term value-based clients. Start off with them as "new" clients whom you can educate properly.

> We tend to view change as threatening. We must view it as opportunity. Every client change represents a potential new piece of business. But you can't just sit back to see what happens. We're not here to put a toe in the water. We're here to make waves.

## FINDING NEW CIRCUMSTANCES

The final tactic for converting clients to value-based pricing is to find some new client, market, or environmental circumstance that supports the reasoning for such a change at this particular juncture.

Some new circumstances will be obvious, but others are more subtle. Yet all can serve as your "transfer mechanism." Here are some examples:

*The Great Year.* The client has had an outstanding year, not least in part thanks to your assistance. Suggest to the buyer that this is a time to consider a more comprehensive and more flexible relationship. Also, never neglect the fact that at the end of any budget year, there are funds often crying to be used or lost. It's tough to put those funds against hourly billing that is not based on any specific amount of hours, but it's relatively easy to put those funds against a clear-cut $100,000 project.

*The Horrible Year.* Your client might have had a disaster, not due to anything you did, of course. There might have been some client defections, unexpected costs, loss of technology, whatever. If the client is happy with your help, however, suggest an easier and less burdensome way to work with you next year, since the fees will be capped, fixed, and otherwise locked in cement. That way, you can't be part of an escalating cost problem, and you can't be cut in a client's effort to address a cost problem. That's win-win.

*The New Buyer.* Most consultants search for arsenic when their buyer is promoted, fired, replaced, transferred, or otherwise misplaced. But this is really an opportunity to educate a new buyer correctly, rather than try to reeducate an old one accustomed to old habits. View a new buyer as an opportunity, and don't allow past practices to continue (hourly fees) without strong resistance (in the form of the buyer's self-interest).

*The Acquisition.* Chaos generally ensues when even the most orderly acquisition is contemplated and consummated. Suggest that this is the time to simplify everything possible, including your billing arrangements. The acquisition might also present an opportunity in terms of the other conversion factors (such as a new buyer) we have discussed.

*The Divestiture.* Although not strictly within the existing client, the new spun-off or purchased unit probably represents high potential for you because you were familiar with it when it was still part of the original organization. Do your best to remain in contact with current acquaintances moving into the new configuration.

*The Competition.* If the competition has pulled a surprise or the competitive marketplace is heating up, suggest that the increasing demands and uncertainties create an unfair situation for the client on any kind of per diem basis. Since ambiguity makes it nearly impossible to calculate hours or time, offer a set fee to create at least some order out of the uncertainty.

*The New Initiative.* Almost every organization regularly trots out a new initiative, hot product, reinvention of itself, or some other strategic change (often fostered by a new leader in a key position or the latest academic's fad). Jump on that bandwagon, and use the initiative as an excuse to alter the past fee basis.

*The Travel Need.* Where travel is a necessary aspect of your project—especially international travel—demonstrate that per diem fees often keep running, although you're just traveling from one place to another. (If you don't charge when you spend two days flying and acclimating to Europe or Asia, you're suffering from more than merely jet lag—you're crazy.) A value-based project fee, including all travel time (although, of course, not travel reimbursement),[2] will remove that unnecessary expense.

> Don't take the position that you have to "slip in" an attempt to convert an existing client to a value basis. Use an opportunity or event to demonstrate why it's the perfect time to do so.

---

[2]There is nothing wrong with including all your projected travel costs in your fee, as long as you feel you have a firm idea of what they will be. That's even a purer billing form, since everything is included.

Within your existing clients who are still on a time-and-materials basis, be alert for opportunities to promote a change to value-based fees. In fact, you can use this "new circumstances" approach with your moderate-priority clients as well.

---

**PRACTICUM**

Take the high-priority clients you arrived at earlier in this chapter and apply the new value, new buyers, and new circumstances factors to each. Whichever ones offer the most opportunity in these areas become the highest of the high priority. They should be on your list for an immediate conversion strategy.

---

## WHAT IF CLIENTS RESIST CONVERSION?

Don't push so hard that you cause ill will if your clients resist converting. Position your intent as serving their best interests, and point out that other clients—and all new clients—have chosen to take advantage of the new arrangement. But by offering them this as an option, you're not taking bread off the table, since the client may still choose to continue along the current path.

If your top-priority clients resist, here is the course of action that might still win the day later on:

1. Don't persist, but do remind. Once a quarter, remind your buyer that the option is still on the table. Every time one of the conversion opportunities discussed in this chapter arises, raise the issue again as the basis for a decision about the new project. There is too much potential profit at stake not to remain persistent, and the more money you make from a client who is resisting a value-based approach, the more money you are actually losing over the long term.

2. Appeal to the buyer's sense of fair play. If you can demonstrate a multimillion-dollar savings or improvement (see Chapter Four for objectives, metrics, and value), and you can show that your total hourly fees added up to 0.001 percent of that improvement (which they well may have), you do have a case to point out that future projects should be more of a win-win endeavor.

Many buyers will be reluctant to allow a disproportionate situation to persist if they envision needing your help on an even larger scale in the future.

3. For some clients, you may be able to cite their own methods as a justification for how you should be treated. Does the client charge for value (everyone from automakers to restaurants actually do), or do they charge by the hour and are themselves unhappy about their own meager profitability?

4. Try to arrive at a halfway point by influencing the buyer to commit to a minimum amount of time, guaranteeing you some basic revenue figure. Point out that you've had to put blocks of time aside in anticipation of the client's needs and often short-term demands and that some quid pro quo is appropriate. It's less of a jump from guaranteed fees based on minimum days to value-based projects.

5. Provide the client with some independent endorsement of the value of project fees over time and materials. Use some third-party articles, trade journals, newsletters, and whatever else you can find that objectively demonstrate to the client that he or she is falling out of step with the times.

6. Revisit at the proper time. The buyer may change, conditions may change, and finances may change. Don't take a refusal as a permanent denial. Simply bide your time and make another attempt when the situation seems better for you.

If you have a strong relationship with these clients and you continue to deliver results, they have the option of continuing as they have been, and there is only a minuscule chance of losing them by asking them to consider a different fee basis. However, you are at great potential risk if you choose not to do this out of fear of losing them, since the more work you obtain from them, the more profit you are leaving on the table.

> You only have 100 percent of your energy and resources to apply. Wasting any amount of this on nonpromising and underperforming business is negligent behavior. You must abandon a portion of your business periodically because no one else will do it for you. The worst clients tend to be the most loyal.

# ABANDONING BUSINESS

This has remained one of the most controversial concepts I've ever introduced but also one of the most powerful in providing consultants with the means to acquire higher-profit, value-based clients.

We become accustomed to certain kinds of business. We tend not to question that business but rather to allow it to accrete, like a stalactite growing from the ceiling of our office. It's always been there. Why fret about it now?

Unless we abandon business regularly, we give ourselves no leeway to reach out for new and more profitable business. Our time is usurped and our energies depleted by business that not only can't be converted to more lucrative arrangements but is actively impeding us from converting (or acquiring) other, higher-potential business.

We tend to rationalize hanging on to certain business with a death grip, reassuring ourselves with platitudes:

- They were there when we needed them. Early business that helped pay the bills is not something we easily forget.
- The job's easy to do. (We don't feel we're really exerting ourselves, so why not? It beats working hard.)
- It's fun. (We love the adulation or the experience or the environment. Our ego is rewarded, and it brightens our day.)
- We have an enduring friendship. (The buyer or others have become friends to whom we feel we owe an allegiance beyond mere business considerations. We don't want to jeopardize that relationship.)
- We're throwing good money after bad. (We've been promised, time and time again, "exposure" for our earlier, inexpensive work, and we still haven't cashed in. Like poker players who have gone too far in a hand they can't possibly win, we're reluctant to cut our losses.)
- We have the time. (The erroneous belief that "something is better than nothing" drives us to accept and perpetuate questionable business.)
- What if other business disappears? How can we then justify cutting this business loose? (Actually, not cutting it loose will cause other business not to appear.)
- We're trapped. (Scope creep and constant concessions have built up a raft of commitments that we honestly won't ever be able to discharge, not

unlike miners who, despite their pay, were forever in debt to the company store. Remember the song "Sixteen Tons"? Okay, I'm older than you.)

- We feel it's a personal failure to lose a client, even if we initiate the departure. (Don't take it personally; it's just smart business.)

> You simply have to let go in order to reach out. There is no way to both hold on to past unprofitable business and to acquire future, highly profitable business. Given that mutually exclusive state, is this really that tough a decision?

Abandoning business doesn't have to be as draconian as it sounds. First, make an objective assessment of all of your business every eighteen months or so. (Do it between fiscal years so you won't be influenced by your own planning needs.) Ask yourself these questions about each single client:

- Am I learning regularly?
- Am I still adding value that others can't?
- Am I being paid as well and is my profit as great as with new clients?
- Am I being stretched and forced to grow?
- Am I introducing new products and services on a regular basis?
- Am I using the client as a referral or springboard into other systems?
- Am I able to experiment or use marketing leverage in this "lab"?
- Am I enjoying this project and having fun?

If the answer to two or more questions (it doesn't matter which questions) is no, plan to move on.

Next, contact the client and arrange for a constructive transfer to another consultant. There is no need to leave the client high and dry. Simply point out the answers to your own questions ("I'm not learning, and I'm no longer contributing unique value") and arrange for someone to take on the project who will see it—at this point in his or her career—as thrilling, subject to further improvement, and lucrative. Remain on board for a time or until the next renewal, or depart as soon as new introductions are made. But get out.

My advice, by the way, is not to subcontract this or otherwise take a "piece of the action," such as a referral fee. Doing so ethically obligates you to be accountable for the outcome and may leave you continually accessible to the client (directly or through the new consultant). Cut the cord, forsake the revenue, and move on.

If the client balks about "abandonment," simply point out that it's really in the client's best interest. You can't afford the requisite time any longer, and the client will be better served with "new blood." You're still around in case of emergency, and you can continue whatever social relationships might be in place if you care to.

Danger: If the client responds with an offer of more money, which sometimes happens (because you've been working so cheaply), turn it down cold. The new amount will still be less than your new margin goals, and your time will be usurped as much as, if not more than, before in return for an insignificant increase in fees. Don't be lured by the client's guilty conscience.

Finally, remain in touch, and use the client as a reference and referral source. Maintain a friendly relationship, although not a business one. You're actually doing the client a favor, and you shouldn't feel the need to skulk out the door.

Unless you deliberately, proactively, and methodically abandon business, you'll be unable to convert any higher-priority clients to a value-based approach, nor will you have the time to acquire new business at the rate or pace that makes sense.

You have to let go to reach out. Let go of those who can most easily go their own way before more important clients let go of you.

## CHAPTER ROI

- Existing clients can be converted to value-based clients, but you must set a careful priority.
- Never take bread off the table: offer the option to continue the current relationship or to change. Sweeten the latter by pointing out that new clients prefer it, and you'd be remiss if you didn't offer it to existing important clients.
- Always offer more value, find new buyers, or look for new circumstances. The change must always be clearly perceived as in the buyer's best interests.

- You can use the test in Exhibit 5.1 to determine the highest-potential opportunities and then devise a strategy around each particular client.
- Approach only a few clients at a time, because the process demands careful and rapt attention. The buyer must clearly see the increased value, so be prepared to demonstrate that improved condition (for example, "unlimited access" to your time and expertise).
- The lowest-priority clients for conversion are also those who are your highest priority for dropping. Every eighteen months or so, you should systematically examine your client base—again using objective templates and criteria—to determine which ones you can let go of in order to reach out to new and more lucrative business.
- All new business should be approached as value-based prospects and should never be given the option of a time-based or time-and-materials arrangement. By also culling out and setting priorities among your existing business, you should be able to convert your practice to an entirely value-based one in a few short years. That alone will represent a dramatic increase in your profits without any substantial increase in your work.
- Don't give up. Try at various times as conditions warrant. They can't say yes if you stop asking them.

*Don't try to convert every client to value-based fees, and don't stop trying if some balk or resist. If you convert one or two high-potential clients, you will have created huge new margins for yourself. Life is about success, not perfection.*

# The Case of the Loaded Loading Dock

I once worked for a training firm that charged either by the number of boxes of training material purchased or the number of people sitting in a room. This is the antipodal position from value-based fees, and it's why I swore I would never get into that business again once I left it.

Essentially, whatever the printing presses, on site long before digital printing, could disgorge onto the loading dock, we were to sell. As the year wore on and we were closer to year-end, the more the dock filled and the harder we sold. To give you an idea, we sold two-thirds of our total revenue in the fourth quarter and two-thirds of the fourth quarter in December.

As you can imagine, many of our clients caught on to our predicament and deliberately waited to buy near the end of the year, fully aware that we were desperate to clear the loading dock. Thus we drove our own prices down, offering "fire sales" that our clients became conditioned to anticipate. That meant that we had to sell even more material to make up for the lower prices.

It was a vicious cycle, repeated each year with the repetition and discipline of penguins marching to the pole to lay eggs that had only a 50 percent chance of hatching.

It dawned on me at some point that we were not driven by our technology, our clients, our markets, or even our products. We were driven by the printing presses. We were actually a production-driven outfit, no less than U.S. Steel or International Paper. This wasn't the professional services future I had in mind for myself!

Don't allow your production ability to determine what you sell or what you charge. In the depths of oversupply of paper, the big paper companies used to reduce prices and take deliberate losses, since that was cheaper than shutting down the papermaking machines!

Don't burden yourself with delivery people, software, inventory, and other stuff that demands that you unload it, use it, or move it.

*Moral: If you live to move materials, hire a moving company, but don't go into consulting.*

# 6

# The Fine and High Art of Using Retainers

## *It's Just the Smarts, Stupid*

There is a difference in my book (and this is, of course, my book) between value-based fees and retainer fees. While both are in the same ball park, the view of the field is different in this regard.

A *value-based fee* is compensation paid by the client in exchange for the consultant's contribution to the ultimate value (improved condition) that the client agrees will be derived. Value-based fees concern projects of finite scope.

A *retainer fee* is compensation paid by the client in exchange for access to the consultant and the consultant's talents for a specified interval. Retainer fees concern time periods of finite duration.

(Just to keep the record straight, a *contingency fee,* which I don't favor for reasons cited earlier in the book, is compensation paid by the client as a fixed percentage of a stipulated financial outcome at a certain point in time. Contingency fees, often called "performance fees," concern percentages of monetary gain.)

I've been engaged in retainer fee relationships frequently. I think they make sense under the right conditions, and they can be a wonderful source of ongoing and predictable income in a profession known for uncertain and vacillating cash flow. However, they can also be dysfunctional and unprofitable if they are not controlled and managed properly.

One final caveat: I am not using the term *retainer* in the traditional lawyer's sense, which is a fixed amount of money from which payment is drawn periodically based on the lawyer's hourly billing rate. That is simply a deposit against hourly bills. "We've retained counsel" actually means "We've paid a lawyer deposit so that they'll show up because they don't trust us to pay them after they show up." If that is what you are intent on doing, go back to Chapter One and start over.

## OPTIMAL CONDITIONS FOR RETAINER ARRANGEMENTS

First, understand that there is no "project" here (there is no "there" there). The client seeks access to your smarts, pure and simple. (Thus it's not unusual for clients who have engaged you for several successful projects to request you on a retainer basis for the future, but it's unusual—although not impossible—to begin a brand-new client relationship on retainer.)

Contrary to the prior sections of this book, the results are not the key consideration here, although they are important. It's the access to your counsel that is the paramount issue. Do not mistake that fact. Your very relationship and the interactions resulting from it become the value, since there are no specific project results in a true retainer relationship.

Most independent consultants find this hard to comprehend: the mere access to your advice and counsel is of significant value to the client. Hence the degree to which that access is used is minor compared to the comforting knowledge that it is there. You are a life insurance policy, in a sense, and the more important the executive life, the more there is riding on it, the higher the premium payment.

Notice that I haven't said that a retainer represents your time. Nor have I positioned a retainer as the value of your presence. It's the client's opportunity to approach you—to approach you, not for you to approach the client—that is the great value here. In other words, don't worry about the nature of the issue, don't worry about the timing, and don't worry about any arbitrary project scope. "If you, buyer, have need for my expertise, just call."[1]

> You must get comfortable with the idea that access to you is of inherent value. If you don't, the retainer will be an albatross, flying after you everywhere, insisting that you show up, engage in work, clean the tables in the cafeteria, and demonstrate that you're doing something.

Here are my criteria for the best conditions—those optimally favorable to the consultant—for the establishment of retainer business.

## Ten Criteria for Lucrative Retainer Agreement Conditions

1. *The Client Is Educated That Access Is the Value.* The client has no intent to use you as a de facto marketing vice president or chief of staff. Nor does the client believe he or she is entitled to see you three days a week, regardless of need. Nor is this a "make work" exercise if you're not actively engaged for a time. The client is paying for your availability and your smarts on an "as needed" basis, no more and no less.

2. *The Client Understands That Access Is Not Instantaneous.* You cannot be instantly available. (Try getting your doctor or attorney to be there the moment you need them.) The idea is to create reasonable expectations of access. In my case, I return all calls within ninety minutes, all e-mail within a day, and all correspondence within a week. Onsite work is subject to mutually agreeable scheduling, although appointments planned in advance will always have top priority and are unshakable in my retainer work. The key aspect of "access" is "responsiveness," not omnipresence.

---

[1] We are going to discuss a little later how to handle retainers that magically begin to generate projects that would otherwise engender a value-based fee. So if that's on your mind, just be patient and read on.

3. *There Is Agreement About Who Has Access.* In most cases, retainers are with a single person. However, there may be times when a team has the access (which costs more; we'll get to that shortly). The people with access must be designated in advance. Otherwise, you can find yourself with a dozen members of the management team demanding your help at all hours and the dreaded "scope creep" has become a demon in what had once appeared to be a very effective retainer arrangement.

4. *Access Must Be Unlimited for the Client.* You can't position some times as more important or convenient than others or declare a block of time "off limits." You would then be driving the client toward certain restrictions, which devalues your access. Actually, when an occasional client calls me on a Sunday night with a special request for advice before an important Monday morning meeting, I'm quite pleased. First, I'm providing tremendous real-time value, and second, I'm doing it from the comfort of my home, not having to make a trip to the client. What could be better than that?

---

If you don't equate "access" with physical presence, you can actually accommodate quite a few retainer clients at once. Why can't consultants telecommute?

---

5. *Payment Must Be in Advance of the Time Frame.* The quid pro quo for unlimited access is payment in advance. If your retainer is for a month, get paid on the first of the month (not thirty days net); if it's quarterly, get paid at the beginning of the quarter. You cannot run the risk of unlimited access for any significant length of time without payment in your pocket. (The longer the time period, the greater the discount offered. For example, if the monthly retainer is $10,000, a quarterly retainer option for that client might be $27,000, providing a 10 percent discount; a half-year might be $50,000—but of course, paid in advance.)

6. *Boundaries Are Established.* You and the client agree on access but nothing beyond that without further compensation. For example, expenses are extra, as would be any subcontracting required. If the client asks that you conduct a survey or run focus groups or serve in court as an expert witness during the course of the retainer, all of those services and the resultant value demand additional fees. While access to you is unlimited, what you will provide after being accessed clearly is not.

**110**

7. *The Time Frame Is Finite and Not Turned On and Off.* If the client doesn't access you for two weeks, that's life. You're providing access during a given, finite time frame, not a cumulative time frame of access. The client can't extend the current retainer by saying, "But we didn't use you last week." You may, at your discretion, provide the client with the ability to formally request a "freeze" or "timeout" if business or personal demands preclude access to you, but I would do this very sparingly, as in "never."

8. *The Procedure for Renewal Is Clear.* Repeat business always beats new business (no cost of acquisition), and that holds true in retainer relationships as well. Establish a time frame (for example, the end of the second month of a three-month retainer or the third week in a one-month retainer) during which you and the client can mutually decide to continue for another time frame (or even a more extended one) or either of you can end the arrangement at the conclusion of the current time frame. It's mutual continuance or unilateral discontinuance. The key here is to allow you to bail out if you wish but also to guarantee the next time frame and advance payment if all is going well for both of you. Do not wait for the end of the retainer period to do this.

9. *Carve Out High-Priority Potential Areas for Collaboration.* You might indicate to the buyer that you've both agreed that sales retention or commercialization in R&D or acquisition evaluation will be the primary focus of your collaboration. In this way, you have the ability to follow up and pursue certain issues with the buyer. Although it may seem ideal, receiving a retainer and not being accessed at all will guarantee just one thing: no renewal business. So if access to you isn't being taken advantage of, you need a basis for "priming the pump." That can be established at the outset so that you have a reasonable premise for contacting the buyer on occasion.

10. *Always Stress That This Is a Collaboration.* A retainer arrangement generally represents a pure counseling role, an advisory relationship, and a partnership. It is far more like coaching than consulting in that regard. It's about ongoing advice, not temporary wins and losses. Keep your eye (and your client's eye) on the larger picture. A retainer does not fail because a new, highly sought employee leaves for the competition, but it does fail if the client either doesn't access your advice or ignores your advice about a strategy for finding and retaining top talent in a competitive market.

Here is a summary of the points just made, distilled down to the three key dimensions for pricing retainers and one prime directive for successfully implementing them.

> Retainers can select a variety of time frames, but they shouldn't be too short or too long. Both extremes weaken the value of the relationship.

## Three Key Dimensions

1. *Time Frame.* The length of the retainer must be stipulated. The client may renew, but there has to be some understanding of the extent. I suggest a three-month minimum, with a decision to renew or not midway through the third month. But you may choose shorter or longer retainers based on the client's confidence, needs, and comfort level. Always try to be paid at the outset of the time period.

2. *Numbers.* Usually you are on retainer to the buyer. However, the buyer may decide to include his or her team or a few colleagues or a trusted subordinate. You must make clear exactly who has access to you. You don't want the client's secretary calling you to review a memo that's going to be sent out. It's difficult to be on retainer to more than three or four people in one company, and try not to accept lower-level people, who will tend to contact you for tactical decisions and problems.

3. *Scope.* What are the conditions of your access? Is it during East Coast U.S. business hours, Monday through Friday, or also West Coast business hours? Does it include after-hours and weekend consultations? Is it solely by phone and e-mail, or will it include mutually convenient onsite visits? You get the idea. What is the extent of your involvement and your availability?

## The Prime Directive

You cannot allow guilt or poor self-esteem to enter this picture. In other words, if the client doesn't use your help for a month, don't go begging for work. Never feel that you owe more than you are providing. An insurance policy is valuable because it's there, not because it's used daily (presumably, life insurance is used only once, and not happily). Understand that your availability and potential access are the value, and you are fulfilling that every day, whether or not you are engaged with the client. While that is nirvana to me, it seems to create overwhelming guilt for far too many consultants.

## CHOOSING TIME FRAMES AND CREATING REALISTIC EXPECTATIONS

Retainers are not ideal for very brief or very long durations unless they are periodically renewed, and even those relationships have problems caused by their longevity.

First, retainers that are too short don't give the buyer enough time to access your help under a variety of conditions, to allow truly valuable applications for your advice to arise, or to let you become adept at this particular arrangement with this particular buyer. I believe that the absolute minimum time frame for a retainer is a month, but two months is far better, and a quarter is ideal. For a single month, the buyer could encounter an event that usurps all of his or her time, and you might not be called on at all. (Even though you could choose to extend the retainer "on the house," it sets a bad precedent.)

Second, however, overly long retainers cause the buyer to question the value if you've become so successful at advising (and transferring your skills to the buyer) that toward the end of the arrangement there is much less contact and much less perceived value on the buyer's part.

I believe that the fairest retainers are probably for ninety-day periods, and they can renew at the end of that time on the same terms (if the client demurs but then wants to renew after the retainer is completed, you're perfectly justified in raising the retainer fee—that's why the sixty-day option is there—as part of the client's benefit). If you feel strongly about six months, so be it; there's nothing written in stone here. But you are probably far better off with two years' worth of retainer that has renewed every quarter or every half-year than you are with attempting two annual ones.

The problems, however, with even long-term, frequently renewed retainers include the following:

- You become perceived as the buyer's "hit man" (or "hit person") and not as an objective observer.
- You have come to represent a single interest and a single point of view. You've probably developed a social or at least personal relationship with the buyer.

> Long-term retainers can turn you into a member of management, which immediately devalues your role as a consultant and therefore ultimately undermines your fee structure.

- One of your initial high-value components, objectivity, is lost when you become so familiar with and immersed in one client that your nose is pressed too tightly against the glass.
- The retainer account may actually become eligible for that bottom 15 percent that requires jettisoning (see Chapter Five) because it's no longer interesting, you're no longer learning, and you no longer bring energy and innovation to the equation.

## Quick Tips for Gaining High-Value, High-Profit Retainers

Here are some guidelines to use to set the optimal conditions for success with a buyer in a retainer relationship:

1. Define access. It doesn't mean constant availability (recall our earlier discussion of scope).
2. Provide unique value to the access. You might provide your home, cell, and car phone numbers, which are normally never provided (nor should they be) to conventional clients.
3. Set your calendar to intervene in silences. If you haven't heard from a buyer in, say, ten days, I'd make a call or send an e-mail, just to remind the buyer that you're there if needed. That gesture can help substantiate your value, even if the client hasn't called you. But don't beg for work. Simply say, "How are you doing?"
4. Ask the client for unique access. Is there a way to circumvent a secretary or voice-mail? Might you have the buyer's home number? Is there an unscreened e-mail address?
5. Go above and beyond in an obvious manner. Let the client know you'll reschedule something noncritical to meet the buyer's urgent schedule.

Review a lengthy report overnight, even though it's an imposition. Talk to a client's customer whom the client is afraid of losing, even if it's not an agreed part of the deal.

6. Don't promise too much. You can't really reduce turnover, improve sales, or increase market share on this basis. (You can take on projects in those areas, but in the next section of this chapter you'll find advice on the best ways to accommodate—and charge—for that.) What you can do is give the buyer peace of mind and improved skills, as well as validation for the buyer's thinking.

7. Remember that as a consultant, you seldom surprise people who know what they're doing. In other words, merely verifying that a position or course of action makes sense to you as an objective outsider is often sufficient. You don't have to help the client reinvent the fax machine.

8. Do some studying. Although I've stated often that consultants are process experts and not necessarily industry or content experts, it nonetheless helps when you become more proficient in the type of business that has hired you on retainer. Read the trade magazines and do an Internet search periodically. Learn your client's lingo, and study your customer's customers.

9. Push back as needed. You're not there to salve the buyer's ego but rather to help make the buyer successful. Take risks. Jeopardize the relationship if it means saving the buyer from himself.

10. Finally, be willing to walk away. It's unethical to sit back and keep the money if you believe that a long-term retainer isn't working. Sometimes you and the buyer made a mistake. Think of future business and future referrals, and suggest that the current arrangement be ended with a prorated refund or credit toward future projects. This is the height of professionalism, and it justifies high fees.

---

Not all retainers will work out well, even when undertaken with great respect and mutual investment in the relationship. If it's not working, it's much better for you to suggest that it end. Always think of future business, not your current bank account.

---

# ORGANIZING THE SCOPE AND MANAGING PROJECTS WITHIN THE RETAINER

One of the most common problems with retainer assignments is that more traditional consulting projects "crop up" in their midst, like mushrooms after a thunderstorm. One day you're on retainer, and the next you're surrounded by projects.

Consultants generally worry that their retainer has become a "catch-all" for projects that in and of themselves would represent more lucrative assignments if taken on in a value-based billing system. And they're right.

You have to make clear to the client that any discrete projects that may arise during the retainer's time frame are not included in the fee for the retainer itself, and this is easier said than done. The major problems and challenges follow, and they shouldn't be taken lightly because they impinge on your effectiveness for the client and, quite realistically, your income.

The client will tend to view you as a resource—almost as an employee—who can be "assigned" as the client sees fit, if you don't counter that notion early in your retainer education. That's why I've stressed that access is the value you are selling (the ability to "pick your brain"), not projects. The client must not be allowed to think that the retainer is showing a return on investment only if you are actively engaged in some activity. You have to draw a clear line in the sand from the outset. For example, if you choose to take on an early project within the retainer at no additional fee "just to get things under way," you're setting a precedent and creating an expectation that will kill you.

As you hear of and/or advise on projects that should be undertaken (for example, something the buyer has asked your advice on indicates that the human resource function needs to be audited and overhauled), and the buyer understands that any projects you undertake are in addition to the retainer, it can be construed that you're actually trying to leverage your retainer into more business. My solution: as you identify potential projects and initiatives that the client should consider, always suggest ways that the client could accomplish them internally or with external resources other than yourself. Don't recommend yourself, but don't rule out that eventual option either. (Some consultants refuse to enter into project work with a client while on retainer, which I find as ridiculous as including projects within the retainer.) If the client wants you even after being presented with alternative resources, you can then legitimately accept the work, for a project fee.

You can lose money on retainers if you consider yourself a one-person "SWAT team" who is all things to all people. Retainers, like projects, have limits and parameters. If you don't establish them and articulate them, you can be sure the client won't think about them at all.

If you accept project work under these circumstances, you're best served if you set out a policy before you begin, and this also has a financial benefit for the client.[2] For example, stipulate at the outset that the project will have the following characteristics:

- Clear objectives, measures, and value (conceptual agreement) to be achieved during a finite interval
- A separate proposal signed off by the buyer and the consultant
- An agreement that the project and retainer work will complement, and not compete with, each other
- A separate payment schedule, which will feature a strong discount for the project work in view of the ongoing retainer project. (My advice here is to give increasingly steep discounts for longer retainer periods. In other words, a project during a quarterly retainer might justify a 20 percent discount, but a project during an annual retainer might justify a 33 percent discount.)

You want to create a win-win dynamic for projects undertaken while a retainer is in force, causing the client to appreciate that the project required additional investment but that the investment is reduced thanks to the retainer relationship.

Because a retainer usually symbolizes an excellent relationship with the buyer and strong mutual trust, it won't be unusual for the client to suggest

---

[2]Obviously, these aren't major concerns for short-term (for example, one-month) retainers. But a project can surface at any time and almost surely will during a ninety-day or six-month period.

project work during the retainer period. In fact, the retainer arrangement might be the natural result of several highly successful buyer-consultant collaborations. Consequently, it's all the more important to separate the two efforts, lest the buyer simply (and logically) conclude that it's far less expensive to pay you a single fee to work on multiple projects than it is to pay you for each project! If you don't take pains to correct this impression—or better, to prevent it—a retainer arrangement can actually ruin what was a fine relationship engendered by those projects.

Retainer scope is also an important consideration. In other words, it's proper to define the parameters of the retainer's "reach." Are you on retainer to the sales department, which your buyer heads, or to anything the sales vice president is charged with (for example, a special acquisition project) or is mulling over (for example, personal advice and coaching on seeking the senior vice presidential position).

The extent to which you are confined to a single buyer (or single source if a buyer has asked you to work with someone) is critical. If your buyer and presumed single source says, "I want to let Ann borrow you over in R&D because she has some people issues that I know you can help with," you're in trouble. There are probably scores of managers whom you can help with "people issues," and you can't afford to be the "people handyman."

Unless you have a "freeze" option on the retainer, the client has to realize that the retainer ends at a certain point, irrespective of the amount of use or lack thereof. Educate the client that a few highly valuable interactions are far better than daily idle chatter. And don't be bashful about bringing it to the client's attention when the retainer is about to end. (This is why I advocate formally discussing the extension or termination of the retainer a month or so prior to its scheduled end date. That way, there are no blurred lines as the end approaches.)

By the way, there's nothing wrong with any project work undertaken extending beyond the conclusion of the retainer period. But keep them separate, so that the client doesn't continue to use you as a retainer resource while you continue to work on the project or as a project resource after the project is over and you continue on retainer.

In brief: you can have simultaneous retainer and project relationships with the same buyer. Keep your criteria clear for which is which, for your benefit and the client's. A retainer that includes unlimited project work will kill you.

> The longer the retainer period, the more critical the need for clarity on potential project work, retainer scope, and other areas of ambiguity. It's a good idea to have a simple, one-page document that outlines the parameters of the retainer arrangement.

## CAPITALIZING ON RETAINER RELATIONSHIPS

Because referral business is so important in our profession, referrals citing you as an excellent retainer resource can be golden. Although it may require several successful projects for a client to be comfortable enough to enter into a retainer arrangement with you, it won't take more than a heartbeat for that client to recommend you to others on that same basis. If you enjoy retainers and the relative freedom and margins they provide, this is a perfect opportunity.

As you become accepted on a retainer basis with new clients, you should continually perfect the relationship so that it makes sense for you and your style. For example, you may want to simply remain on retainer, or you might seek to use retainers to leverage into additional project work. Both are legitimate strategies.

I suggest that if you do frequent retainer work, you develop a one-page "working agreement" in addition to your proposal that you and the client approve after the deal is signed but prior to work beginning. Doing this has the advantage of keeping the simple document out of the potentially trivializing grasp of the legal department and allows it to serve as an informal template that you and the buyer use to guide the retainer relationship. An example of such a letter is presented in Exhibit 6.1, but it's meant only as a guide and not as the last word. Customize it to your particular comfort and situation.

With the current power of modern technology, retainers are far easier, more realistic, and less labor-intensive, yet more effective, than ever before. You can, as your career progresses, move exclusively into retainer work while significantly reducing your travel. This is no small matter for veteran consultants. Here is how to market that service.

**Exhibit 6.1**  Sample Letter of Agreement for a Retainer Relationship.

Letter of Agreement for the Retainer Relationship Between Alan Weiss on Behalf of Summit Consulting Group and Grace Jones, Vice President of Marketing for Acme Corporation

1. The retainer is for the six-month period from July 1 to December 31, 2008.
2. Your access to me is unlimited during the retainer period and under our single fee. My business and personal contact information (phone, fax, e-mail, street address) appear below for your exclusive use. You will provide me with personal and direct contacts to you to expedite our communications.
3. The retainer fee will be paid upon commencement and is nonrefundable for any reason. However, you may request a "freeze" of the calendar at any time in intervals of thirty days, which will be added to the end of the retainer period. The ultimate limit of the retainer period will be March 31, 2009, under any circumstances.
4. The retainer fee represents access to my advice, counsel, and coaching for you, personally, in your capacity as vice president of marketing and also for your special assignment to choose a new advertising firm.
5. Any specific projects that you and I agree I might undertake on behalf of the company shall be in addition to this retainer arrangement and will require a separate set of objectives, metrics, and fees expressed in a separate proposal. We agree that a specific project is represented by an initiative that requires more than my advice and counsel to you, as indicated by a clear set of business objectives (for example, improved retention of sales talent) to be achieved. I will always suggest alternative

A simple working agreement, tailored to your style and preferences, is an ideal discussion point at the outset of the retainer relationship. I often call the points in the agreement the "rules of engagement."

methods to engage in such projects with internal resources or other third-party resources at your request.

6. During the month of November, we will discuss the potential of extending the retainer for a similar period at its conclusion. Either of us may decline. If we both decide to proceed, that decision will be made by November 30, 2008, so that I can allocate proper time. The new start date would be January 1, 2009, or at the conclusion of any "freeze" time we have agreed on.

7. You and I will periodically review this working agreement as the retainer progresses and we learn from our work together. We will remain flexible, but we agree that any revisions or changes must be agreed on by both of us.

8. Any expenses incurred during the course of the retainer will be billed at the end of that calendar month as actually accrued and will be due upon receipt of the invoice.

9. The value of our relationship is in our personal, trusting, and unrestricted contact, not in frequency or onsite visits. Let's maximize our efficiency by phone and e-mail, and meet personally only at times when we can best accomplish our objectives in person. This will reduce your expenses as well as maximize the flexibility of our interactions.

10. Trust is the essential element. I will regard all of our discussions as strictly confidential, covered by nondisclosure agreements, and not to be repeated without your explicit permission. In return, you will keep me apprised of the effectiveness of my help and advice and suggest ways to improve our partnership at any time.

## AGGRESSIVELY MARKETING RETAINER RELATIONSHIPS

Once you have the experience of several retainers under your belt, you may want to include the service as a focal point of your marketing. (Don't forget that if you engage in executive coaching on a value-billing basis, you may well have created a retainer arrangement without realizing it.) This means that you may want to undertake the following marketing efforts:

- Include testimonials in your press kit and on your Web site that stress the benefits of your having been on retainer (in addition to your overall quality).
- Place "typical results" achieved from your retainer work, specifically, on the Web site and in your press kit.
- Conversationally mention your retainer work in speeches. For example, "When I was on retainer to the executive vice presidents of several trade associations, I found that their common challenge was increasing membership in a strong economy when they were all attending to their own businesses."
- Write articles on the value of retainer relationships, or mention those relationships (as in the speech example) in your other articles.
- Where appropriate, include a retainer option in your proposals—generally most effective when the prospect "doesn't know what he or she doesn't know" and realizes that help is required to begin sorting out the numerous challenges and opportunities facing the organization.

---

You have the option of occasionally, frequently, or solely engaging in retainer relationships. This is not a client, market, or competitive factor. It's a question of how you choose to structure your practice.

---

- Consider structuring some of your pro bono work on a retainer basis, even though you're not being paid; that is, become an adviser to the pro bono client, rather than engaging in a particular project or serving in a particular capacity.
- Become an "authority" on retainers so that others seek you out; if the profession considers you an expert, clients will too.

How many retainers can you take on at one time? I don't know, and the answer really isn't important or even necessary to know, for the same reason that it's dangerous to have a business plan of "25 percent growth" or "$5 million in revenues." The danger is that you stop aspiring when you hit it, even if you could have done much better.

I've been engaged in three major retainers at once, on top of project work for other clients. I found that not only was it not taxing, but the retainers provided a nice change of pace from my more traditional project-oriented work (not to mention a nice fixed source of income). The longest retainer I was ever involved with was for five years with Calgon, and I think that was an aberration resulting from an exceptional CEO, terrific chemistry, and a surfeit of needs in a very tough, competitive marketplace.

My experience and observations indicate that a consultant can develop a pure retainer practice, with project work the exception, rather than the other way around. This is much more likely and appropriate when one's career is in a mature stage, but it's certainly something that can be anticipated and planned for at any stage.

To conclude, here are the traits and abilities that I think are important for the consultant who wants to foster and build more retainer relationships, above and beyond those traits we need in any case merely to be effective consultants.

**Traits of a Successful Retainer Consultant**

- *Rapid Framing Skills.* The ability to recognize patterns, universal challenges, and common problems expressed by your client enables you to use relatively few pieces of advice to resolve what may seem like a myriad of issues.
- *Nonjudgmental Stance.* You must be able to refrain from commenting on how you would do something or why your client is his or her own worst enemy, and instead focus on clear evidence and observed behavior, which can be validated and confidently addressed.
- *Empathy but Not Sympathy.* Sympathy is feeling *what* the other party feels, while empathy is understanding *how* the other party feels. You need to empathize in order to gain trust, not sympathize and merely commiserate about misfortune or bad rolls of the dice. You must provide avenues toward success and not rationalizations for failure.
- *Rapid Responsiveness.* Although you're not on immediate call and don't need to carry a pager, you should be able to respond to phone requests within a couple of hours and e-mail requests the same day. Some issues really can't wait, and if you have a particularly hyper or type A client, you may be able to save a great deal of grief by responding as promptly as possible—heading things off at the pass rather than waiting around the bend.

- *Push back.* Your client will sometimes be wrong, based on the facts. Tell the client in a straightforward manner (this is why it's so much better to be paid in advance). Don't equivocate. Tough love is better than pity or cowardice. Confront the behavior and help change it. A little of this will go a long way.
- *Expertise.* Easily identified expertise makes the investment desirable rather than dubious. "I have one of the best consultants in the business on retainer" is what the client should be telling anyone who asks. That's why retainers are easier to obtain by veterans who have built a brand than by newcomers entering the profession.

---

Not every consultant is an effective retainer consultant. Consulting on retainer is not simply an elongated project. It's a more intense and personal relationship, requiring a higher degree of communication skills.

---

## CHAPTER ROI

- Retainers are not always the best alternative, but they make a great deal of sense when the client wants access to your smarts. The key is to position having that access as the value you are providing.
- Projects may arise that will require a separate proposal and fee. Don't confuse a retainer with the responsibility to accept every project that might come along as a part of that retainer.
- Establish realistic expectations with the buyer early, and stipulate them in a letter of agreement before the actual work begins. That way you can establish "rules of engagement" short of the legal department.
- Quarterly and semiannual time frames are probably ideal, although monthly and annual retainers can work well in specific circumstances. Anything longer or shorter is problematic.
- Make sure you create conditions that are maximally supportive of the retainer arrangement. Organize the scope and the parameters so that they are crystal-clear.

- Exploit and capitalize on the retainer success—you may choose to move your practice partially or predominantly in that direction.
- Arrange for retainer renewals well before the period is over. Either party can unilaterally end it, but both are required to extend it.
- If you don't include retainer work as a service offering, you aren't providing a full range of opportunities for your client and your practice.
- Retainers are often the least labor-intensive of all client work and relationships; they are also highly profitable.

*Your mind and your talent are assets that represent value in themselves. Why not charge for access to those assets? After all, the ultimate brand is you.*

# Ethics and Fees, Fees and Ethics

## *A Midbook Practicum*

Since the first edition of this book was published and more and more practitioners and firms have adopted value-based fees, I've been receiving thousands of inquiries about ethical considerations. These are encouraging, since they are well thought through and very well intentioned. I've summarized the most frequently asked questions here. Since I believe ethics are a central issue of our work, I thought it would be appropriate to place this in the middle of the revised book.

**Q:** Can I charge different fees for the same work to different clients or even within the same client organization?

**A:** You can and you should. Value-based fees are based on the value being delivered to the client. Let's suppose you are using a common coaching methodology without any change at all (although that's rare; we'll use an extreme for our example), with two different people.

The first is a call center manager with ten subordinates, no direct budget responsibility, and call content dealing with general inquiries for directions and basic technical problems. The goal is to improve her talents for providing employee feedback and reducing average call response time. The annual improvement is estimated at about $100,000 and higher morale.

The second is a vice president of sales with 150 people in the operation and a sales goal of $24 million. He has a budget of $4 million, and the goals are to improve his ability to retain and develop top talent. The estimated impact on the business of achieving those objectives is $1 million on an annualized basis.

Using the same methodology and perhaps the exact same time investment, you're achieving far different results for the organizations. There is nothing unethical about charging based on your contribution to that larger return,[1] and the client's return on investment will still be superior. The problem with hourly billing is that you'd be receiving the exact same rate for vastly different client results.

**Q:** When do I exceed high value and simply become very expensive, seeking "whatever the traffic will bear"?

**A:** When the client's ROI becomes so low that there is a question about the wisdom of the investment, you're probably overcharging (or underestimating value—be careful). I think a 10-to-1 return on a *conservative* estimate of value is very powerful, and don't forget that the buyer has agreed to that estimate of value during the conceptual agreement stage. I've worked with consulting firms in the manufacturing field that believe that a 3-to-1 return is very significant for their clients, so you can see that this is very persuasive ground.

There are few places, if any, where the client is generating 10-to-1 returns. So long as you can demonstrate that kind of dynamic, quantitatively or qualitatively, you'll never be accused of "gouging."

---

[1]Here's the phrasing I use: "My fee represents my contribution to the value you receive from the successful completion of this project, providing a dramatic return on investment for you and equitable compensation for me."

**Q:** Aren't I obligated to choose the lowest fee that I feel comfortable with while meeting the client's objectives?

**A:** No, not at all. The only thing that matters is whether the client feels well served. If your accepted fee is $140,000 and you could have charged $155,000 or would gladly have done it for $125,000, *it doesn't matter.* It's all profit (it had better be if you're doing this correctly). So long as the buyer is happy, you're under no ethical, moral, or legal obligation to provide the lowest possible fee.

Market conditions and buyer emotions determine fees, which is why some people look for the best deal with a new car, some people pay the full sticker price, and some pay *over* sticker price for a car they want to own before anyone else.

**Q:** If I'm on retainer and the client barely calls me, shouldn't I extend it or offer to do other work?

**A:** Only if you believe your client is a child and doesn't understand the business. Do you expect your insurance company to extend your coverage for free just because you haven't made a claim?

A retainer is paid for access to your smarts on an as-needed basis. Once again, you can't allow yourself to be caught in the time trap. The buyer is an adult. He or she may access you regularly or rarely or merely take solace in the fact you're there if needed, which by itself is a good investment. Understand what you are being paid for. You are not obligated to perform when someone simply wants to ensure access.

**Q:** Isn't there actually a law that mandates equal fees for equal services?

**A:** You can't discriminate in terms of a buyer's ethnicity or height, but you can be discriminatory about the fee you charge for differing value as perceived by the buyer, which is why people are paid disparately in all kinds of jobs (Diane Sawyer made considerably more than Charles Gibson for a long time as they sat next to each other cohosting *Good Morning America* on ABC).

What most people are confused about is the Robinson-Patman Act, advanced by Congressman Wright Patman in the 1930s, which forbade different prices for commodities used in interstate commerce if the result was to decrease effective competition. That has nothing to do with consulting services based on value delivered to the customer.

**Q:** My client has asked me for a sort of "frequent flyer" discount, since we've done business before. Is this proper?

**A:** It's proper to set whatever fees you like in terms of preferential treatment for repeat customers, high volume, pilots, tests, and so on. I wouldn't go around offering reduced fees, but if a client makes a legitimate request, you should consider it for the sake of the long-term relationship.

For example, I always offer a 10 percent courtesy discount if the full fee is paid upon acceptance. I find that a good business practice: it guarantees that the money is in my pocket and I have use of it, and I'm much freer to speak my mind without the threat of a future check being withheld.

**Q:** The client tells me that state tax must be withheld from my fee, under a new law being phased in, and that to fail to do so would be unethical and not in keeping with the spirit of the law. What do I do?

**A:** First, see your tax attorney, and make sure he or she is superb. This is no place to look for bargain rates.

There is a movement to try to tax out-of-state services, which is already assessed on products in some but not all states. The idea is that there would be reductions in tax in your home state, but my impression is that the overall burden would increase for all of us.

At this writing, there is no such requirement in place, and no such interstate agreement has been concluded nationally. Educate yourself about the law and your home state's regulations. I suspect that you do not have to pay such a local tax legally or ethically. California is currently the toughest state in this regard, and I've never had a client attempt to withhold any taxes from my consulting or speaking fees in that state. There are other criteria, such as whether you have a local office or representation, so obtain an expert opinion.

**Q:** A long-time consultant has told me it's not ethical to charge and accept money for work not yet completed, much less begun. Is that true?

**A:** No. Let me say it another way: NO. All kinds of organizations accept deposits and advance payments all the time, from catering companies to law firms (it's called a "retainer" there, albeit a different kind). The way you *account* for money will depend on whether you are on a cash or accrual basis and what your financial adviser recommends for your particular circumstances, but you can take money from anyone at any time.

That's a long-time, but not a highly successful, consultant giving you that advice. Always consider the source.

**Q:** What is my ethical obligation for a client who has paid me but keeps canceling or postponing services and events? How much of a liability do I have to carry and for how long? Must I return the money at some point?

**A:** No, never return money. I would provide the client with great leeway—say, a year—subject only to your availability. But it's quite proper to tell the client that he or she has six months left before the fee is forfeited.

As I've pointed out before, clients are adults, and sometimes they sacrifice plans because other priorities have arisen. The best you can do is remind them, be flexible, but also be businesslike in creating an end point. It's quite proper to put into your proposal wording to this effect: "You may cancel and reschedule this project and its components without penalty, subject to mutually agreeable dates. However, we cannot be accountable for the original objectives in the event of more than a ninety-day delay, and all obligations on our part will cease after a six-month delay unless otherwise agreed in writing by both parties."

I hate boilerplate, but those lines are very effective, *especially* when you have a limited window of opportunity to make a project work.

**Q:** Isn't the client really better served—with a clear idea of ongoing expenses—by an hourly rate that can be tallied at any given point in time?

**A:** *Au contraire.* The most unethical aspect of fees are time-based, because the client is best serviced by quick resolution and the consultant is best compensated by slow resolution. It's a conflict that I'm astounded continues to exist and is most egregious with the large, production capability–driven firms, which make money with scores of consultants billing maximum hours every week for years.

If you can solve the same problem (or improve the same situation) in twenty minutes as you can in a month, the client is best served by the twenty minutes, since the gains start sooner and the disruption in minimized. Therefore, and this is counterintuitive to many people, the consultant should be paid *more* for less work. That's because work is an input and is unimportant in the fee equation; business results are the output, and they determine value.

I've found that the consultants who have the hardest time moving away from time-based billing are those who have the least confidence and belief in the value they deliver. Hence they look for a substitute, which turns out to be the clock and the calendar. And that's simply pathetic.[2]

**Q:** What happens when my buyer changes? I had one who was fired, and his replacement demanded that the project cease and all payments be refunded for work not performed.

**A:** A deal is a deal. Your proposal should state that the agreement is "non-cancelable for any reason." Not only can you keep what you've been paid, but the new buyer has an obligation to honor the contract for any payments due in the future.

If the buyer insists that you stop work, you should still demand the rest of the payments. Though it may be awkward to sue, you can take a small business to small claims court or have your attorney fire a shot across the bow. Write to the CEO of a larger business and indicate that it may be embarrassing that a new manager has decided unilaterally not to honor a legal contract and is taking advantage of a small business. You have nothing to lose, and the ethical obligation here is your client's, not yours.

**Q:** What do I do with a client who is in deep financial trouble, has gone to 120-day payments to vendors, or has asked that I "be patient" until the company gets back on its feet?

**A:** Ignore the request and the policy (and this is why you should *never* have a friend for a client). You can't pay your mortgage with an IOU, and the gas station is unconcerned with promises.

Inform your client that you are a small business, very vulnerable to cash flow, and you expect all your clients to conform to agreements, contracts, and proposals. Hence, while you sympathize with the client's plight, you must insist on payment as agreed.

---

[2]The big firms, on the other hand, are calcified in their accounting methodology and audit backgrounds and continue to take advantage of their clients while—improbably—denying themselves the true revenues they could be demanding if "billable hours" weren't their mantra.

Whatever you do, *stop work* until you are paid. Do not feel bashful about pressing the matter and involving your attorney. There is always money (the owners and executives are paying themselves). If you're not ethically bound to give money to every charity that approaches you, you're certainly not ethically bound to provide charity to your clients who are screaming poverty.

**Q:** Am I ethically bound to provide lower fees to nonprofits?

**A:** Let me say this about that: No. Nonprofits have money, sometimes, a great deal of it. And although they are proficient at sobbing and crying about the paramount nature of their cause and the difficulty in supporting it, you'll concurrently find that they are spending a huge amount of the cash they generate on administration, not the cause they espouse. I'm not being cruel, just pointing out a simple fact: nonprofits must spend significant money to support the infrastructure that generates new funds.

You are a part of that support and deserve to be paid for your value. Peter Drucker was fond of saying that the Girl Scouts was the best run organization in America, for-profit or nonprofit. The CEO of the United Way at one point was paid $450,000 a year. Teachers' union officers are paid six figures, sometimes four times what the average teacher in the union makes.

Don't go soft on nonprofits. You're helping them reduce costs or increase revenues just as you are for anyone else. If you want to contribute to charity, write a check.[3]

**Q:** When a buyer pays the fee for me to coach someone else, who is my client?

**A:** This is an important and often misunderstood issue. When a buyer asks you to work with someone else, you must establish whether the buyer wants feedback from you, wants feedback from the coaching subject, or does not require feedback. You must then make this clear with your subject. That is, you cannot report on progress (or lack of progress) to your buyer without the consent of the subject. There must be full disclosure of the nature of the project and reporting. The ideal situation is to provide

---

[3]This is additionally important because donated time or reduced fees are *not* deductible under IRS standards, whereas monetary contributions are.

no feedback to the buyer and allow the buyer to judge progress from observed behavior.

**Q:** When a government entity states that it will only accept request for proposal (RFP) responses that cite hourly rates, can I be successful if I tell them that I feel that this is not an ethical approach for me?

**A:** Probably not. My basic advice is not to respond to RFPs because they present predetermined alternatives ("We seek a three-day leadership training program featuring role plays delivered by someone with experience in military environments . . .") and are evaluated by low-level people paid to conserve money. And in triplicate.

However, if you feel you must act, respond to the RFP as best you can using hourly rates, but also attach your own proposal, exceeding the value sought by the RFP and providing value-based fees.

The ideal is to become a sole source provider—by dint of a book, intellectual capital, travel, unique experiences, or some other advantage—and to avoid competitive bidding and RFPs altogether.

**Q:** Am I ethically obligated to meet or beat a lower fee from a competitor offering the same services?

**A:** No. First, the services may be the same, but the value each of you is providing is different by virtue of your being different people. Second, if you're in a close race, your relationship with the buyer should carry the day.

Even in government, something called the Farr Act allows purchasers to choose a more expensive alternative if the value is deemed proportionally greater than that of lower bids.

**Q:** Is it ethical for a prospect to show my proposal to other consulting firms being considered and theirs to me?

**A:** No. You should stipulate in your proposal that it is for the buyer's use only and may not be shown to nonorganizational personnel without your written consent. Moreover, you should put a copyright notice on your proposal if you even suspect that this may happen.[4]

**Q:** Can I ethically raise fees for the same client and the same service due to inflation or increases in materials costs?

---

[4]Technically, under the law, anything you write is automatically copyrighted and owned by you, but the written © symbol may remind the buyer of this fact and prevent others from spreading your property around.

**A:** Of course. You can increase fees at any time without a reason for renewal or new business (but not, of course, during a contractual assignment), just as the phone company or postal service does.

However, beyond ethics, always keep pragmatics in mind. Ideally, current clients should get the best deal you offer, and newer clients should be paying more. Older clients should not be subsidizing your new business, and a veteran client who finds that you are offering better fees to newer clients will bail out on you faster than a skydiver in a jump zone. (And you will not have a chute.)

**Q:** When a client says, "If you can lower your fee right now, I can shake hands with you," is it right for me to do so, especially when I desperately want the business?

**A:** Sure—but always arrange a quid pro quo. You'll be glad to lower your fees if the client pays 100 percent of the discounted fee up front or allows you to remove some value from the project or throws in some value for your benefit, such as referrals and introductions, or takes on more of the labor with client personnel—you get the idea. If we merely lower fees, the client will wonder, "How low will this guy go?" and press onward. Demand concessions, and you'll get the business and retain the respect.

**Q:** Is it an ethical obligation to tell subcontractors what fees I'm being paid and what percentage I'm paying them?

**A:** Is it your obligation to tell the plumber what you earn each year and adjust plumbing fees accordingly? I don't think so.

Subcontractors are hired hands, almost always people who love the work because they are inept at marketing and creating their own work. Treat them as hired help, and pay an hourly or daily rate. This is a buyer's market, since there is a plethora of competent delivery capability all over the place.

I tell subcontractors that my books are pretty bad and that they shouldn't waste their time on them. So far, so good.

**Q:** Must I file and pay taxes in each state in which I do business?

**A:** Not as of this writing, though that may change. Try not to have any kind of permanent presence, such as an office or alliance partner whom you visit regularly, and use your financial adviser's help. The state in which you are incorporated or reside may have an influence. But thus far, I've never had reason to do this, and all my clients have happily complied and never assessed or withheld taxes.

**Q:** Is it OK to charge for expenses that are agreed on but not actually expended? For example, can I charge for airfare even though I used frequent flyer miles?

**A:** Absolutely not. For some reason, many professional speakers feel that this is an alternative way to raise money, probably because their fees are so low and they have no idea how to raise them, with the result that they have low self-esteem *and* cheat on their expenses.

Let's be clear: you shouldn't ask for an expense reimbursement for anything that didn't cost you money. If you stay with a friend, don't charge for a hotel; if your spouse drives you to the airport, don't charge for a cab; and if the airplane ticket is free, don't lie and try to be reimbursed.

Charge for your value, not by cheating on your expenses. In cases when you've agreed on a fee that is inclusive of expenses, you need not make any changes, since there is no specific expense reimbursement. But even then, if you're using free air miles or driving instead of taking a plane, my advice is to reimburse the client. When you feel you have to augment your income by deception—which this is, have no doubt about it—then you're committing fraud and undermining your own worth.

**Q:** Is it proper to accept bartered services instead of a fee or in lieu of part of a fee?

**A:** Yes, but. You can accept tickets from United Airlines if that is a client of yours, or rental cars from Hertz, or televisions from Samsung. However, these are *taxable* forms of compensation and must be reported. If you fail to do so, you are violating the law intentionally, which is also unethical (let alone subject to fines and even imprisonment).

This is why you may deduct charitable giving only in excess of the goods and services received in return and why charities provide documentation to that effect for the IRS. The underlying premise is the same: if you receive something, it's worth something, and that's taxable income.

**Q:** Is there anything wrong with accepting cash in return for a discount?

**A:** My immediate question is "Why the discount?" I assume it's because you're not going to deposit and declare the money in standard fashion, thereby attempting to avid taxation on it.

See the preceding response. Cash is a messy form of payment, since there is no paper trail. (What if the client claims, for tax purposes, that you were paid $25,000 in cash, and you claim, for tax purposes, that you received only $10,000? Who's lying, and how do you prove it?)

There is no legitimate reason to accept cash unless you are selling products at the back of a room during a speaking engagement. And even then I'd recommend that you accept payment only by credit card and check. In many such instances, you're also responsible for the payment of sales tax, and the revenues, including cash, must be accounted for.

(*Note:* Providing a fee discount for full payment in advance is quite different and acceptable. In this case, you have immediate use of *all* of your money, and you've ensured that problems with the client beyond your control will not impede your cash flow.)

**Q:** Surely there can't be anything unethical about raising fees when people pay by credit card, since I'm paying a processing fee, which I may pass on to the customer, right?

**A:** It's not unethical and it's not illegal, but it is tacky. Paying 2 to 3 percent for credit card processing is a cost of doing business. You're talking $2 or $3 on every $100. If you have a $25,000 project, it's $500, but you have $24,500 profit, and the client has been accommodated.

Credit cards are becoming increasingly common, and it's no longer unusual to be paid for speaking engagements, expense reimbursements, and even modest consulting work by credit card. I'd suggest that you obtain merchant accounts for all the major cards, find the best (lowest) interest rates that you can, and get on with your business. You're running a consulting practice, not a candy store.

**Q:** What about assessing penalty fees when payments are overdue? Many companies charge me 1.5 percent per month for overdue amounts or slap on a flat $35 charge.

**A:** If you have a strong relationship with the buyer, you shouldn't have to worry about overdue payments. Similarly, if you secure full payment in advance, you're home free, except for expense reimbursement.

Here's a hint: make all invoices "due on receipt" and not "thirty days net" or some such silly thing. Next, send your invoices well in advance of the due date for installment payments. Also, have in your proposal that "expenses will be billed as accrued at the end of each month and are due on the presentation of our statement." I'll give a client a thirty-day grace period on expenses—because I'm not looking at expense reimbursement as a revenue source, nor am I dependent on it for my cash flow—but after that, I go right to my buyer and say, "We have a problem."

**Q:** Can I set up payment terms beneficial to me for taxes? For example, near the end of the year, can I deliberately defer payments into the next year if I don't want to increase this year's income? Is that ethical?

**A:** It's both ethical and legal, usually. Check with your financial adviser, who can examine what it means for your personal accounting structure (cash versus accrual basis, for example). You can always arrange deferred payments or installment payments or, even easier, just delay work or billing until the next year.

Having said that, let me remind you that payment in hand is always a better alternative, even if it means higher taxes. Paying higher taxes on increased revenues is a *pleasant* problem. (It's when you're paying higher taxes on the same income as last year that you have to throw the rascals out of office.)

A great many things can happened to interfere with even the best-intentioned and most tightly constructed agreements. Every time you forestall payment, you are risking no payment. The probability may be low in your estimation, but I can guarantee you that the seriousness is quite high. I've dealt with a great many desperate consultants, speakers, and coaches who had relied on "secure" contracts—and in many cases had already spent the expected money—who found themselves washed up on the shore of reneging clients. In this business, in the end, a client determined not to pay you will not pay you, and the cost of trying to recoup is prohibitive.

My advice: always take the money as soon as you can.

**Q:** Is it ethical to abandon long-standing clients who cannot or will not pay higher fees, especially when their fee basis originated many years ago?

**A:** I advocate dropping at least 15 percent of your business every two years, and this is one major reason. Cast it as being in the client's best interest: "We've been together a long time. I don't feel I can raise your fees, but neither can I continue to give you the priority attention you deserve.

I want to recommend someone else to you who can fit within your budget and do a great job."

And everything I just said is absolutely true. You can't reach out until you let go, and you're not going to attain the next fee level as long as you're carrying all that low-fee baggage from your past. Do both the client and yourself a favor and move on.

## CHAPTER 7

# Seventy Ways to Raise Fees and/or Increase Profits Immediately

---

## *Act Today and Receive the Bass-o-Matic Free of Charge!*

After six chapters on strategy, rationale, and large-scale tactics for improving your fees, I thought it would be nice to examine some street-level tactics that can be employed immediately. (With apologies to all those excellent "guerrilla" and "street fighter" books, I don't believe that fee setting is a matter of ambushing clients in alleys or garroting them from the rear.)

You might want to use the techniques in this chapter as a template, to test your aggressiveness in setting fees. Or you might view them as a buffet, from which you can draw the nourishment that best augments your current diet. Or think of them as an exercise ritual . . .

That's enough of that. The point is that none of us, despite our smarts and successes, is doing everything we can to maximize our income commensurate with the value we are providing. And while the preponderance of this book deals with the longer term, there is a high probability that you may be leaving money on the table today—right now, as you're reading this—in terms of proposals that are too modest, negotiations that aren't handled assertively, and opportunities that are being lost.

If you leave $50,000 on the table each year, that's a half-million dollars over a decade that you will never, ever be able to recover. If it's $100,000 a year, . . . You get the picture. Now is the time to plan for that extra million in the not-too-distant future.

So if you were to review this book twice a year to ensure that your fee strategies are moving in the right direction, you might also review this chapter monthly to ensure that you are not missing something right under your nose. (If you have staff of any kind, it's important that they familiarize themselves with this chapter, because it has implications for everyone, from business acquisition people to receptionists.)

Since I've been working on the art and science of fee setting for over twenty years and I didn't want to provide anything less than a comprehensive array in this chapter, some of the material has appeared in part and in different forms elsewhere. The two primary sources are the first book in this series, *The Ultimate Consultant,* and my booklet (which started it all) *How to Maximize Fees in Professional Service Firms.*

> If you follow my philosophy of the 1% Solution,® you only need apply one technique to raise fees every day for seventy days to have potentially doubled your income in that period.

And now, on to the techniques. You might want to read a batch at a time and think about them, or highlight or take notes as you go through them.

Overlaps and partial duplications are deliberate, since I don't want to miss a nuance that might apply to some consultants and not to others, depending on how I present them and in what context.[1]

1. *Establish Value Collaboratively with the Client.* It's imperative to reach agreement with the buyer as to the real worth to the organization of achieving the business outcomes specified in the objectives. This should be done interactively (that is, not by e-mail or letter) and result with the buyer literally nodding in agreement as you summarize the quantitative (retention improvement) and qualitative (better teamwork) worth, which you can then reiterate in your proposal.

2. *If Value Differs, Fees Can Differ.* Just because you're doing the exact same thing for two different clients doesn't mean the fee must be the same. Coaching a vice president running a $200 million division and coaching a manager running a $350,000 sales center have two vastly differing outcomes, even if the coaching regimen is the same in each case.

3. *Base Fees on Value, Not on Task.* Never base a fee on your doing something. Always base it on the client's achieving something. Tasks (surveys) are commodities. Value (market share) is a unique client improvement. Also, never base fees on per capita (number of people in a workshop or survey) basis, which tends to drive the client to limit participation.

4. *Forget About What's Happened Before.* It doesn't matter if the client has always paid by the day for a certain type of help or if the client places limits on fees for consultants. No one needed a fat pen until Mont Blanc produced one. If you allow yourself to be guided by the client's history, you're helping neither the client nor yourself.

5. *Never Use Time as the Basis of Your Value.* The toughest obstacle for consultants to overcome is to disregard their time. They tend to believe that the client will abuse their time or that the time a client demands is time lost elsewhere. In truth, clients don't abuse time if there are clear, delimiting objectives, and the time you would be spending with your feet propped up

---

[1] I have a friend, Greg Godek, who wrote a book called *1001 Ways to Be Romantic.* Someone mentioned to me that he thought there were really only 987, because of fourteen purported duplications. I told him that if he were able to master the 987, he probably wouldn't miss the other fourteen, nor would his wife.

watching a *Seinfeld* rerun doesn't count. Conversely, you can't feel guilty just because you only had to show up four times to complete a $74,000 project (which has happened to me frequently). You must shake the "time ghost." Your value is in your talent, not in your showing up.

6. *Practice Stating High Fees.* That's right, practice saying, "It will be between $150,000 and $225,000" out loud. When you say these things matter-of-factly, the client assumes that he or she is out of step if the amount sounds high. If you giggle or turn red, you lose a certain amount of credibility.

7. *Think of the Fourth Sale First.* Fees are cumulative, not situational. Don't be greedy. Even on a value basis, the goal is to develop a relationship and implement successful projects that will lead to years of work. View your larger clients strategically, and anticipate how you can be of help over years on a variety of projects, not just for the present on a single project. Over 80 percent of my business has been repeat business, and most of the rest has been by referral. The cost of acquiring new business from scratch seriously decreases margins.

8. *Don't Use Round Numbers, but Don't Be Ridiculous.* It's probably best not to position options at $100,000, $125,000, and $150,000, but it's also ridiculous to cite $123,687.90. The client is going to want to see the worksheet that generated that kind of precision. Remember, if the client walks away thinking that the value was a bargain and you walk away feeling that you were paid well, there is no third consideration.

9. *Engage the Client in the Diagnosis; Don't Be Prescriptive.* The client perceives much greater value when you and the buyer are jointly diagnosing the issues, instead of you prescribing some off-the-shelf medicine. Internists make much more money than pharmacists because they are so much more valuable in diagnosing illness. And when the patient is involved in the diagnosis and the ensuing course of treatment, the quality and success of the treatment are greatly enhanced. One simple way to do this quickly is to provide a "process visual" and let the buyer decide where the organization belongs. See Figure 7.1 for an example.[2] Ask the buyer to profile the organization for each factor.

---

[2]See my book *The Great Big Book of Process Visuals* and its successor, *The Second Great Big Book of Process Visuals,* for examples of such visuals and potential joint diagnostic tools.

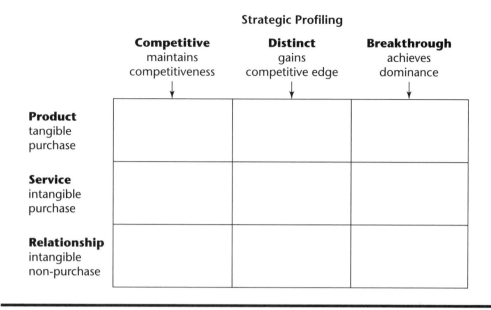

**Figure 7.1** Strategic Profiling in which the Buyer Joins in the Diagnosis.

There is an intrinsic value in merely involving the client in discussions of how to approach the project. Value is based not just on what you contribute but also on your embrace of the ideas and desires of others.

10. *Never Voluntarily Offer Options to Reduce Fees.* In a frenzied attempt to close business rapidly, many consultants build in automatic fee reductions, based on numbers, multiple assignments, and other factors. The only option I ever recommend is a small discount if the client pays the entire fee up front, at the time of project acceptance, and that's mainly for two reasons: you have use of your money from the outset, and the client cannot cancel the project.

11. *Never Deal with a Purchasing Manager or Accounts Payable.* If the buyer suggests that "finance will take it from here," insist that you and the buyer absolutely agree on the fees and the payment terms. Emphasize that the hand-off is fine if "finance" merely implements the paperwork and generates the

checks but that in your experience, such people often try to show their worth by pressuring for a "better deal." Obtain firm agreement on your agreement while you and the buyer are *together.*

12. *Add a Premium If You Personally "Do It All."* Often a contract will have a provision that says the consultant will do everything required, but if subcontractors are used, the fee will increase to accommodate the extra expense. Presumably, the extra help will speed project completion. I do just the opposite. I tell the client that the fee is for the entire project and I'll decide whether subcontracted help is needed. However, if the client wants me to do all of the work myself in order to keep a single "filter" in place or guarantee a single qualitative source, there is a 10 percent premium on the fee. In other words, it costs more if I'm the only one to work on the project, not less. I'm the talent; the subcontractors are not.

13. *Remove Fees from All Printed Materials.* Purge any reference to fees in your printed, Web, and other promotional materials. Make sure that old testimonials do not inadvertently provide a fee schedule (for example, "Joan was expensive at $5,000 per day but a bargain in the long run!").

14. *If Forced to Consider Fee Reduction, Reduce Value First.* Sometimes reduction of fees is a reasonable request. On those occasions, never reduce fees without making a commensurate decrease in value. Take out the international part of the study or remove the post-survey discussions with management or eliminate the written reports. Sometimes a client will say, "We can't afford to lose that" and will concede the fee, but in any case, you don't want to be seen as someone who has a padded fee awaiting reduction.

15. *Always Make It Clear That Expenses Are Extra.* Except in cases where you are deliberately including expenses in the fee, state orally and in writing that the quote is "plus expenses." Many clients will claim that they thought the fee included everything, whether they did or they didn't, and you might be salivating sufficiently on the edge of a yes that you agree. Don't. It could cost you thousands on the bottom line.

16. *Always Provide an Option That Exceeds the Budget.* Sometime you'll be told the budget, and it's reasonable, so always provide one option that is above the limit. There will still be two or more options within the budget limitation, so you're not risking anything but just may be laying the groundwork for higher profits. I lost a piece of business once to a competitor who came in

"I'm told you're very expensive by my colleague who referred you," said the buyer I had just met at a New York bank.

"I'm not that expensive," I replied, "if you consider the return on investment that this project will provide. It's no different from the returns you seek for your investors."

"Well, we boast about being the best, so I guess that means we'd better acquire the best help around, right?"

There's nothing like a referral system that already educates a prospect about what to expect or a prospect who is already positioned to appeal to his or her own clientele as a high-value choice.

over budget but offered far more than the buyer had specified. I didn't have to learn that lesson twice.

17. *As Early as Possible, Ask the Question Guaranteed to Result in Higher Fees, or QGTRIHF: "What Are Your Objectives?"* Always begin with objectives, because they focus the buyer on results (not on costs) and give you the opportunity to pursue real needs (not wants). There is nothing easier, or more valuable, than starting the process by asking, "Can we begin with what you'd like to accomplish as a result of this project?"

18. *Broaden Objectives as Appropriate to Increase Value.* If a buyer says, "We need better market share in the Northeast," I always ask, "Wouldn't you want greater market share everywhere?" If the buyer says, "My team needs better delegation skills," I inquire, "What about the skills of their reports in accepting delegation and the culture of the organization in supporting empowerment?" It's relatively easy to broaden the objectives—and, consequently, raise the fees—by asking a few innocent questions.

19. *Ensure That the Client Is Aware of the Full Range of Your Services.* Prospects will sometimes jump to a conclusion about your "specialty," or they may have been misinformed by a reference source. If you're talking about a

customer survey, for example, don't be reluctant to drop into the conversation that "one survey we conducted took place immediately before we ran a strategy retreat, which provided contemporary feedback for the strategy process."

> Few things limit fees as much as stereotyping. That's why the concepts of "develop a niche" and "specialize or die" are so constricting. The fewer competencies you yourself promote, the fewer the client's opportunities to pay you.

20. *If Something Is Not on Your Playing Field, Subcontract.* A good rule of thumb is this: if the predominant aspects of the project are not within your competencies, refer it elsewhere. But if the predominant parts are within your competencies, subcontract what you can't handle. It's the overall relationship that counts, not individual mastery of every implementation element.

21. *Always Ask Yourself, "Why Me? Why Now? Why in This Manner?"* If the buyer has a raft of choices, you're less valuable, but if you're one of the few with the expertise or reputation, you're much more valuable; if the client can wait without a problem, that's one thing, but if the window of opportunity is closing, that's quite another; if the client can do this internally, that's easy, but if an external consultant is mandatory, that's different. By asking these questions, you'll know your intrinsic value in setting the appropriate fee.

22. *Use Proposals as Confirmations, Not as Explorations.* Don't submit a proposal until you have conceptual agreement on objectives, measures of success, and value to the organization. Otherwise, the proposal becomes a negotiating document, and the options you have listed will be the point of departure to negotiate downward. I hit over 80 percent of my proposals, but I send out far fewer than most consultants because of my method of using them.

23. *When Asked Prematurely About Fees, Reply, "I Don't Know."* Don't be cornered. Simply tell the buyer that you can't quote a fee until you have more information—in fact, it would be unfair to the prospect to do so—but you can have the options ready within twenty-four hours. When consultants allow

themselves to be forced into fee quotes prematurely, they almost always quote too low, and the prospect expects to negotiate down from there.

24. *If You Must Lower Fees, Seek a Quid Pro Quo from the Buyer.* In the real world, you'll sometimes want a piece of business and will accept a lower fee to get it. Even then, suggest an accommodation whereby the client guarantees to provide referrals or videotapes one of your presentations for your use or provides products and services free of charge or at cost or places you in front of a related trade association. There is usually some barter arrangement that is attractive to both parties.

---

Don't use other people if you don't have to. There is no inherent benefit in numbers or bodies. No matter how much you charge, every additional employee or subcontractor on a project will reduce your profit margins.

---

25. *Don't Accept Troublesome, Unpleasant, or Ugly Business.* A prospect who is unethical, ornery, nasty, or otherwise unfriendly won't magically metamorphose as a client. Bad prospects are bad clients, and the only thing worse than no business is bad business. No matter what the fee, these clients will cost you more than you keep.

26. *When Collaborating, Use Objective Apportionment.* You may divide the client business into acquisition, methodology used, and delivery, for example. That means that if I sell the client, my technology is used but you deliver; I get two-thirds and you get one-third. Use whatever formula you like (some people feel the acquisition aspect deserves more weight), but use one that's clear and objective so that everyone understands the ground rules for revenue sharing.

27. *Any Highly Paid Employee Must Bring in New Business.* Whether on salary, bonus, or commission, high pay is justified for new business acquisition. Delivery, research, and support are commodities for which you should subcontract. In fact, it's a buyer's market, since those abilities are in huge supply. Don't pay people for delivering your business acquisition unless it's on a pay-for-performance basis.

A prospect kept gently inquiring about costs during our initial two meetings, and I parried each time by pointing out that I didn't know enough yet (we hadn't reached conceptual agreement). Her continual gentle pressure was met by my continual but firm resistance.

Finally, I had gathered enough information and commitment to put together a proposal. The buyer again inquired about fees, and I said that she would have my proposal, options, and fees within forty-eight hours.

On a whim, I then said, "You've been very curious about the fees. Is there a budget you want me to stay within, so that I can formulate my proposal accordingly?"

"Well, yes," she admitted. "We've allocated only $150,000 for this project."

I had estimated that my options were going to range from $75,000 to about $110,000. "I'll do my best to stay within that allocation," I responded with all the calmness I could muster.

I provided improved and even more effective options at $128,000, $141,000, and $172,000. She chose the second one. She was relieved, and I was probably $31,000 to $66,000 wealthier for the commensurate increase in value.

28. *Seek Out New Economic Buyers Laterally During Your Projects.* This is part of the "springboard" from Chapter One. The time to market is always now, so be on the lookout for opportunity as you are implementing. This is neither unethical nor illegal. It's simply smart business.

29. *Respond to "Scope Creep" with "I'll Send a New Proposal."* Whenever the client requests work clearly outside the objectives of your original agreement, accept it graciously provided that you can send a new proposal—with new objectives and new fees—to cover the additional work. Regard your

original project objectives as "lines in the sand," and don't allow them to be blurred.

30. *It Is Better to Do Something Pro Bono Than to Do It for a Low Fee.* Don't ever be pegged as a low-priced option. If there's something you're dying to do or a cause you feel more than merits your attention, do it free of charge as part of your pro bono work. Don't allow yourself to be pegged as a "cheap resource." Rule of thumb: *never* do pro bono work for a profit-making entity.

31. *If You Do Something Pro Bono, Send an Invoice.* Show the pro bono client what your actual fee would have been, and then waive it, showing a net of nothing due. That way you've established your fee for that particular project in the mind of that "buyer" and of anyone else on the board, on the committee, or in the room. (*Note:* This does not constitute a "donation" or a tax-deductible item under current IRS rules, so don't attempt to use the invoice to justify a deduction.)

32. *Fees Have Nothing to Do with Supply and Demand, Only with Value.* Don't listen to the "experts" who tell you that you can raise fees when demand exceeds supply, which is a formula to work harder, not smarter. You want to work smarter, not harder. Every year, ask your trusted advisers and clients to help you assess the value you're providing. You may be the worst judge and the biggest impediment to raising your own fees.

33. *Raise Fees at Least Every Two Years.* Actively and aggressively increase your fees for the same kind of value you've provided in the past about every two years or so. Your customers, clients, and suppliers are doing the same. Even in times of low inflation, other expenses mount. If you use occasional base fees—for a keynote speech or a strategy retreat, for example—raise these by at least 10 percent every two years.

34. *If You Are Unaware of the Current Range of Market Fees, You Are Undercharging.* When you network and talk casually to clients, try to find out what the general ranges are for a variety of projects. This kind of market intelligence will help you implement your strategy, whether you choose to be the Mercedes of the market or the Volkswagen. Just don't choose to be the Tata, the baby Indian car that costs less than many wristwatches.

35. *Stay Acutely Sensitive to Margins.* It's not what you make but what you keep that's crucial. You may actually be increasing your fees while increasing your expenses at a faster clip. (This tends to happen as we become flush and invest more in marketing and client acquisition.) Analyze how much you

are keeping, and adjust your fees or your expenses accordingly to maximize margins.

36. *Psychologically, Higher Fees Create Higher Value in the Buyer's Perception.* (I've called this the "Mercedes-Benz syndrome elsewhere in this book.) Buyers believe they get what they pay for, which is why McKinsey, IBM, Rolex, and Ferrari don't enter into price negotiations. No one says, "This is the cheapest consultant I could find, and I'm proud to have him!" Instead they say, "This person is costing us a fortune, and we were lucky to get her, so listen up!"

37. *Value Can Include Subjective as Well as Objective Measures.* When an executive says to me that a given result would be "priceless" or "invaluable," I move on. That's good enough. A high-level buyer's relief from stress, anxiety, unpleasant situations, poor image, safety concerns, and similar pressures is worth a great deal. Go with that.

38. *Use Other People Only When Absolutely Necessary.* Use subcontractors if (a) you don't have a requisite skill, (b) you need "legs" because you can't interview all over the country on the same day, or (c) you're bored with the nature of the work. But don't use them as a show of force or because you think doing so adds credibility. What it does is decrease profit, no matter how much you've boosted the revenue line.

---

The higher-level your buyer, the more you can afford to include subjective measures and the buyer's personal metrics. The lower-level the buyer, the more you must seek quantifiable measures and commit them to writing.

---

39. *Introduce New Value to Existing Clients to Raise Fees in These Accounts.* Suggest that a client consider using the traditional customer and employee surveys as a device to get customers together with employees who never otherwise see them to create a greater sense of accountability. Offer to combine the annual performance evaluation process directly with the periodic succession planning system. Don't simply sit back and do the same thing every year.

40. *Do Not Accept Referral Business on the Same Basis as the Referring Source.* If a colleague refers business to you from a client paying by the hour or the

day, don't accept the same terms. Immediately educate the buyer that you work differently and so your arrangements will be somewhat different. This will protect your fee ranges, avoid your having to refuse the work, and prevent you from being branded as a per diem consultant.

41. *Ask the Comparison Question.* When a prospect says, "That's more than we intended to spend" or "We never imagined it would cost that much," point to a copy machine or computer and ask, "What's your annual cost for warranties on this equipment? It's more than the sum total of this project. Are you really so willing to invest more in preventive maintenance than you are in human development?" (Of course, you should make whatever case it is that benefits your project.) Do some homework, and work out these comparisons in advance—you can use ruined postage, cafeteria subsidies, carpet cleaning, all sorts of things. It works wonderfully for putting your fees into perspective.

42. *When Forced into Phases, Offer Partial Rebates to Guarantee Future Business.* When the client insists on a phased approach to a complex project (for example, needs analysis, design, pilot, implementation, or monitoring) that the client won't buy into all at once, offer a rebate from the fee for the prior phase on the succeeding one if the buyer commits before the prior phase is completed. This tends to dissuade buyers from looking for alternatives at every new phase, using your work from the prior phase.

43. *Cite a Time Frame for the Proposal's Acceptance.* Tell the buyer that the fees—and any discounts you may be offering for one-time payment, for example—can be honored for thirty days, after which a new proposal will be required. After all, you have the right to manage your business and your time investment, and the client can't suddenly determine, ninety days from now, that you should proceed full steam ahead. Force the client to make a decision within a reasonable time if his or her investment is to be protected.

44. *At Least Every Two Years, Consider Jettisoning the Bottom 15 Percent.* All of us are burdened by business that made sense at one time but no longer does, business that is accustomed to too much service for too little money, and business that is comfortable but unchallenging. We can't reach out unless we let go, and we must let go of nonproductive, low-potential business. I've seen large firms dragged down by these anchors. Refer the business to someone who will appreciate it and handle it even better than you.

45. *At Year-End, Always Emphasize Early Payment.* Clients will often have "money to burn" in the fourth quarter of their fiscal year, which is returned

to the corporate coffers if unused. Make it clear that your accounting system allows for advance payments in the current fiscal year to be applied to future business. This is an ideal way for a client to tap the budget for next year's work, thereby improving next year's margins (a return at no expense). Remember that some clients operate on a fiscal year that differs from the calendar year, so you should find that out very early.

46. *Practice Saying, "I Can Do That for You."* When a buyer trusts you, the buyer will often remark about things that have to be accomplished outside of your project. For example, it might concern a facilitator for a strategy retreat, a mediator in an acquisition, or a presenter for an awards dinner. If the need matches your competencies, casually suggest that you could do it if needed. But don't do it for free. As always, provide the buyer with some options. Often the buyer won't realize that you are as multifaceted as you are.

47. *Start with Payment Terms Maximally Beneficial to You Every Time.* For example, explain that your policy is to receive the full fee paid in advance. If the client finds that unacceptable, offer 50 percent on acceptance and 50 percent in forty-five days (no matter what the length of the project). If you start with nothing down and gradual payments, I can guarantee that you'll wind up searching for your fees well after the project is over, which means you've received much less money than someone else getting the same fee paid in advance. Beneficial terms to you equal higher profits.

48. *Suggest Key Objectives Beyond the Project.* One of my buyers began talking to his own staff about how to use my help in the next year, well beyond the current retainer. I realized that I had offered sufficient inducement to have him think long term. Don't be blatantly self-promotional. Simply suggest, "Here are three things to accomplish next year that would exploit current successes still more" or "You're not in a position to assign some resources against this new market in the months ahead."

49. *If Payments Are Late, Pursue the Buyer.* Don't fool around in accounts payable if a scheduled payment or expense reimbursement isn't received. Immediately go to the buyer and state, "We have a small problem." The buyer will always be in a better position to expedite things internally than will you from the outside. Consider this a joint problem, not your personal misfortune.

A participant in my mentor program was having a very tough time raising fees for his sales skills workshops and training. We had practiced all of the right moves, all of the rebuttals, and all of the value propositions.

Then I noticed that he had in his briefcase a set of promotional materials that I had never seen. "Oh," he said, "I didn't want to bother you with this. It's just the stuff I send out to initial inquiries."

As I glanced through it, I found a fee schedule based on type of workshop and days. He had forgotten that it was in there.

Check your materials, Web pages, and all other promotional sources to ensure that you are not inadvertently providing a con-stricted payment schedule.

50. *Offer Incentives for One-time Full Payments.* You never know until you ask. By offering a modest (5 to 10 percent) discount for payment on acceptance, you just may put a six-figure check in the bank tomorrow. (*Note:* Some organizations have rules in their accounts payable department that any accepted proposal or contract that offers a discount mechanism must be accepted with the discount.)

51. *Be Clear on What the Client Owes for Expenses.* I had created a $3,500 slide presentation for a sophisticated workshop based on my consulting results before it dawned on me that the client was responsible for that expense. I'm glad I had the breakthrough before the project ended! If you've created something unique that was required for that client and did not simply use your generic materials or equipment, chances are that it might be reimbursable.

52. *Send in Expense Reimbursement Requests Promptly.* I actually had to counsel a consultant with dreadful cash flow problems who had nearly $100,000 in outstanding expense reimbursements unsubmitted going back

over a year. Send these in every single month, and never agree to a period longer than a month. If you don't like detail, too bad—I don't like wasting time at the dentist, but I prefer that to my teeth rotting. Hire a bookkeeper by the hour if you must, but submit reimbursement requests zealously, with receipts, to avoid questions and delay.

53. *Read the Fine Print; Then Push Back.* Many clients will send you a generic contract accompanying their approval to begin the project per your proposal. The problem is that the contract will often supersede your proposal by demanding the right to cancel on short notice, pay expenses within 120 days, and set other conditions beneficial only to the client. Read the fine print, and respond to your buyer (not the purchasing people or the legal department, who may have actually sent the offensive document). Tell the client that you have just learned that the two of you have a few unexpected conflicts to work out. At worst, you can probably compromise on the most odious parts.

54. *Never Accept Payment Subject to Conditions to Be Met on Completion.* Conditions change. Buyers get hit by beer trucks. The project is never quite finished. If you allow yourself to fall into this trap, you deserve what you get (or what you don't get). You don't buy an oven with the agreement that you'll finish paying after it has cooked its last meal. Don't allow yourself to be fried in this dilemma.

> Manual laborers get paid when their work is done, knowledge workers when their work is beginning. You don't pay for a book after you've completed reading it, and you don't pay for software after you've mastered it. You're not even paying the car manufacturer or house builder over time; you're paying the bank. Do you really want to be in the loan business?

55. *Focus on Improvement, Not on Problem Solving.* Everyone can solve problems, and problem solving is a commodity. But few people can systematically raise the bar and improve the performance of already stellar operations. Yet that's where the value is. It's a question of the all-stars improving still

further. Orient yourself to innovation, not problem solving, and the worth of your project will be commensurately higher.

56. *Have the Client Absorb Expense Billing.* Explore whether the client will establish a master bill at a frequently used hotel, provide tickets through the client's travel agent, and provide limo service for local pickups. Many clients will, and an administrative assistant can take care of everything. Not only does this help cash flow by preventing payments and waits for reimbursement, but it also reduces the number of invoices a client sees and reduces the total costs associated with your project (since the expense amounts are usually absorbed within corporate accounts). Consequently, you improve your cash flow, and you look better as well.

57. *Provide Proactive Ideas, Benchmarking, and Best Practices from Experience.* Don't become "industry-bound." Demonstrate value to the buyer by bringing to bear experiences in other industries and under other conditions that can contribute to improving the current client's condition. Allow your "weaknesses" to become your actual strengths.

58. *Quote in U.S. Dollars Drawn on U.S. Banks.* If you are an American based in the United States, whenever you propose any overseas business—even for a U.S. company—stress that all funds are to be paid in U.S. dollars drawn on U.S. banks and that your fees are quoted in U.S. dollars. If you don't, not only will the currency translation hurt you severely, but U.S. banks often charge as much as 25 percent to convert foreign checks issued in non-U.S. funds.

59. *Practice Stating and Explaining Your Fees.* Practice your responses so that you're neither sweating profusely nor losing eye contact. Like a basketball player who bounces the ball three times before every foul shot to get into a "routine" or a baseball batter who take five practice swings, you need to get into a "groove" that allows you to conversationally say, "It's $75,000. Can we proceed?"

60. *Always Be Prepared to Walk Away from Business.* Few tactics increase your fees as much as this one. Never be anxious. If you're at an impasse, simply say, "I've enjoyed meeting with you, but I don't think I can undertake the project, given what you're offering. Let's stay in touch." Often you'll be stopped before you're even out of your chair. But just as the client can say no, so can you. Don't be afraid to reject business that's not in the form most advantageous for you.

While playing hooky from a boring speakers' convention poolside at a Dallas hotel, I met a woman whose husband was a speaker. She said he travels constantly, having worked 220 days the prior year.

"If I may ask," I said, "what does he charge?"

"Oh, $1,100 dollars a day."

"Well, if he doubled his rate, he would make the same amount but could work just half the time."

"Oh!" she said, worried. "He could never demand that high a fee!"

If that's what they both believe, then they're absolutely right.

61. *Make Sure Your Fee Increases Exceed the Inflation Rate.* A great many consultants forget that even in periods of modest inflation, there *is* inflation. You are allowed to raise fees if you so desire, just as ExxonMobil or Siemens might.

62. *Push Toward Being the Bentley of Your Field.* At the beginning of your career, it's fine to be more competitively priced to draw business. But as your career trajectory continues, you should be building the contacts, referrals, and expertise to demonstrate that you are the class act in the field.

63. *Build Strong Brands and Nurture Them.* People are attracted to brands and pay far less attention to price. You've all heard, "If you have to ask how much it is, you can't afford the purchase." Brands draw clients who don't care about the fee, only the results and being associated with you. Never forget that the strongest brand is your own name.

64. *If You Are Active Globally, Consider Both Differential Rates for Overseas Work and Being Paid in Local Currency If That Helps.* Right now, for example, the dollar happens to be very low against the euro and pound sterling. If you were doing business in London, it might pay to open an account and be paid in pounds or in Paris in euros. On the East Coast of the United States, for

example, you might add 50 percent to all fees for Europe and Latin America and 100 percent for Asia and the Pacific Rim. Do the reverse if you're located in Sydney or Hong Kong.

65. *Never Allow Local Taxes to Be Deducted from Your Fees.* Consult your attorney and financial adviser, but in 90 percent of the cases, there is no justification for the withholding of local taxes.

66. *Accept Wire Transfers from Clients.* Credit cards carry interest charges, and cashing foreign checks takes time and often has a fee attached. If you accept fees via wire transfers, there is usually a small charge from the bank, but you will get the money faster and have use of it.

67. *Use Multiple Invoicing If a Client's Level of Authority Is Surpassed by Your Proposal.* There is nothing unethical, illegal, or immoral about sending two $50,000 invoices instead of one $100,000 invoice.

68. *Keep Boilerplate Out of Your Proposals.* Once "the third party shall hold harmless in the original jurisdiction" appears, the proposal is going to the legal department, and your entire project and fee basis could be challenged. Use plain language and rely on your relationship with the buyer for honorable behavior.

69. *Never Allow Accounts Payable to Do Anything but Send You the Check.* Don't let yourself be relegated to the accounting staff to be "set up in our system." Never fight with them over terms. Their job is to enforce existing procedures, not to help exceptions. Have your buyer sign off on everything, and ask the buyer to expedite the payment.

70. *Look in the mirror and say, "The fee is $176,000."* When you can do that without giggling, you just may be there.


# CHAPTER ROI

- Maximizing your profits means improving the top line and controlling the expense line. What you keep, not what you make, is the key.
- Use the guidelines in this chapter as a template that you can apply to your business on a periodic basis. There will always be room for improvement because none of us do all things equally well or apply them uniformly. If you have a staff, use this list as a conversation point at meetings and strategy sessions.

- We control much more of the profit dynamic than we think we do, but the way we educate the buyer, insist on our rights, and have the confidence to forge our own policies will determine how successful we are at protecting our bottom line.
- Remember that you are providing value, not "taking business." Your contribution to that value justifies an equitable payment to you. There is a name for this: it's called "capitalism."
- Whether or not you believe you are worth the fee, you're right.

*If you can't find several ways to increase profits from these seventy suggestions for raising fees, you aren't really interested. If you haven't highlighted and noted at least a few of the options, you may just be reading and not learning—which is never enough.*

# The Case of the Rebounding Retainer

For several years, I was on retainer to the CEO of a $600 million subsidiary of one of my largest clients. The CEO had access to my smarts, if you will. He could call at any time and ask about anything on his mind, providing it was within my competency. Nutrition, for example, was off-limits, since my life is the quest for the perfect cheeseburger.

The president would call me about once a week or less. On occasion, he would call me on Monday night during half-time of *Monday Night Football. He* didn't like football, but he knew that I did!

Once or twice a year, he would call on a Sunday, apologize to my wife for the intrusion, and ask a question that had arisen and was urgent for a board meeting the next morning. One Thursday he called about a critical violation of company ethics and asked if I could possibly facilitate a retreat that weekend since he was bringing in the entire field force to address the issue. I dropped what I was doing, reoriented my schedule, and took care of it.

Every year around November 1, we would casually discuss the next year's retainer and agree on a handshake to continue it on the same basis: $10,000 per month or $100,000 total if paid in one sum on January 2. Each year, he paid the $100,000 right after the New Year.

In the fourth year of the agreement, we chatted as usual on November 1.

"Same deal?" I asked nonchalantly.

"No, not next year," he said, not looking me in the eye.

I was stunned and immediately began desperately thinking about what I had taken for granted or missed or trampled. I was literally speechless.

Stepping into the silence and clearly enjoying himself, the CEO continued, "Make it $130,000, because you've been far more valuable than the present retainer."

The buyer has unilaterally raised my retainer by 30 percent! I had neither the intent of raising or lowering it. But that's the amount of value he perceived from our infrequent discussions and occasional emergencies. Like an insurance policy, he was happy to pay just to know I was there.

*Moral: How many of your clients perceive that degree of value, to the extent they want to pay you more than you charge, and how can you best achieve it?*

## CHAPTER 8

# How to Prevent and Rebut Fee Objections

## *Since You've Heard Them All Before, How Can You Not Know All the Answers?*

I'm constantly aghast at salespeople who wring their hands, rend their garments, and give up the fight when a prospect reacts with the quite normal reaction of "I don't think I need that." If you've been in the sales arena for longer than a month and haven't heard every imaginable objection, you've been embedded under a rock.

We, as consultants, know what our prospects' objections are going to be. There is no excuse not to be prepared for them. That doesn't mean that we'll be able to convert every single contact into a sale, but it does mean that we should be able to engage the buyer in a more prolonged dialogue and provide

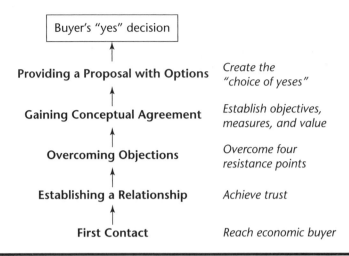

Buyer's "yes" decision

Providing a Proposal with Options — *Create the "choice of yeses"*

Gaining Conceptual Agreement — *Establish objectives, measures, and value*

Overcoming Objections — *Overcome four resistance points*

Establishing a Relationship — *Achieve trust*

First Contact — *Reach economic buyer*

**Figure 8.1**  Filters to Be Overcome to Reach a Buying Decision.

ourselves with more opportunities with the decision maker to influence his or her ultimate choice.[1]

There is a succession of "filters" (see Figure 8.1) that we must negotiate to achieve a positive buying decision. Some require "footwork" and maneuvering, such as getting through or circumventing feasibility buyers and committees to reach the economic buyer. Some require careful questioning and discerning listening in order to reach conceptual agreement.

But one of the most critical and most often bungled steps is dealing with early buyer resistance in the form of quite natural objections and rejections of the consultant's value or potential impact. The reasons include the following:

- We tend to take rejection personally and strive to avoid placing ourselves in a position of possible rejection.
- We provide a sales spiel or other selling retort instead of a true response to the buyer's real objections.

---

[1]Once again, I must emphasize that this chapter and its techniques apply only when dealing with the economic buyer.

- We don't recognize the generic nature of the objection and offer rebuttals that address our comfort areas and not the client's discomfort areas.
- We panic.
- We actually believe the buyer may be right.

> It makes as much sense to ignore the buyer's discomfort to focus on our own areas of comfort in rebutting objections as it does to focus on how well the project suits our own needs instead of the buyer's.

## THE FOUR FUNDAMENTAL AREAS OF RESISTANCE

There is a wonderful apocryphal story of a man encountering a friend on the street, searching the ground under a streetlight. "What are you doing," asks the man.

"I'm looking for my lost car keys," responds the friend.

"How did you happen to lose them here?"

"Oh, I didn't lose them here. I think I lost them a block away when I entered the restaurant."

"Then why are you searching here?"

"The light is better here."

It doesn't matter where your light is better when you're trying to find the reasons for the buyer's resistance. What matters is where the buyer actually lost your reasoning and value.

There are four major generic areas of prospect resistance and potential objection. We know what they are.[2] We might as well get good at responding to them.

---

[2]The origins of these four areas are murky, and many people take credit. I first heard them from Larry Wilson, the founder of Wilson Learning, in the early 1970s. His collaborator, I believe, was Dr. David Merrill.

## Resistance Point 1: I Don't Trust You

Perhaps the most common and most fundamentally understandable resistance is that the buyer has no reason to trust the consultant. The credentials might not be strong, the route of entry might be problematic (for example, direct mail or cold call), or the consultant might have other traits that undermine credibility: poor appearance, lack of maturity, poor vocabulary, inadequate promotional materials, and so on.

I don't trust people who call me on the phone at night to try to sell me securities. I do trust my accounting firm, which was referred to me by a trusted third party and which carefully considered whether we were right for each other. We've now worked together for fifteen years, and I have referred other potential clients to the company.

This is the primary reason that I've advocated "marketing "gravity"[3] for all consultants, so that they are known to potential clients, are referred by current clients, and possess an inherent level of trust from a cohesive body of work in the field. Not only is the creation of a name, brand, and reputation a quick route to establishing trust with any potential buyer, but it also considerably shortcuts the process of negotiating the various "filters" between consultant and potential buyer.

When the buyer has no inherent trust—and it's important to understand that this is not created by something the consultant does but rather is the default position unless you actively change it—it is folly to provide "benefits" about money, timing, or value. The client won't listen. And it's impossible to reach conceptual agreement without trust.

It is mandatory for a consultant to establish a trusting relationship with the economic buyer. That will never occur if you choose to work through middlemen.

## Resistance Point 2: I Don't Need You

This obstacle means that the prospect may very well trust you and even like you, but there doesn't appear to the buyer to be any need. That might mean

---

[3]See the first book of this series, *The Ultimate Consultant,* for details on creating marketing gravity.

that the prospect doesn't see anything requiring fixing or improvement. This is the most common plight of consultants who are merely introduced to a buyer without any specific reason other than "You two should spend some time together." A friendly buyer does that based on the advice of a third party but sees no intrinsic need to be filled by the consultant.

This is also why so many consultants have come to me with the same fundamental question: "What do I say after I've said hello?" They've managed to meet a buyer but haven't managed to move the buyer. In fact, many people who don't understand these dynamics make statements such as "I can't understand it—we get along fine, but he doesn't seem to want to hire me!"

---

It's not the buyer's job to tell you about "needs." In well-run organizations, there may well be no pressing issues. It's the consultant's job to demonstrate need in improving the client's condition though new and better performance.

---

What's not to understand? If there is no perceived need, working on greater trust doesn't help. It's incumbent on consultants not to launch arbitrary torpedoes of methodology, technique, approaches, and alternatives, hoping to hit a moving target. It's far better to listen carefully and to ask precise, prompting questions to discover need (see Appendix B), to suggest need, and to create need.[4]

This phenomenon is why I've strongly suggested that the major value of consultants is to raise the bar to new heights, not just to fix problems. Even the best of organizations can steadily improve; thus there is always a need that can be created, even if there is nothing obvious to be fixed.

The consultant must be able to identify preexisting needs, create needs, or anticipate needs. This is why a "sales pitch" (elevator speech) about an alternative is completely ineffective.

---

[4]No one "needed" frequent flyer programs, global positioning systems, or drive-through banking and burgers, but we certainly need them today. A luxury tends to become a necessity after just one successful use!

# Resistance Point 3: I Don't Feel Any Urgency

This is the near-legendary excuse that "the timing isn't right." Every consultant has had hot prospects that could have closed immediately if only the timing had been better. And many of those consultants keep those prospects in their forecasts—or, worse, actually spend the money they're anticipating from the project—for quite a long time.

But the timing never gets better.

If a client doesn't feel a sense of urgency, then enhancing trust levels or heightening need isn't the logical response. After all, I may like you, believe in the fact that we have room to improve, or have a condition that needs remediation. But I've lived with this condition for a long time, and I don't see why I have to do anything (that is, spend money) at this juncture.

Prospects typically resort to "no urgency" or "poor timing" for three reasons:

- When they are afraid of disrupting the organization ("Let's leave well enough alone")
- When the return doesn't justify the investment ("I can't see justifying that expense until the problem is costing us far more than it is")
- When the perception is that everyone has to put up with this and the prospect is not unique ("This is a 'necessary evil' that would be impossible to eliminate")

In this general resistance area, the consultant must create urgency. This can be accomplished by these methods:

- By pointing out competitive actions that will threaten the client
- By identifying a unique and limited window of opportunity to address the issue
- By showing that the prospect is incurring far more damage than perceived
- By demonstrating a far greater return on investment than the prospect believed possible
- By showing that the prospect is not on a plateau but that the condition is actually causing a decline that is increasing in its degree and speed

> When prospects tell me "the timing isn't right," I tell them the timing is never going to be right. There is no ideal time to intervene in most organizations. So what's the real nature of the reluctance?

"Not the right time" is a specious argument because there is always time to devote to business matters—the issue is where it is invested. Time is never a resource issue; it is always a priority issue.

## Resistance Point 4: I Don't Have the Money to Pay You

This is the most commonly cited rejection by consultants, and it's mistakenly assumed as the primary objection of most buyers. It is not.

If you've been reading carefully to this point, you've probably come to agree that most resistance is not about money; it's about trust, need, and urgency. If there is trust, perceived need, and sufficient urgency, *money can almost always be found.* After all, few buyers wake up in the morning and say, "What a beautiful day. I wonder if I can hire Alan Weiss?" And few budgets contain discretionary funds for consultants to be hired for concerns unanticipated, unappreciated, and unheard of.

Most consulting budgets must therefore be created, meaning that the money originates in other areas. It is appropriated from other budgets and other sources. There is never any money, in the sense of quickly available, earmarked funds, for consultants.

So the money objection is the easiest, most common, and most misunderstood. It is almost always an excuse, a cover-up for one of the first three areas not being satisfied. Yet consultants, upon hearing "I'd love to, but we have no budget," quietly and complacently fold up their tents, leave their cards, mutter "Let's keep in touch," and disappear into the night.

It's time to have some backbone and buy some floodlights. When a client does say, "We need to do this and I want you to do it for us but I don't have budget," the consultant can help the client find the funds. When the first three needs (or possible objections) have truly been addressed, the client and consultant can collaborate on finding funds and developing payment terms that are mutually satisfactory (for example, pay half in this fiscal year and half in next or provide stock as partial compensation or take the funds from the annual convention budget and hold the meeting locally rather than overseas).

We're going to discuss some techniques to counter specific points of objection and demurral, but keep them in the context of the four major areas. Your approach should be determined by which of these areas is causing the buyer's resistance at any given time. There may be occasions when all four are working against you, but that is relatively rare. The probability is that one or perhaps two are most on the buyer's mind and that the fourth—no money—is rarely an objection in actuality (although it may be the one verbalized).

If a prospect admits to need, trusts you as a professional and competent resource, and believes the time is right to act, the money will be found. Consequently, the budget is always the worst place to start, because it derails the conversation from the actual and pivotal reasons for the client's rejection.

Worse, focusing on the budget prompts the consultant to lower fees rather than address the true issues behind the resistance. If that's not a double whammy, I don't know what is.

"No money" is as specious as "no time." There is always money—the question is, will it go to you? This, too, is a priority issue, not a resource issue.

Remember that objections are signs of interest. A truly apathetic, uninterested prospect would ignore you or refuse to return calls or have an intermediary stall you. But objection is a sign of interest and provides a springboard for you to catapult into an investigation of the prospect's reasoning.

Treat objections as opportunities, not threats. And think about this: if there is no time, how did the buyer find the time to talk to you?

## MAINTAINING THE FOCUS ON VALUE

Here's an ironclad rule: if you're in a discussion about fees and not value, you've lost control of the discussion. Prospects often want to go immediately to a discussion of costs. It's important to understand the psychology of this tropism. The buyer wants to deal with fees—costs—early because they provide the easiest excuse to be rid of you. You're not dealing with a real objection but instead with a very effective technique (if not correctly countered) to immediately end further discussion.

The rebuttal to this immediate focus on fees is not to do it. Once you agree to talk about fees, you have enabled and empowered the prospect to focus on the cost side of the equation, not the outcome or value side. If you become a willing accomplice to this tactic, you might as well leave your card and disappear into the night. It ain't going to get better. You must create clear results so that ROI is readily apparent, not ambiguous results where only fees are readily apparent.

Here are the major rebuttals to use when the prospect immediately wants to know what you charge:

- "I don't know what the fees would be, since I don't know what you need or even if I'm the right consultant. Can we spend some time talking about your situation first? That will put me in a better position to answer that question."
- "It would be unfair to you to attempt a response. We've just met, and both of us need to explore and learn a few things first. Let's table that issue until I can provide a thoughtful proposal, which won't take long if I can ask you a few questions now."
- "It would be unethical for me to give you a response this early in our talk. I don't know what you need or whether I have the competency to respond to those needs. Let's explore those areas, and then we can talk about value and investment when the scope of the project is clear."
- "The range will be from $5,000 to $1,000,000. Seriously, I have no idea. Let's explore what's involved and see whether a relationship even makes sense for both of us. If it does, I'm sure we'll find some mutually beneficial way to work together."
- "What's your budget? [The prospect doesn't know or won't say.] Of course you can't say, and neither can I. We both need to learn more if we're going to have a responsible and cost-effective solution to the issue. So why don't you begin by telling me what you're trying to accomplish, and I'll see how I can help."

> The prospect can't discuss fees if you refuse to do so. No prospect that I've ever met has ended the conversation at that point. This dynamic is controlled by the consultant, not the buyer. But the consultant usually surrenders the field as soon as the dreaded "How much do you charge?" is uttered.

The key for the consultant is to sidestep this issue using one of my suggested rebuttals or a combination of rebuttals. Under no circumstances should you agree to discuss fees before all the following steps have been completed:

1. You have met the economic buyer.
2. A trusting relationship has been formed.
3. The four generic resistance factors have been overcome.
4. Agreement has been reached on objectives, measures, and value.
5. Agreement has been reached to entertain a written proposal with a "choice of yeses."

It may seem that this postpones the discussion for a very long time, but believe me, the refusal to discuss fees any sooner always leads to higher fees.

> *Alan's fourth theorem of fee dynamics:* the earlier a fee is quoted, the lower the ultimate fee will be; the later a set of fees is quoted, the higher they will be.
>
> *Corollary:* when a set of fees is quoted at the ideal moment in the sales process, the buyer will tend to migrate up the set to higher fees in return for perceived higher value.

# BORING IN ON THE SUBJECT

It's embarrassingly common for a consultant to negotiate all the shoals and rapids of project negotiations and arrive at the proposal stage only to find the buyer with a near-fatal case of sticker shock. That occurs when the client, despite having stipulated to seeking several millions of dollars of savings and improvements in the project results and believing in the consultant's ability to achieve them also believes—quite seriously—that the fee will be around $5,000, while the consultant's most inexpensive option, which the consultant considers a "good deal," is $55,000.

How can this happen so far into the discussions and after conceptual agreement? The cause is twofold:

1. Some consultants fail to develop a sense about the client's philosophy of return on investment and overall spending.
2. Some clients are totally out of touch with investment needs.

The reasons for the second condition are these (which you can use as red flags should you want to test for willingness to invest early):

- The client has never used consultants in the past and so is totally unfamiliar with investing in external help.
- The client used very inexpensive and inexperienced consultants in the past, which has caused an incorrect "education" and precedent.
- The client has tight cost controls and a zealous focus on the expense side of the business; doesn't see ROI, only costs.
- The client tends to focus overwhelmingly on the short term.
- The client's firm is losing money and in desperate straits.
- The client is a small business owner, weighing personal and business expense needs.
- The client sees the consultant as "too new" or not totally credible and feels that the consultant is getting a chance to prove himself or herself, so the fee can be commensurately low.

When these signs are present, you need to ascertain what the buyer's budget expectations are. Don't forget, few buyers have set aside funds for consultants, so the money has to be found somewhere. And if you're not skilled in determining the budget conversationally, you must find out formally.

Some clients are hard to read. Others are deliberately deceptive. When you're the least bit uncertain, find out what the budget is. You won't die, but you might be shocked.

Here's how to do that. After conceptual agreement is reached but before the proposal is even created, ask the buyer a variation of the following question: "You've been very kind, and I'm in a position to offer a proposal with some investment options for you. Since there are options for achieving these goals, is there a budget amount you'd like me to stay within?"

Another approach is this: "We've made fine progress, and I don't want to waste your time or mine as we go forward. Is there a budget—or even a rough amount in your mind—that represents the limit of your investment in this project?"

And here's one more, which I call the New York (direct) approach: "We're ready to move to a proposal, but before we do, my experience has shown that it's important to understand any constraints on our approach. What is the budget you've allocated, now that we've reached this level of agreement?"

My suggestion is to ask these questions *after* conceptual agreement because you will have the best chance to convince the buyer that a significant investment is justified at that point. But do it before the proposal so that you don't waste your time if the buyer's expectations are simply ridiculous.

There are three common responses to my three questions, and they in turn deserve certain reactions from you:

*Common Response 1:* "What is this? The wedding reception approach? So the more money I have, the better the reception? I don't want to disclose what I'm prepared to spend." This usually indicates that you don't have a very trusting relationship. You should respond, "I've come to respect you and don't want to waste your time. My judgment at this point is that the investment range is going to be $35,000 to $65,000, depending on how much certainty you're seeking. Is that in the ballpark?"

If the client tells you to go ahead, then you've prepared the buyer, and there can't be sticker shock. If the buyer says the range is too high, part as friends.

*Common Response 2:* "Our expectation is that the project should cost somewhere around $20,000." If that's realistic, respond, "We can work within that, and I'll get the proposal to you tomorrow." If it's unrealistic, say, "I don't think we can do it for that amount. We're probably talking about $35,000 at the low end to $65,000 at the high end. Do you want to discuss this further?"

This allows for total honesty. The client might say, "OK, I'm prepared for a slightly worse case, go ahead." If not, part as friends.

---

Note that any discussion of budget at this point is always based on the investment, since the objectives and their values are already established. This is far superior to discussing fees at the outset, when they are simply isolated costs.

---

*Common Response 3:* "We're willing to spend whatever is reasonable to make this happen." Your reply here should be, "Thanks, I'm sure you'll find the investment well within reason in view of the benefits we've already detailed. The proposal will be here tomorrow."

Asking about the budget is perfectly fine, provided that you do it at the right time and are prepared for the three types of responses. Here are the conditions:

- You have been talking to the economic buyer all along.
- You have achieved conceptual agreement with the economic buyer.
- You are uncertain of the buyer's understanding of the level of investment required.

Note that if you are speaking professionally in addition to your consulting and a prospective buyer asks about your appearing at an event, ask very early what the budget is. Many infrequent or novice buyers of speaking services have no idea about fees, which vary tremendously in the field.

# OFFERING DISCOUNTS

I offer discounted fee under certain circumstances, and I'm not talking about returning a coupon or buying a special appliance. I offer discounts when I find that the project calls for phases (not options, which I always provide) and I want to encourage the client to use my help through all of the phases. A phase is a timed step or sequence, each succeeding one dependent on the successful completion of the prior one. Typically, a project might require an information-gathering phase, then recommendations for intervention, then creation of the interventions, then the implementation, and then follow-up and monitoring. While I'd prefer to include all phases in one project, it's sometimes impossible to do so, since you can't predict needs further down the line until earlier steps are completed.

In this case, I suggest offering the client another form of a good deal. Offer the client the rebate of a percentage of the phase 1 fee if you're hired for phase 2, and so on down the line. What's the right percentage? Who knows? But I keep it to 50 percent or below. (The higher the fee for phase 2, the higher the percentage rebate—don't make the mistake of looking at the fee for phase 1 for the rebate percentage!)

*Example:* The client has agreed to a phase 1 needs analysis among customers for a $35,000 fee. The second phase would be the development of a better customer response system, based on the customer feedback and priorities. You're estimating that phase 2 would be in the range of $125,000 to $175,000. You tell the client that should you be chosen to implement phase 2 of the project, you will rebate 50 percent of the phase 1 fee. That means that you're still netting $90,000 to $140,000 on phase 2 while greatly reducing the chances of another consultant being brought in or the client deciding to do it internally.

Of course, if you think that you're a "lock" for the continuing phases, there's no need to offer a rebate, or you can offer just a token one. But I always like to "think of the fourth sale first," so I believe rebates are a good idea in these situations, particularly with new clients with whom you don't have a track record. If you think of the totality of the several phases as the real project, then the rebates can be reasonable reductions against the very large total investment.

> Don't give rebates unless phases are in the best interests of the
> project and the client. When they are, offer the potential rebate in
> the proposal itself so that it's committed to writing in the same
> document that the client is accepting as the basis for phase 1 work.

You might want to use the designation *rebate* or *discount* or *professional courtesy.* The key is, it's a tool to be used when appropriate. I find that I tend to offer rebates relatively rarely, but with great effect when I do.

## USING "SMACK TO THE HEAD" COMPARISONS

There are times when the client will balk at a fee, even when you know darn well that the fee is entirely reasonable and the good deal is terrific. You'll also be certain that the buyer can afford it, and the reluctance will sometimes start to get on your nerves. This often happens after a proposal has been presented and you believed that all such contingencies were long since dealt with.

You'll be very frustrated. So the answer is to get a metaphorical large board and smack the buyer upside the head. Here's how you do that. Find comparisons that will embarrass the buyer into giving up his or her resistance. Some buyers are simply maneuvering for a deal; some have an ego that won't be sated until they get a concession; some are transferring other issues in their life (a fight with a spouse, a lost promotion) to you. No matter. Whatever the cause, don't fall for it. Fight back.

I've found the best comparisons to be the following, but any imaginative consultant can easily add to my list (in fact, it's fun to do so):

- Point out that the client is spending more on copy machine warranties and repair than the total cost of your proposal.
- Demonstrate that spillage and ruined product cost ten times the proposal's most expensive option.

- Ask what one lost customer a week is costing.
- Ask what the cost of a very bad hire is.
- Cite the cost of each talented employee who leaves the organization (including replacement, lost business, training, succession planning, and so on); don't skimp.
- Ask the cost of the client's most recent gaffe in connection with a failed new office or a poorly received new product.
- Cite what the savings would be if R&D commercialization time were cut by 25 percent.
- Ask what the board of directors' reaction would be if the board considered the cost of the current problems versus unwillingness to make this investment to solve them.

You get the idea. Have these ready, because you never know when you'll need them. The most agreeable and friendliest client can spring an unexpected fee objection, even after conceptual agreement and receipt of the proposal. It's your own fault if you're not prepared to fight back.

> Most embarrassing comparisons will hold true from organization to organization, so the preparation of a few "beauts" will serve you reliably over the course of time.

There are several sources to use to develop your "smacks upside the head":

1. In your preliminary discussions leading up to conceptual agreement, make some gentle inquiries into the costs the prospective client is incurring in some of these areas. Listen for voluntary disclosures (for example, "Do you know we're spending $175,000 just on software 'fixes'?").
2. Use Internet search engines to turn up statistics and facts on common issues. For example, find out the average costs of turnover, lawsuits, recruiting, and so on.

3. Tear relevant items out of your daily reading. *The Wall Street Journal* and *BusinessWeek* are forever publishing information on the costs of accounting, legal, computers, and other areas.

4. Remember that many of these are generic, and you can use them from client to client. Save your best ones to use in key situations. I'm forever pointing to the copy machine "culprit" sitting in a corner as an example of the client's being willing to spend more money on equipment maintenance than on human development.

5. Use your prior client engagements as examples of investments and ROI. The closer to your current prospect in type or situation, the better.

6. Provide a calculation of what's lost if no action is taken. Steady bleeding can kill the patient as surely as trauma can.

7. Demonstrate that attempting to resolve this internally is impractical and even more expensive (and it always is) because of time taken away from other tasks, turf battles, lack of external best practices, lack of residual talent, and so on.

The embarrassing comparison will take care of most of the flimsy and capricious objections to fees. Sometimes you just have to pack a strong metaphorical weapon.

## IGNORING THE COMPETITION

I've often stated that if you don't know what the competition is charging, you're probably charging too little. But I don't mean to imply that you should peg your fees to those of the competition. The former is merely market intelligence. The latter is simply foolhardy.

Don't allow any buyer to tell you that the competition is charging so much and that you should come in below that. Don't listen to the argument that "this is what we've paid in the past and expect to continue to pay" for consulting services.

The whole point in developing a relationship prior to conceptual agreement is to ferret out these kinds of (sometimes) legitimate expectations and (sometimes) devious devices to depress fees. You are not like past consultants (which is why you're there), and you don't do what the competition does (which is why you're there). Telling a Mercedes dealership that the Buick place down the street charges much less will get you an uncomprehending stare or a firm "So what?" Telling an airline that you're accustomed to paying the amount of tolls on the New Jersey Turnpike to drive from New York to Philadelphia and that you expect an equivalent airfare will get you escorted away. Telling a theater that your budget only permits you to pay $2.50 will not gain you admittance to the show. So why should you listen to similar irrational arguments regarding your services?

Educate your buyer immediately and repeatedly that what's gone before is history and what goes on around you is irrelevant. The only thing that matters is the "good deal": Is the client achieving a great return on a reasonable investment? You'll be happy to demonstrate that via a proposal at the appropriate time, if the buyer can cooperate with some information at the moment. But you're not interested in comparisons and arbitrary parameters.

After all, this must be a win-win relationship. What if you told the buyer that prior buyers paid a minimum of $600,000, that consultants who do what you do receive an average of $450,000 per contract, or that you're simply not prepared to accept anything less than $475,000 because that's your expectation? You'd be thrown off the property, probably under armed guard. So why allow the client to express equally absurd expectations?

---

Reverse the client's logic about expecting low fees—that you're expecting high fees—and you'll hear equally moronic lines of argument. Point that out and move on.

---

Don't dignify bizarre positions. Educate the buyer correctly from the outset. Ignore the competition and the competition's poor strategy. Now is the time to be your own person.

The only person deciding what your profit level is should be you. It's a mistake to allow the buyer to do that, and it's insane to allow the competition to influence it in any way at all. So stop doing that.

# CHAPTER ROI

- There are four fundamental resistance points: no need, no trust, no urgency, no money. You must address the correct one. Seldom do all four come into play, and lack of trust is usually the fundamental problem. Lack of money is usually a red herring.
- Always focus on value, not fees; otherwise you've lost control of the discussion. Don't hesitate to ask about the buyer's intended budget, especially if certain red flags appear during early conversations.
- Offer rebates or discounts on multiphase projects, when such phases are truly called for and are in the client's best interests.
- Prepare yourself with embarrassingly harsh comparisons for times when an otherwise agreeable buyer has fee issues that you know should be brushed aside.
- Remember that an objection is a sign of interest and provides you with an opportunity to further your progress.
- Ignore the competition, since neither the buyer nor the competition should establish your profitability levels.
- Remember that most of the fee-setting dynamic is actually under our control and influence, and you should guard against sacrificing this strength.
- The best way to support high fees is first to believe in the value you're providing and then to convince the buyer of it.

*There is no such animal as a "new" objection. We've heard them all before, every one. If the prospect has successfully rebutted your position, the buyer is simply better prepared than you are, and you haven't established a "good deal."*

# The Case of the Perverse Purchasing Agent

I had concluded a deal with a handshake with Tom, the general manager of a division of a Fortune 25 company. He told me to start in two weeks and meanwhile he'd put through the paperwork to get the deposit we had agreed on. I summarized our discussion in an e-mail that afternoon.

Two days later, I received a call from Margaret, who identified herself as the purchasing manager for the site and said she was calling to negotiate my contract.

"You must be misinformed," I said. "I already have an agreement with Tom."

"No, you are misinformed," she corrected, "since he is not empowered to negotiate terms with vendors."

"I'm not a vendor; I'm a consultant."

"You're a vendor to me, and you will provide me with an hourly rate that I'll compare against the average hourly rates

183

of the consultants we've used over the past year. If your rate exceeds it by more than 10 percent, you'll be asked to reduce it by that amount."

"I'm not doing that."

"Then you won't work here."

I hung up and dialed Tom. I told him that we had a problem.

"What is it?" he asked. "Do you need more money?"

I thought about that for a few seconds and then decided to tell the truth about Margaret.

"I've heard prior rumblings about her, but never so specific," he acknowledged. "I'll take care of it; you just proceed as planned."

When I turned up two weeks later, Margaret had been fired. I had no regrets. Her job was to support top management, not enforce bureaucratic rules to impede relationships and progress.

*Moral: Never argue or debate with anyone in accounts payable, purchasing, human resources, or other low-level support functions. Always go back to your buyer, with whom you have a peer-level relationship.*

## CHAPTER 9

# Setting Fees for Nonconsulting Opportunities

How to Make Money While You Sleep, Eat, Play, and Make Money Elsewhere

I'm constantly surprised at how stupid I was two weeks ago. Once upon a time, I would have said "two years ago." I like to think that today's shorter time frame is not so much a sign of my increasing dementia as it is one of exploding opportunities in this profession. (A speaking buddy of mine, Joe Calloway, told me he wants to call his original clients and just cry, "I'm sorry for that nutty advice I gave you years ago, but it was the best I had at the time! I want to return your money!" I'm with him until that last sentence.)

There is nothing wrong with the position that holds that one is a consultant and not interested in the peripheral and tangential activities that may distract one from the work at hand. Fair enough. But if you're at all like me and you believe that consulting is simply an input to a much greater end—our lives, loved ones, and legacy—then why not explore the myriad opportunities that a successful consulting practice can generate?

Remember, wealth is about discretionary time. Money is important because it is the prime determinant of discretionary time.

Basically, there are a lot of ways to make money in the profession, but like the nature of our consulting fees, there are also a lot of ways to charge incorrectly and shortchange ourselves in terms of receiving fair compensation for our value. It's not unusual for a consultant in my mentor program to ask whether he has a right to charge a high fee for speaking to an organization that has been attracted to him by a book he has written. "After all," he (incorrectly) reasons, "they can get most of this out of the book, so I don't think I'm bringing much extra value."

If that's what you believe, then you're right.

If you're of the "pure" consulting philosophy, you might want to skip this chapter. On the other hand, you might want to read on and see what you're missing. And if you're a big believer in maximizing your income, especially in non-labor-intensive pursuits, then pick up your highlighter.

## KEYNOTE SPEAKING: DON'T CHARGE FOR YOUR SPOKEN WORDS

The intent of this discussion is to provide help in how to set fees for speaking activities. If you're interested in how to begin a professional speaking career, or how to craft a speech and get onto the lucrative speaking circuit, see my book *Money Talks*.

No one is worth very much for an hour of his or her time. As in consulting, it's the value that you provide during that one hour that will support your speaking fee.

A keynote speech is usually forty-five to ninety minutes in length. It is ordinarily a general session speech, delivered to the full assembly and not to concurrent sessions or breakout groups. Technically, only the opening speech is the keynote speech (sounding the "key note" for the conference); the others are plenary speeches delivered during the course of the conference.

The least expensive speakers delivering keynote speeches are paid about $3,500 by major trade associations and large organizations, and the most expensive are paid from $75,000 to $200,000. These latter people have included Colin Powell, Norman Schwarzkopf, Bill Clinton, and certain athletes.[1] The typical highly regarded noncelebrity keynote speaker is paid between $7,500 and $15,000 at this writing.

At the lower end of that scale, speaking just once a month generates nearly $100,000 a year of what is essentially pure profit. Speaking twice a month at the higher end yields well over $300,000. Do I have your attention?

There are also more traditional training opportunities, which may involve concurrent sessions, workshops, and so on and may take several hours or several days. I favor keynotes, since they are the least labor-intensive and command the highest fees, but longer training sessions are also viable options for any consultant.

In terms of your fees, I think there are three main considerations.

## Factor 1: Establish Your Value

Your materials, Web site, conversations, and other promotional efforts should focus on value—not on topic, not on delivery, and not on methodology. Recall the value package concept from Chapter Three (repeated here in Figure 9.1).

Your speaking approach must accentuate the client's future. The more of your past that is relevant, unique, interesting, and attractive, the more you can potentially contribute to the client's future. The intervention—the speech—is merely the transfer point.

If you can keep this process in mind, you'll have no reluctance charging for your worth. If you concentrate solely on the nature of your intervention

---

[1]I believe that the unofficial record was set by former President George H. W. Bush, who in exchange for delivering a speech in Tokyo accepted stock options that subsequently generated several million dollars for about an hour's work.

| Consultant's Past | Current Intervention | Client's Future |
|---|---|---|
| • experiences | • coaching | • higher productivity |
| • education | • survey | • lower attrition |
| • accomplishments | • redesign | • higher morale |
| • development | • workshop | • improved image |
| • travels | • retreat | • better performance |
| • work history | • etc. | • greater market share |
| • beliefs | | • greater profit |
| • victories/defeats | | • more growth |
| • risks/adversity | | • more innovation |
| • experimentation | | • problems solved |
| | | • happier customers |
| | | • superior service |

Process Flow

$\longrightarrow$

**Figure 9.1** Transforming Consultant Past to Client Future.

(a speech, workshop, seminar, or training session), you'll constantly wonder how you can charge more than a modest amount. And you'd be correct.

Be crystal clear on the value you provide in your speeches. Educate the prospect. Do you help improve sales, increase retention, deal with culture changes, enhance customer service, develop strategies for growth, or foster teamwork? Those are certainly more valuable objectives than "providing a speech" or "helping motivation."[2]

---

The best "motivational speakers" provide pragmatic techniques for people to apply in order to improve their lives and their jobs. The worst provide empty aphorisms and "affirmations," which evanesce in the cold light of day.

---

[2]In fact, "motivational speakers" have a justly deserved poor reputation for much froth and little substance. We had all better be motivational in our talks, but we had all better be providing solid techniques for improvement as well.

A perfectly fine speech can be crafted based on your consulting experiences, challenges, and results.


## Factor 2: Develop Options

The "choice of yeses" extends to professional speaking. For example, I can turn virtually any keynote speech into a solid five-figure assignment by providing options to the buyer such as these (I've made up the numbers just to provide a comparison):

- Deliver the keynote according to the buyer's objectives: $8,500
- Talk to selected participants first by phone to include their observations in the remarks and customize my approach to their issues: $2,500
- Talk to the division executives (corporate officers, board of directors, trustees, others) to include their views, remarks, and further tailor the presentation: $3,000
- Conduct a brief survey to compare industry practices to the client's practices and highlight the distinctions: $5,000
- Appear at subsequent workout sessions with smaller groups to respond to their questions and interpret the keynote remarks down to operational concerns: $2,000
- Provide a copy of my book (tape, other product) for every participant to bridge the remarks and their application: $1,000
- Create a page (with pass code) on my Web site just for attendees: $2,500
- Provide a CD of the speech to all participants: $1,000 (for one hundred people)
- E-mail coaching of selected participants for up to ninety days: $7,500

You might create more and better options. But these alone add up to $33,000. Any combination will land you somewhere in the teens or twenties. And since you're a consultant to begin with, you can provide and complete these options much better than a pure speaker, who does nothing else for a living. In other words, the options allow you to build on your innate strength.

Most speakers will not offer these options. Some buyers will tell you they can't afford them. So what? This is a sideline for you, and one that you can embark on within your own parameters. And you'd be silly not to build on the very value that you bring to the equation.

### Factor 3: Use Speakers' Bureaus Only on Your Terms

Bureaus are brokers between the client and the talent (you) for which they expect 25 percent of the deal (some want 30 percent and more, indicating that there are still a lot of people who don't connect fees and value). Bureaus can be highly effective, since they bring business you would not ordinarily have acquired, and your own marketing cost is nil. However, they can be deadly and dangerous for consultants.

Bureaus will want a "fee schedule." For example, your keynote fee may be $7,500, your half-day fee may be $9,000, and your full-day fee may be $12,000. This is what bureaus market. That's OK if they allow you to negotiate further with the client, providing options as I've suggested. But many bureaus won't allow you to do that out of a general paranoia, and your fee would be restricted to the $7,500 less the 25 percent commission, or $5,625 net. That means that the annual revenue from speaking just once a month drops to $67,500—still a decent figure, but considerably less than the $90,000 it might otherwise have been.

---

A bureau relationship should be like a client relationship: mutually trusting, mutually beneficial, and mutually supportive. If it's not, walk away. You don't need bureaus; they need you.

---

## HIGHLY LEVERAGED PRACTICES FOR WORKING WITH BUREAUS

If you're going to deal with bureaus, and you're a professional consultant who is speaking, not a professional speaker who can't and doesn't consult, then follow these guidelines in your bureau relationships:

- Don't pay more than a 25 percent commission. Commissions on "spin-off" business (subsequent business generated by your appearance) should provide the same commission to the bureau for a finite period (one or two years, for example), although some bureaus reduce commissions on spin-off business. However, never pay that amount for spin-off *consulting* business. For this, pay a maximum of 10 percent.

- Demand to speak to the buyer and negotiate the actual fee yourself. Bureaus almost always deal with meeting planners, who are rarely economic buyers. Consequently, their demand is to conserve money, not to invest in value. (Obviously, this is a middleman dealing with a middleman.) After all, the higher the fee you negotiate, the higher the bureau commission.

- Develop a relationship with the bureau principal. If the two of you can't work together as peers, walk away.

- Be clear that subsequent consulting work that might arise out of your speaking is not subject to the bureau's speaking commission. You might agree to pay 10 percent or less, but the thought of paying the bureau 25 percent of a $200,000 consulting fee is not fair, justified, or sane. Make sure that this is clear before you speak, as most speakers' bureaus do not understand consulting at all.

- Do not invest in bureau promotional initiatives. The reason bureaus get 25 percent, ostensibly, is to market you. If they also insist that you pay for placement in their catalogue, on their Web site, or in special mailings, take a hike.

- Do not allow any money to be held in escrow. When the client pays the (typically) 50 percent deposit to hold the date, the bureau should keep half (the 25 percent commission) and send the other half to you. The final 50 percent should be paid directly to you no later than the presentation date itself. Any other arrangement is simply unfair to you.

The most desirable professional speaking will come directly to you (avoiding bureau fees) via your normal "marketing gravity." (I speak about thirty times a year—and used to speak fifty times annually—which is the rate I've sought to maintain, with only five or six assignments coming from bureaus.) That requires that you educate prospects about your availability as a speaker in your promotional materials, Web site, articles, networking, and so on. You will always be more valuable as a consultant who speaks than as a speaker who consults.

Keep your fees high. This is not your main source of income, and people believe they get what they pay for. The more unique you are as a consultant (book published, international work, media interviews, and so forth), the more valuable you are as a speaker. Finally, like consulting, speaking is about marketing, not methodology. You can always improve your platform techniques (and there are only 57,000 coaches who will be happy to help you), but unless you market yourself, you'll be speaking to yourself.

I once addressed a small group for six hours, and before I began, the CEO asked his assembled team what they believed I was charging him. They hemmed and hawed and arrived at a range of $2,500 to $5,000. "He's charging me $18,500," bellowed the CEO, "so listen up!" Buyers have egos too.

## PRODUCTS

One of the biggest errors I made when I first published *Million Dollar Consulting* in 1992 was to advise that products should wait until the consultant has a firmly established reputation. Actually, products can help branding and the creation of that reputation.

However, since I'm talking here primarily to successful consultants, products are an important part of the repertoire in any case. And they possess the wonderful attribute of providing income while also promoting your consulting.

---

The buyer said to me while walking out of the room, "By the way, can you send along four hundred copies of your book with an invoice?" I managed to say, "Yes, sure," before I realized that I didn't know which book the buyer wanted.

---

Here is a brief description of some of the product options available to successful, innovative, and aggressive consultants.

## Commercially Published Books

You can buy your books at a discount *not from the publisher* (who offers about 40 percent off) but rather from one of the book wholesalers, such as Ingram.[3] In this way, you can qualify for more than 40 percent off, get another 2 percent off for prompt payment, and generate royalties for yourself (since the wholesaler buys from your publisher). If your hard-cover book retails for $30, you can net $12 to $15 on your own sales using this route. (Always sell at full retail.)

## Self-Published Books

This is where the serious money resides, but two factors are absolutely critical: First, the book must be good. Most self-published books are terrible, and they look as though they were produced by someone who can't even use a computer properly. Second, they should be expensive, not inexpensive. While I have some booklets that sell for $7, they are also used as free marketing vehicles when necessary. However, my large margins come from books that sell for $75 to $150. Value-based pricing can apply to books (as you've probably understood when paying for one of those large, gaudy "coffee table" editions). You can self-publish a hard-cover book with an initial print run of two thousand copies for about $8,000, and subsequent press runs will cost about half that. That means that you're making about $25 on a $30 book. You're better off with low volume and a high margin than with high volume and a low margin, since you're not in the book fulfillment business.

## CDs and Albums

Plan some of your speeches with the intent that they will be recorded for a possible product offering. (In other words, don't use the client's name repeatedly, don't cite the date, and refrain from using contemporary but transient examples.) You can offer the client free copies if you need cooperation.

---

[3]Ingram Book Company, P.O. Box 277616, Atlanta, GA 30384; (615) 793–5000).

Record the audience reaction as well through careful microphone placement.[4] These single CDs are ideal marketing devices as well as potential products. Keep each to about sixty minutes (the maximum is usually eighty minutes or so), which is "drive time" for a commuter. Edit them with professional introductions, elimination of "dead spots," and so on. They cost about $2 apiece to duplicate. However, once you have several on related topics, you have a four- or six- or eight-CD album, which you can accompany with a workbook, set of pamphlets, or manual, and a product emerges that can sell for $150 or more. Don't record tapes in a studio; they sound stilted and demand perfection. Talks taped live are more fun, more energetic, and forgiving of errors because they are live. You can also create analogous MP3 downloads for purchase from your Web site or by providing download links. The iPod has made these very popular. Streaming audio can be used on your Web site for demonstration purposes, marketing, and so on.

## DVDs and Albums

I've found that video is less desired than audio, which is less desired than print. However, video can augment your product offerings nicely, costs only about $10 for duplication, and can be created during your normal speaking endeavors. Sometimes the client will make the recording for the client's own purposes, and you can get a master by waiving any fee for agreeing to the arrangement.[5] This, too, always needs a live audience. In addition to what you talk about, make sure your dress is conservative and doesn't betray a date or time. I sell videos on marketing, product development, and actual samples of one of my keynote addresses. You can combine these with audio, print, and related materials to build quite impressive—and expensive—products. You can also use this as streaming video on your Web site. You can find audio and video to sample at my site, http://www.summitconsulting.com.

---

[4]Hire a professional recording firm. It will cost you less than $1,000, and the resulting quality will be well worth that small investment.

[5]I always allow audio- and videotaping free of charge, provided that I'm given two master copies with permission to use them for product purposes after the client name and proprietary information have been removed. If you prefer to do it yourself, a professional video team can be hired for less than $2,500, using two cameras.

> The key to product sales is margin. This is not a business in which you want "loss leaders"—you're not Kmart. Moving $40,000 of product is just silly if it earns you a paltry $2,000.

## Other Stuff

Focus on high-margin, relevant materials. I've actually seen consultants sell all kinds of tchotchkes, such as T-shirts, coffee mugs, bumper stickers, paperweights, and assorted dust collectors (although professional speakers are far more prone toward this nonsense than professional consultants). However, even items such as calendars, daily planners, and project templates are suspect, because they don't command high prices and are generally not terribly practical. If you have manuals, templates, worksheets, and related guides, which have an intrinsic and immediate application, these can be valuable products. For example, a brief pamphlet or set of instructions on behavioral interviewing, assessing recommendations, rebutting the most common objections, or using PowerPoint might be very well received among the appropriate client groups.

There are at least seven questions regarding potential products for sale that should always be answered in the affirmative before you proceed:

1. Is there sufficient margin per sale?
2. Can I sell this product to both existing clients and nonclients?
3. Will this product reinforce my marketing plan?
4. Can I create this product cost-effectively and kill it cost-effectively if it proves to sell poorly?
5. Can I fulfill orders expeditiously and efficiently?
6. Will this product remain relevant and timely for at least a few years?

If you're selling products, accept credit cards and plan for lost shipments as a cost of doing business. Use an International Standard Book Number (ISBN)[6]

---

[6]You can apply for an ISBN number through W. W. Bowker at http://www.bowkerlink.com.

so that you can distribute via Amazon.com, other Web sources, bookstores, and other retail outlets. Create a separate secure and user-friendly section of your Web site just for product sales.

## EXPLORING NEW LUCRATIVE FIELDS

You've heard me say before that there are a lot of ways to make money. I just never imagined how many there were. Actually, we're presented with them almost every day, but we fail to set fees for them for a variety of reasons:

- We don't take the time to recognize their intrinsic worth.
- They're things we do "naturally" and unthinkingly.
- The positioning is wrong.
- We assume that a fee is our only source of remuneration.

I've never written about these elements before because they best apply to mature, successful consultants whose name, brand, stature, and positioning have created a powerful attraction. Like a bank loan that becomes available only once you're so successful you don't need it or a speaker's bureau that wants to represent you only after you've made a name for yourself on the speaking circuit, these alternative sources of income arise when you're already doing well financially.

However, you're still willing to accept the bank's line of credit and the speaker's bureau's business, so why not embrace new sources of income that can provide for retirement, kids' college tuition, vacations, charitable donations, or simply discretionary income?

> If you are providing any kind of service, help, or advice on a continuing or even periodic gratis basis, ask yourself, "Why am I not charging for this?" There will often be a completely spurious reason (or no reason at all, other than your own lassitude).

Here are some alternatives for assigning fees to activities ranging from the unmistakable to the unlikely.

## Remote Consulting

I used to receive calls all the time for "informal" help. They were sometimes from managers I had never met in nonclient companies, sometimes from other consultants, and sometimes from, well, unanticipated sources (such as the person trying to patent an adhesive device I couldn't even begin to fathom but who needed an entrepreneur's assessment of whether he was receiving competent legal help; he wasn't). The easy problem was one of time. I could just turn these people away when I was very busy—and take time with them when I wasn't.

The tough problem was quality. Very few of these issues could be resolved (or sometimes even understood) within the bounds of a single phone call. My ethical quandary was whether to give incomplete advice on a quick basis or provide a more qualitative response at the sacrifice of still more of my time.

I decided that the best interests of the callers were served by the close attention required for a highly qualitative response, accompanied by a relationship of some duration allowing for trial and error, feedback, and further fine-tuning of the resolution.

---

**VIGNETTE**

An individual called me last week who represents the quintessential dilemma I once had but now address quite easily.

"I've read your book on speaking [*Money Talks*]," he said, "and I want you to be my mentor. I'm calling you because I'm determined to make this happen."

"You mean you'd like to join my formal mentor program?" I asked.

"No, money is tight. But I'm willing to work for you, help you, do whatever it takes under your terms. You haven't met anyone as determined as I am. I need to work with you to accelerate my career."

---

"I don't have employees, I don't need help, and my conditions are simple: you can join the program as others have in your position. That's it. No options."

"But," he yelled, "you don't know me. Give me a chance."

"That's exactly the point," I said. "I don't know you. Why should I favor you and not someone else? That's why there is an objective set of criteria for joining my program. But there are free articles, indexed, on my Web site, and a free newsletter. You're welcome to avail yourself of those resources."

The conversation took two minutes. I know that I helped him by not enabling his entitlement and victim philosophy or the mistaken notion that passion alone justifies free help. And I know I helped myself.

Remote consulting can take various forms; let's look at three of them.

## Coaching

Coaching is designed for managers and professionals working for organizations. In other words, they are not independent entrepreneurs. They usually require help with a single issue, although sometimes they are seeking longer-term career advice.

My suggestion is that you provide coaching help for set intervals (for example, thirty-day periods) during which the individual can phone or e-mail you. Meetings are never in person. Phone calls are at mutually convenient times or on the basis of your returning the call within some satisfactory time frame (for example, twenty-four hours or less). You might choose to limit contact to no more than one phone call a week or some other standard if you wish (or provide options at different fee levels). You assess a fee for the time interval, rather than each transaction, so that the individual has in fact "retained" you for a limited duration and with certain restraints.

Coaching is a very hot topic, partly due to real need and partly due to pure ego ("Of course I have my own coach!"). But it's often done best on an anonymous basis and when certain situations present themselves. That's why coaching by phone and e-mail can be so effective for the process, economical for the client, and lucrative for the consultant. (You don't need to go to any "coaching university" to be an effective coach. Who certifies the certifiers?)

I've promoted the coaching option on my Web site so that I could refer people to it easily without long discussion. Payment is always in advance. If you were to charge even $500 for a thirty-day interval and had three people being coached a month, that's $18,000 of pure profit annually derived during your "down time" that can pay the mortgage on a vacation home or tuition at a fine school. Of course, if you were to charge $1,000 and averaged four coaching clients a month, your annual profit would be $48,000, which could pay for your home mortgage or send two kids to college.

## Mentoring

I define mentoring as providing rather intimate, one-on-one assistance to other entrepreneurs. (If you were an actuary, it would be for other actuaries, or if you were a pottery maker, for other pottery makers. There has actually been a farrier in my mentoring program who has mentored other farriers.)

You might find that coaching and mentoring are similar or identical, and that's fine. But I've made the separation for the purposes of differentiating my services and assigning proper fees for the value provided.

As you've become more and more successful, greater numbers of people come to you for advice. Sometimes you see yourself as "giving back to the profession," sometimes as doing a good deed, sometimes as harried, and sometimes as unfairly imposed on (see the preceding vignette). No matter how great our ego, the luster of being sought out as a "star" begins to dim when people insist on free advice and intrude on our time.

Hence mentoring. Many executive coaches have set up coaching "certification" programs. I've seen facilitators do the same, as have people in quality control, expert witnessing, and technology consulting. I've tried to create a broad program to encompass entrepreneurs of all kinds, but about 75 percent of the participants have been consultants of one stripe or another.[7]

I also believe that mentoring takes place over a longer period of time (my program is six months). You can charge a considerable amount of money for your remote involvement, which the participants nevertheless consider a bargain. I've tried to structure my fees so that they can be charged on a credit card and so that the client can recover them easily through higher fees or additional business so as to recoup the expense fairly quickly.

My particular program requires an investment of $3,500, payable at the outset (and more sophisticated and more expensive versions of the program have emerged). That's an extremely reasonable fee for my kind of high-powered help, and it hasn't been unusual for participants (who are at every level of the profession, some just beginning and some already earning in the high-six- to low-seven-figure range) to double and triple their income.

> The key to any remote relationship is a "good deal" for both parties. I've found that the removal of a personal interaction can be more than compensated for by rapid responsiveness and adaptations to learning styles.

You may choose to mentor one or two people at a time or a dozen at a time, depending on your own objectives and work schedule. But since this is truly *remote* consulting, you can always return a mentor's call or e-mail from the road. At this writing, more than six hundred people have been through my program at $3,500 each; about 30 percent have reenrolled between one and

---

[7]I actually now hold an annual mentor summit, open to all present and past participants in the program. It's averaged more than seventy people per meeting, all of whom pay their own expenses.

ten times; and another hundred people have been through either my guided program at $6,500 or my total immersion program for $9,500. These are fees I've kept constant from inception in 1996 or whenever the newer programs were introduced. I'm sure some of you are doing the math at this point.[8]

## Situational Consulting

I've been called by people for a long time who have an immediate and urgent need for help on a very clear and well-defined issue. They don't need coaching, and they don't need mentoring. They just need some quick answers.

I used to do this for free, but I came to resent it. After all, I was helping people make hundreds of thousands of dollars, avoid legal problems, attract new clients, and improve their image, and often as not, they were calling on my toll-free number!

I now tell people that I can't do justice to their issue with a quick response to a rapidly stated quandary. I explain that there's a modest fee, in return for which we spend up to an hour on the phone (cumulatively) and exchange unlimited e-mail for up to five business days.

---

> **VIGNETTE**
>
> A guy I'll call "Roy" whom I barely knew from a professional association we both belonged to phoned me out of the blue. He was working on a major proposal, had heard that I was the consulting guru, and asked for my opinion about the work and his fees.
>
> His fees were ridiculous, under $200,000, and we quickly moved them to $410,000 over two years (I'll never forget that figure). I helped him with the reasoning and how to present the proposal.

---

[8]People ask how I arrived at $3,500. At the time, it was the monthly payment on my Ferrari. I figured that a dozen mentorees a year would pay for the car. Today, my Bentley costs $4,500, but I've held the original price on the mentor program because I'm a sentimental guy.

He called two weeks later to tell me he got the business. He said that something was in the mail for me. I subsequently received a gold star paperweight with one of his aphorisms on it.

Although I refrained from throwing the paperweight through my window, I didn't refrain from committing to myself that I would never provide such help gratis ever again. And I haven't.

If you were to charge $1,000 for this value and provide it twice a month, you'd bring in $24,000 a year, which would pay the lease on many luxury cars. You will also, perhaps even more important, drive away the "energy suckers" who want to "pick your brain" until they have every last crumb consumed.

---

Charging for your value, no matter how brief in duration or confined the issue, not only serves to gain pure profit but also drives away the parasites. Such cleansing is important in nature.

---

## AND NOW FOR SOME PERSPECTIVE

I'm not saying that you should abandon all pro bono work or refuse to offer free assistance to anyone you please. I am saying that there's no need to give away the store, that success does not demand self-immolation, and that people realize that there is no free lunch. Or at least they should realize that, and we can help them. I speak at least a dozen times a year for free to professional trade association chapters in my profession.

You may choose not to take a personal fee but to suggest other forms of remuneration. Here are some alternatives that I use:

- Make out the check to a favorite charity or cause
- Provide a favorable review of one of your books to be posted online

- Volunteer for a cause you are leading or backing
- Return the favor with referral business
- Return the favor by helping with some tedious work
- Participate in a sample taping you're doing for a product
- Promise to help another person develop business, skills, or marketing when he or she is ready
- With permission, use the opportunity to test new material and approaches

I'm not mercenary, but I am pragmatic. I've found that most people who seek and accept free advice seldom put a premium on it and rarely fully implement it. They know that if they screw up or need further help, there's always more to be had at the original price.

Consequently, I can make a case that you're helping people more when you require that they invest—no matter how modestly—in their own success and take some accountability for implementing your help. There's nothing like paying money to force someone to analyze the return on that investment!

When we are successful, it's too easy to enable others who simply want the "shortcut" version of our success without the hard work, the dues, and the discipline. I tell people all the time that I can't control their discipline or their talent. I've found that those who want things for free usually can't control those factors either.

One more criterion: when you are doing work that you dislike and wonder how you got "roped into it," it's time to start charging. Just as you're justified to charge more for difficult and fractious clients, you're certainly justified to charge for previously free work that is now driving you nuts. If the other party refuses to pay, you have ample cause to walk away. I've had to tell too many people in my life that I was helping them out of my good nature and that I didn't expect argument and debate as a result. (The people who tend to complain most bitterly in the aftermath of elections are ineluctably those who didn't bother to vote.)

There are a lot of ways to make money. You may not choose to make money doing all of them, but you owe it to yourself to at least examine them in terms of your overall life goals and business objectives. You could probably, right now, be making another $100,000 to $500,000 on your bottom line if you intelligently engaged in nonconsulting activities and remote consulting.

> At least once a year, examine your business and your talents for the potential of additional nonconsulting and remote consulting income. If you don't do that, no one else will do it for you. Yet it is a huge area for lifestyle improvement.

## CHAPTER ROI

- There are a lot of ways to make money, whether for yourself or for a cause or charity that is important to you.
- In addition, charging fees for nonconsulting services often provides the relief needed from those who constantly bang on your door wanting your expertise for free.
- Speaking is a primary money generator in addition to being a wonderful marketing tool. For those interested, it can be a second profession and a very lucrative source of income. But fees here, too, should be based on value and assigned over options. Training and workshops are allied endeavors.
- Products provide wonderful passive income, as well as additional branding. They also yield excellent marketing advantages.
- Nonconsulting services and remote consulting provide as much or as little opportunity as you care to pursue. Their great power is in generating income during "down time" without travel, wear, and tear. The probability is that you're already doing a great deal of this for free, which is fine if it's a conscious choice but deadly if it's a "necessary evil."
- Diversifying your income also provides flexibility to weather economic ups and downs, client defections, and your own wish to decrease labor intensity.
- The bottom line: even a modest amount of nonconsulting income can make a tremendous impact on your life goals.

*Passive and remote income will keep you off airplanes and remove the burden on your retirement planning. This is because it tends to be an annuity that persists long after you elect to reduce your activities. In the trajectory of your career, you should be implementing passive income opportunities* now.

## CHAPTER 10

# Fee Progression Strategies

*Why You Fall Behind When You Stand Still*

I t's fascinating how we rigorously update our computer software, seek out the latest cell phone technology, and constantly improve our Web sites and press kits but tend to ignore our fee practices as if they were fossils best left undisturbed.

This chapter is intended to provide a holistic view of fees and when and how to raise them. We've been through the tactics, the rebuttals, the options, and the preparation. Now we're going to examine the process as an ongoing strategy. Although we'll start with early career planning to provide continuity— and this might appeal to newer consultants—it's difficult to engage in a comprehensive strategy early in one's career when putting food on the table seems more important than negotiating with a client. (In the early days, a closed deal of any kind is a successful negotiation!) I'm also anticipating that some sophisticated, mature, and successful people from other careers are reading this book as they enter the consulting profession and intend to use the successful practices of others.

I think it's critical for the successful consultant to view fees as part of a process that continues throughout one's career. For example, you don't raise fees when times are good and lower them when times are bad, any more than you would increase marketing when times are bad and abandon marketing when times are good. Successful consultants embrace and apply pervasive strategies, not short-sighted tactics.

---

**VIGNETTE**

A member of my mentor program who successfully added professional speaking to his offerings was asked by a client to speak for one hour on each of two consecutive days in San Juan, Puerto Rico.

"What kind of a deal should I give my buyer?" he asked.

"What do you mean?" I responded.

"Well, should I give a discount for the second day or apply it to both days? Or should I waive expenses? Or should I do one day for free if the buyer pays for my wife's expenses?"

"What kind of deal has the client requested?"

"Oh, the client hasn't asked for anything."

"Then send the buyer a bill for the full fee for both days and for your expenses after the event. And keep your mouth shut except when you're actually addressing the conference."

---

# ENTRY-LEVEL FEES

One of the worst strategies that I've ever encountered at entry level is to price low in order to get business. Since this book is for advanced consultants and flourishing practices, I won't spend too much time on this, but since early fee strategy often determines later fee levels, it's important to understand the influence (so that you can undo it, if you must).

Ironically, but completely understandably, the tendency to set low fees to attract business actually reduces business and establishes a horrible precedent that is difficult to overcome.[1]

---

Poor fee strategy at the beginning of one's consulting career creates all kinds of problems later in one's career. It's easiest to reach the roof from the top floor, not from the basement.

---

Here's what I mean when I refer to fees that are too low on a value basis: if the client would have paid, in terms of value, $70,000 for a project and the consultant's actual fee was $58,000, that's fine. But if the consultant's fee was $24,000, that's not fine, despite "exposure," the promise of future business, or the prestige of landing that client. That's because those factors *would also have been garnered at the higher fee.*

The invidious nature of low fees early in one's career creates the following problems, which must be overcome and eventually undone:

• The client and all the client's referral business will tend to view the investment required for the value you deliver in that type of work at the level you cited. Being viewed as a bargain is not, in and of itself, sufficient if you are not well paid. That's not a "good deal" for both parties.

• You, yourself, begin subliminally to believe that you're at the level the market will bear for that type of value, although what you've really achieved is a self-created, artificially low market level.

• When you raise prices as a result of determining that more of the project value should be reflected in your fees, your increments will be based on a very low starting point, meaning that it could literally take you years

---

[1]Note that because my focus is on value-based fees, I'm not referring to fee schedules or per diem amounts when I talk about fee levels but rather to the value that the consultant is comfortable using as the basis for his or her fees.

to make up for the lost opportunity. It's tough for people to move fees from $50,000 to $150,000, even when the client believes the latter fee is more than fair.[2]

> Early fees are not a function of one's experience (or lack of it) or limited perspective. They are a function solely of how the consultant educates the client and whether or not the consultant believes that his or her contribution is worth the fee being charged for it.

- Your margins are much lower, preventing you from investing in the kind of marketing and promotion that build reputation and brands and that in turn support still higher fee levels.
- You tend to take on too much business and the wrong kind of business to create more profit. Ironically, this actually reduces profit, since you become engaged in activity and labor-intensive work rather than intelligent marketing and high-margin work. Many would-be consultants become mired in the training business because they used training to put bread on the table, found themselves in a very low-margin and price-sensitive business, and sought to maximize their "billable days" rather than break out of that morass. (Subcontracting is even worse: the big "seminar houses" are notorious for paying as little as $300 to $400 per day. Welcome to Catch-22.)

That's enough on the early problems for our purposes, but it's important to lay the groundwork for what follows. We've all made mistakes, and it's important to understand how it is we came to be where we are. Remember

---

[2]Professional speakers often find themselves in worse traps when, having listened to bad advice, they find themselves at low fee levels, which can be raised slightly but would need to be tripled or quadrupled to actually bring them in line with their value. Few bureaus or clients will accommodate that degree of increase, meaning that it takes years of slower increases—and lost profits—to achieve a representative market level.

Value-Based Fees

this: it is extremely hard to convince a client, no matter how pleased, that your fees should be raised if the client doesn't perceive any increase in commensurate value.

## TRANSITION TO A "GOING CONCERN"

I love the accountants' term *going concern*, which indicates that a business is, essentially, breathing, eating, and ambulatory without life support. I use the term here to indicate that once the practice is established and the bills are being paid, there is a new phase—and new strategy—to consider.[3]

Some of you are in the going-concern phase, because you've never bothered to market or expand your horizons so that you enter the "word of mouth" stage (to be discussed shortly). These are the hallmarks of the going-concern phase:

- Referral business has begun and is not unusual.
- About 70 percent or so of all business is repeat business.
- There is still a tendency to reduce fees if competition is perceived or if any degree of buyer resistance is encountered.
- Fees are about 50 to 65 percent of where they could be and are not methodically examined.
- Some business is turned away, but not much.
- The business is still far too labor-intensive, and margins are relatively low.

This is often the phase in which consultants don't want to "rock the boat." The problem is that by not rocking the boat, they stay adrift, without propulsion or direction. The going concern should be a transient phase, not a permanent home.

---

[3]Most accounting authorities feel that a small business has become a going concern after about three years, when the founder has run out of original friends and contacts and has had to generate new business to support the operation. About 80 percent of all new businesses fail within the first three years.

In this phase, the consultant should begin to formulate the basics of a fee philosophy. The positions to be reconciled may include the following:

- What kinds of work will I encourage, what kinds will I accept, and what kinds will I phase out as unprofitable or unattractive?
- How can I increase my own comfort level with value pricing and educating the client about the advantages of single fees?
- To what degree can I create and offer options in almost any setting and on any project?
- What are the minimum fee levels at which I'll work?

It's always safe to be aggressive with fees, because we almost always underestimate our value and are competing with larger firms that must charge high amounts simply to cover their overhead. High fees can, when necessary, always be lowered (by reducing value). By contrast, low fees can seldom be raised, no matter how much value we can demonstrate.

A rough rule of thumb is that in the going-concern phase, an aggressive consultant should be at least at the average fee levels being paid in the profession. In other words, if strategy work is being delivered for $150,000 to $300,000, then the consultant should be in the low $200,000s. See the fee progression presented in Table 10.1.

As you can see in the table, there are some predictable progressions that consultants go through in terms of fee practices. The idea is to accelerate or even leapfrog the intervening steps. The going-concern phase is probably the first legitimate opportunity to do so, since entry level is really a matter of getting grounded and determining whether the profession is for you. But if you've succeeded over three years or so and you are indeed a going concern, there's actually no reason to labor your way through the ensuing phases.

On the assumption that most of you reading this book are in the intermediate phases, I'll continue to describe them so that you can identify yourself and plan your leap to the ultimate phase.

**Table 10.1** Fee Progression Across Categories.

| Phase | Business Sources | Business Qualification | Fee Integrity | Fee Levels | Nonconsulting Fees | Margins |
|---|---|---|---|---|---|---|
| Entry Level | Friends and former business contacts | Accepts almost anything | Client determines the fee | Rock bottom | Irrelevant; don't exist | Slim to none |
| Going Concern | Referrals and early marketing | Accepts most business, plans to cut out some | Extreme flexibility | Below average or average | Probably not a factor or very low | Small to average |
| Word of Mouth | Referrals and marketing | Must be high margin with strong potential | Determines value-based fees and is firm | Demands a premium above average | Strong fees and firm | Above average |
| Brand | Referrals, name in the market, publicity | Selective, only consistent with strategy | Maximizes margins in every case | Far above average and firm | Near the top of the profession | Very strong; near the top |
| The Ultimate Consultant | Key buyers seek you out | Selects only those of interest | Not even discussed | At the very highest levels | Not even discussed; very expensive products | Extraordinary |

---

> Word of mouth means that people cite you and recommend you
> without any direct impetus from you at that moment. The beauty
> of word of mouth is that it is exponential in growth. You should there-
> fore assign fees that meet the expectations of people referred to you.

# TRANSITION TO WORD OF MOUTH

The word-of-mouth phase occurs when people begin speaking of you of their own volition. It may be due to the nature of work performed or your marketing activities or through that odd dynamic of peer pressure to which many people succumb (I can't tell you how many people have said, "Oh, yes, Summit Consulting Group—I know your work" when they couldn't possibly).

In this phase, consultants begin to apply stronger qualification criteria to potential business. Value-based fees are the norm for consulting work, and there is a conscious drive to create high-margin business rather than more business. The fee levels therefore tend to be above average for the services provided, and the quotations are firm. The consultant in the word-of-mouth phase would rather walk away from business than accept poor-margin business. The need for exposure and potential contacts has been largely overcome by the effectiveness of the marketing effort.

At this stage of one's career, there is probably the first real opportunity to establish major retirement and investment plans, pay off long-term indebtedness, and take spontaneous vacations or make significant impulse purchases.

My experience is that the word-of-mouth phase is where many consultants plateau. They begin to get "fat and happy," and complacency sets in. Even though most consultants are relatively young when they first hit this phase, their learning stops, and they assume they're going to continue to grow simply by supporting the same practices that helped them get where they are. This is the phase of the deadly "success trap," as shown in Figure 10.1.

These plateaus can occur at the word-of-mouth or brand phase but most often occur at the former, when consultants are beginning to enjoy the "good life" and assume that this is as good as it gets.

> There is a key juncture when value-based fees begin to be used correctly and word-of-mouth recognition grows, that represents a potential and lethal trap. The consultant says, "I've arrived," when the journey is only beginning to get interesting.

At the word-of-mouth phase of success, the consultant should actively seek to improve and climb the curve in a number of ways:

- By creating brands around intellectual property, approaches, products, and ultimately the consultant's name[4]

---

[4]See the second book in this series, *How to Establish a Unique Brand in the Consulting Profession.*

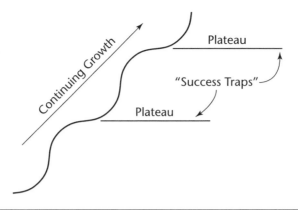

**Figure 10.1**  The "Success Trap" at Word-of-Mouth and Brand Phases.

- By refining the criteria for accepting new business
- By attempting to maximize margins at every opportunity and walking away from business that does not present a "good deal" under more and more favorable terms
- By creating reliable sources of nonconsulting and remote consulting income, which themselves are near the top of the fee structure for their categories
- By examining failed attempts to attract more lucrative business and higher fees or losing out to very large concerns and learning how to build on your own unique value propositions
- By viewing wealth and balance as critical factors in your life and seeking to reduce your labor intensity across the board

This phase in the progression may therefore be the most crucial; it's like the stationary bike on which we think we're working out well while not really moving anywhere. Just breaking a sweat doesn't necessarily represent progress.

## TRANSITION TO THE BRAND PHASE

In this phase, the consultant has achieved successful branding. There are actually two types of branding: (1) branding of approaches, products, methodologies, and other "tools of the trade" and (2) branding of one's own name.

## Branding of Approaches, Products, and Methodologies

Examples of brands of this sort are The Telephone Doctor®, The Coach, The Teambuilder, The One Minute Manager®, and The Strategy Quadrant. They attract spontaneously generated publicity from sources outside consulting, which use your branded models with attribution, and from the media, which might use your approaches as widely known and quotable examples.

At this stage, the consultant can be highly selective because a great many potential projects and references are in the pipeline, many originating from the consultant's marketing gravity and branding but many more resulting from the brand names themselves (for example, "Get me the guy who wrote *Managing Call Centers for Profit*"). In every case, without fail, margins should be maximized, and part of the value is in the consultant's known and accepted approaches. This puts fees far above average in the profession, with the buyer expecting as much.

Nonconsulting fees can be escalated quite aggressively, since products can proliferate under an umbrella brand and others will seek the consultant out to increase product offerings.[5] Speaking fees, for example, can readily go to the low five figures.

My brands (all of them registered trademarks) include Million Dollar Consulting®, Million Dollar Consultant®, The Odd Couple (with Patricia Fripp), The 1% Solution: Tools for Change, and Life Balance: Blending Life, Work, and Relationships. However, ultimately, people say, "You have to work with Alan Weiss."

---

> Branding should be done with a strategy toward involving one's name as the ultimate brand. Since this cannot be duplicated by anyone else, no fee comparison is possible.

---

[5]In fact, the consultant should be aware that less is more. Too much low-margin, low-value product can cheapen one's overall brand, while a few very high-margin, high-value offerings can enhance the brand and generate tremendous profits.

An intermediate step that is quite successful and quite subtle in progressing from brands based on activities and products to a brand based on one's name is creating eponymous brands. For example, "Parkinson's Laws" quickly became associated with their creator and author. Norman Augustine, CEO at Martin Marietta, created "Augustine's Laws." If you have a strategy brand that's known as "Accelerated Strategy," there's no reason why you can't migrate to "Ackerman's Accelerated Strategy" to begin incorporating your name. "The Negotiating Seminar" can easily become "Jay Randolph's Negotiations Made Easy." This can be an easy route to the second type of branding. Note that most people can't name the author of many a best-seller that has become a catchword: think of *The Tipping Point*.

## Branding One's Own Name

This is the most powerful brand and shouldn't be confused with the eponymous tactic just described. This is a case where Tom Peters or Peter Drucker (or Bain or McKinsey on a corporate basis) *is* the brand.[6]

Note that after the Enron scandal and the dissolution of Andersen Consulting, the remaining organization that had split off from Andersen was successful using Accenture as the brand, not the original name.

When someone says, "Get me Jane Sanders," it means that the decision is literally yours as to whether you will accept work that is being offered to you, rather than seeking out the work or even collaborating on whether you and the buyer are right for each other. In this case, the buyer is saying that the work is yours if you deign to accept it. This dynamic maximizes your margin in every case. You are very near the acme of the profession, and your margins should be near the top.

While the "success trap" discussed in the prior phase doesn't represent as much of a threat here, there are two considerations in terms of fees that should be kept in mind. First, there are, comparatively, many consultants

---

[6]Tom Clancy, Stephen King, and Danielle Steele have done this as authors. Virtually every actor must do it. Picasso and Warhol did it as artists. Many, but not all, politicians do it. Once again I refer you to an earlier book in this series if you want to learn more details about branding in this profession: *How to Establish a Unique Brand in the Consulting Profession*.

When I was called in originally by the Federal Reserve Bank, I was told that the buyer wanted to consider me for a particularly tough and rewarding project. As I attempted to discuss the issues and determine objectives and metrics, I had to keep stepping back to answer questions about my prior work, experiences, and philosophy.

The conversations were always cordial, however, and I finally said, "How many other consultants are you considering?" since I was afraid that this process could take months. "Oh, only you at the moment," said my contact, "but we don't know anything about you, so we wanted to get comfortable before we started working together."

"Well, how did you find me and why did you call me if you know nothing about me?"

"We told one of our client bank executives about our project and needs, and he said, 'You must get Alan Weiss for that project. He's the only one for that job.' So we called you."

At no point were fees ever discussed in all of the preliminaries. The client wasn't sure who Alan Weiss was exactly, but they knew they had to have him.

---

at the product and approach branding phases and few at the personal name branding phase. My belief is that consultants who have branded their methodology and approaches tend to get stuck in that position and don't make the transition to personal name branding. That's why I've included the subtle transition step of eponymous naming. I don't believe you can progress to ultimate consulting unless your name becomes a brand.

Second, I don't think enough consultants seek to stretch what brands they do develop to encompass an ever-wider range of offerings. Singular brands and limited breadth tend to confine the consultant to a niche where learning, growth, and improved fees are not naturally forthcoming.

Consequently, I think it's important to continue to progress beyond the branding phase, no matter how lucrative and rewarding it may seem at the time.

A member of my mentor program who has progressed from high school coach making $30,000 a year to Fortune 500 coach making over $300,000 a year called to ask about starting his own mentor program and conducting public sessions based on a book he published. "Don," I asked, "how will you market this? People flock to high-priced workshops and mentor relationships only if they have a need and feel that the presenter has value. Are you sufficiently known? Your book is not exactly a best-seller." He wisely decided to spend more time building his brand. It doesn't matter what you think of yourself; all that matters is how your potential clients perceive your brand (assuming that they perceive it at all).

---

The ultimate consultant doesn't worry about fees and margins, much as in the early part of one's career, but for very different reasons.

## TRANSITION TO THE ULTIMATE CONSULTANT

This entire series is based on achieving and reveling in a stature of the profession that I've called the "ultimate consultant." I've assigned that status as the highest level of my progression, even though one continues to grow, experiment, and benefit in this phase.

Fee Progression Strategies                                                **217**

The ultimate consultant is sought out directly by buyers. There are no "middlemen" or feasibility buyers. The consultants select the projects that are of most interest and greatest mutual benefit. Fees are not discussed and may take the form of long-term retainers, deferred compensation, and other devices. The fees and margins are among the very highest in the field. Nonconsulting and remote consulting fees can be whatever the consultant decides to make them.

Ironically, the ultimate consultant and the entry-level consultant both need focus very little on fee levels and margins. But in the latter's case, it's because the consultant's business is desperately needed and so there is no thought of negotiation. In the former's case, the consultant's business is not needed and so there is no thought of negotiation.

Relatively few practitioners may reach ultimate consulting, but that doesn't mean we shouldn't be prepared for it. People believe they get what they pay for, and it's important that we behave in a manner consistent with our value. Therefore, the ultimate consultant

- Does not discuss fees
- Dresses and acts as a peer of high-level buyers
- Is never "hired" but agrees to collaborate with the buyer
- Is known by name
- Fosters products and approaches that build on name recognition
- Seeks high margins, not high volume
- Creates an aura of "Do you think we can get him?"
- Decides, along with the buyer, whether the project is a good fit and hence worth accepting
- Does not negotiate or build relationships with low-level people or HR

---

The client, competition, economy, government, methodology, project, and timing do not control your fee. You control your fee. The good news is that there is only that single variable. The bad news is that there is only that single variable.

---

Where are you currently in your fee progression and career progression? The operative word is *currently*. You should be acutely aware of the strategies required to progress and move ahead. Your value is increasing with your age, experience, and longevity in the business. Your fees should be increasing commensurately.

## THE BOOK'S ROI: ALAN'S AXIOMS FOR THE "GOOD DEAL"

If you've taken this book off the bookstore shelf to glance at these final few pages, forget it. You're not going to be helped without reading the prior two hundred or so. But for those of you who have come with me this far as active participants, I'd like to make some final observations and provide some final provocations.

### 1. You Are Entitled to Be Compensated for Your Value

We live in a capitalist system, which works better than all others. People believe in such a system that they get what they pay for. However, the first sale is to yourself. You must believe that you are entitled to fair remuneration, and you must appreciate your own value.

Creating shared success with the client is the best way to create shared value, at any time in one's career but particularly early in that career. The "good deal" occurs when the client believes you've been a bargain in terms of the results you've helped produce, and you believe you've been paid very well.

It is never too early to begin branding what you do, how you do it, and who you are so that perceived value is even higher. The only source for a fee is perceived value. There is no limit to perceived value and hence no limit to fees. The worst limitation is probably in your own mind.

### 2. Basing Fees on Time or Materials and Not on Value Is Simply Crazy

There is no law of supply and demand in the consulting profession. Good times and bad times economically don't matter, nor does the number of competitors, nor does your own available time. What matters is the results you generate.

The essential need in breaking away from time-based fees is to understand that your value is never a matter of your "showing up." Nor do you have to justify yourself by being in the buyer's presence. In fact, there are ethical conflicts in basing your payment on the number of times you're physically present.

Lawyers, architects, CPAs, and most consultants have educated their buyers incorrectly for several hundred years. Since the evidence of that miseducation is so apparent in low incomes and poor profitability, why on earth should we attempt to perpetuate it? It's up to us to educate the buyer correctly about value and fees based on that value from the initial meeting. But again, we have to believe it ourselves.

## 3. Buyer Self-Interest Is Based on Results

People change their behavior based on self-interest. Self-interest is most affected by results, not task, by output, not input. That's why "deliverables" are only a commodity that will be comparison-shopped by most buyers. A report, a training session, or a coaching regimen are simply tasks performed. But improved morale, faster customer responsiveness, and more effective leadership are highly valuable organizational outputs.

Buyers will change their behavior—spend money when none is budgeted or spend more than was anticipated—not because a training session seems better but rather because customers might buy more. They're not that interested in a better interviewing procedure, but they're mesmerized by saving $300,000 a year in lower new-hire turnover.

The consultant brings his or her past experiences, through an intervention, to dramatically affect the client's future. It's that final part that merits high fees: the future. The consultant's past is only an input, and the intervention is merely a device. Fees should be based on future improvement, not on past technique.

> The discussion with the buyer should always be about future results, not the consultant's past or methodologies. The client's improvement will provide strong self-interest for the buyer to change behavior. The consultant's talent and devices will not.

## 4. Conceptual Agreement Is the Linchpin

The ability to reach agreement with an economic buyer on objectives to be met, metrics to assess progress, and value to the client is the centerpiece of fee strategy. This creates a return-on-investment mentality instead of a cost mentality. It's critical to establish clear outcomes at a fixed investment and not to surrender to vague outcomes at clear costs.

The consultant's unique value (Why me? Why now? Why in this manner?) is also an important consideration, which is why a unique relationship with the buyer is so essential to forging trust and reaching conceptual agreement. Measures may be objective or subjective, quantitative or qualitative, so long as both consultant and buyer agree on their reasonability and desirability.

There are some formulas to apply if you must have more comfort. But the formulas will usually depress fees and not boost them. This is art and science, and a successful consultant is adept at both aspects.

## 5. Existing Clients Can Be Converted to Value-Based Fees

The key here is to create a strategy based on picking selected targets that represent strong potential. Don't attempt to convert everyone, and be prepared to abandon some business.

In converting clients, offer new value, find new buyers, and find new circumstances. Make sure that existing buyers see more value in converting the relationship and that new buyers are educated correctly from the outset (and not by the old buyers). There is nothing immoral, unethical, or illegal about reaching out laterally to new buyers during ongoing projects.

Abandon business that you've had forever and don't know why, that isn't generating a sufficient margin, or that is just no longer interesting. You're doing neither your client nor yourself much of a favor by hanging on to it.

## 6. Retainer Business Is Discrete and Sound Business

Retainers represent access to your "smarts." Be sure that the conditions are carefully spelled out and that you're not mixing project and retainer work together. Ensure that the buyer's expectations are the same as yours.

Choose intelligent time frames with favorable fees. Organize the scope and numbers of people who have access to you. Focus on the renewal aspects, making sure there is an "overlap" to create a smooth, ongoing retainer relationship, not a succession of stops and starts.

Coordinate project work and retainer work for the same client through separate proposals and payment schemes.

## 7. There Are Scores of Ways to Raise Fees and Margins

Every day that you interact with prospects and clients, you are encountering dozens of ways to increase your fees and your bottom line. Learn all the techniques you can, and build them into your conversation and promotional materials.

This might be something as simple as not disclosing any fees early in the conversation by practicing "turnaround" questions to avoid being pinned down. Or it might be something as nuanced as suggesting options very early, to prepare the buyer for a "choice of yeses."

If you were to apply just two techniques a month intended to raise your fees or margins, you would probably double your profits without growing your business over the next year. If you also developed more business, you would probably increase profits by a function of four or five times. Every day you may be "leaving money on the table" by not focusing on your fee tactics.

> You have the opportunity to focus on and apply successful fee tactics every day. If you don't do this, you have decided to reduce your margins over time. That's a heck of a way to run a business.

## 8. You've Heard All the Objections Already

You know what all the fee objections are because you've heard them all before. It's criminal and negligent not to be prepared for them, not merely with rebuttals but with effective counterarguments.

There's nothing wrong with asking about the buyer's budget—in fact, it can be a very effective tactic early in the discussion. Offering rebates will help you acquire successive phases of a multiphase project. Using comparisons to equipment, damaged goods, vending machines, and so on can embarrass the buyer into realizing that investments must be made in people.

Ignore the competition. The client's self-interest will serve to overcome any objections. It's not about what the competition does; it's about what you do with the buyer.

## 9. Nonconsulting Activities Are Lucrative

You can and should charge substantial fees for speaking, coaching, products, licensing, and so on. Although you may choose to ignore peripheral areas and remain a "purist," there really is no need to be so narrow.

As you succeed in the profession, it makes sense to try to reduce undesirable travel and to increase passive income so that your career trajectory is maximally beneficial to your chosen lifestyle. Products and other non-consulting income streams make that possible.

Consider the options open to you, and strive to create high-margin products and services that place the least demand on your personal time. The more successful you become as a consultant, the easier it is to market in these areas.

## 10. Identify Where You Are in the Fee Progression Strategy

Consultants tend to move from an entry-level stage through other, more advanced stages if they manage their careers and their fee structures accordingly. This doesn't happen automatically.

Where are you in the progression, whether you use my words and standards or your own? What are you doing to prepare for the next phase? How can you tell if you've been in the present one too long already?

Unless you're growing and improving, you're losing ground. You can control your own growth and success if you create a strategy for doing so.

*This book has been about achieving your life goals by helping clients achieve their business goals. It's as simple as that. It's time you began getting paid for it. That's the "good deal."*

# The Case of the Fee Feng Shui

I was sitting at a conference table on a June day with the president and top team of a $200 million manufacturing operation. My proposal had been discussed in my absence and accepted. Now the decision was when to begin.

The summer was the company's busiest season, and the president thought it prudent to wait until the fall when things slowed so there would be the least disruption to the operation. In the summer, there were part-time workers, overtime, rushed orders, and so forth. I thought he was right, in that I didn't want to start the project amid chaos.

However, I also knew that he wasn't about to make the deposit until we actually began and that too many bad things can happen in four months. Then the vice president of human resources, of all things, seated directly across the table from the president, said, "You're right, but it's a shame we can't start now in that the eventual changes are supposed to help us operate better in busy times and slow." The rest of the team studied their fingernails.

I saw the president make a "What can you do?" gesture and begin to gather his papers when I said, "Why not have the best of both worlds?" Everyone turned to me expectantly.

"I can start observing now," I hastily improvised, "so that I can appreciate the nature of your busy season but stay out of the way except to debrief at times with you folks. Then, in the fall, I can incorporate all I observed firsthand into the change efforts, and we won't have to wait until *next* summer for me to make adjustments."

The HR woman said, "That works for me." There was a murmur of, well, murmuring.

"Why not?" asked the president rhetorically. "Sounds like a plan."

"I'll send you the paperwork and plan to return next week," I summarized, and off we all went. Four months later, 9/11 occurred. Our work was far into the planning stage, I had been paid, and the president said, "Let's keep going forward with the implementation, which we all need to take our minds off these horrible events."

Although nothing as dramatic as this tragedy will usually interfere with your plans, *something often does.* Use the dynamics of the group, setting, or circumstances to argue for immediate acceptance and launch. I had four clients in my pipeline who already paid deposits or full fees prior to beginning detailed work, and all four decided to continue, even though I offered to return the money.

*Moral: A check in the hand is better than one hundred handshakes without a check.*

## CHAPTER 11

# Technology and Fees

*Greater Wealth in the Brave
New World*

Over the course of my career, nothing has provided more support for increased and more diverse fees than emerging technologies. Nothing else comes close, because factors such as globalization, remote work, and more varied offerings are all dependent on constantly improving technology.

## THE SERVICE ENHANCEMENT

We have the opportunity today to provide brilliant, timely, and precise services for our clients because of improvements in communications. Let's look at some examples.

### Response Efficiencies

It's now possible to respond to client and prospect inquiries very quickly via cell phone, computer, or automated systems.

The beauty of the arrangement is that you are no longer tethered to a phone line, and you can return calls at your convenience, enabling you to manage more clients simultaneously than ever before. Clients accustomed to voice mail are not surprised to have to use it, but by returning the call rapidly—yet still at your convenience—you provide a wonderful level of service (or response to prospects) that is singular. Yet you are not required to hire expensive staff or special equipment to do this.

I return all my calls within ninety minutes during Eastern Time Zone business hours. Everyone finds that impressive, if not unprecedented. (If I'm tied up in a strategy session, I have someone call in for me, usually my wife; when we travel overseas together, someone does this for me for $100 a day.) Buyers are highly impressed by rapid responses, assuming, correctly, that they will receive the same kind or service if you are hired. And you're able to guarantee service during the consulting project that is of high value and justifies higher fees.

I carry an IPhone in my briefcase (which works without any alteration overseas), and all of my cars have phones or chips built in to the audio system.

Similarly, e-mail provides a rapid response even when traveling, from laptop (which I prefer) or PDA (acceptable for urgency only). You can review documents and even submit proposals without the "tether."

## Decreased Labor Intensity

Aside from simply raising fees, there are other ways to increase profit margins. One is to work less for the same fee, which means you have additional time to take on more work or simply enjoy life.

Your ability to use the Internet, e-mail, and phone (and its variations, such as Skype) greatly enhance your potential to provide more with less. Although this book series is for veteran consultants, I'll advise you all that a good "modern" home office should have a top-end computer,[1] laser printer, color printer, scanner, copy machine (with enlargement and reduction capability), multiline phone, postage meter and electronic scale, and credit card

---

[1] I am a Mac addict. They are fast, idiot-proof, compatible with anything, and the greatest time-savers I've encountered.

capability (plus whatever your unique needs also demand). One critic of one of my books stated that the equipment was too expensive. If that's what he thinks, he shouldn't be reading these books.

Your letterhead, invoices, and other documents can be sent electronically in perfect color, just as you can receive and print those of your clients and prospects. Think about this: most clients don't like wall-to-wall meetings and feel overwhelmed. If you suggest that you can reduce *their* labor (always position this in the buyer's self-interest), why should they object?

In this technological age, there is no excuse for continuing to create labor-intensive projects that require frequent trips and long visits. If you educate the buyer correctly, you will net a small fortune by reducing your physical workload, as well as dramatically improving the quality of your life.

## Marketing Enhancement

Economic buyers do not troll the Internet to purchase consulting services, period. Please don't cite the rare exception that only proves this rule. (And *never* listen to a technological "expert" for marketing advice. It's like asking an insurance agent for the best investment vehicles. "Oh, it's insurance? Really?")

For you and me, our Web sites are credibility statements. They are places buyers go *after* they have decided that we are potentially of value to them. Therefore, this is your repository of expertise. Using your Web site as a "passive" press kit and publicity site is highly effective. Be sure to include all of the following on your site:

- Typical results your buyers can expect to derive
- Case studies (challenge, intervention, result)
- Testimonials[2]
- Position papers
- List of articles published
- Client list

---

[2]Basically, the site should say here's what the client gets and here's who says so. The rest is just support. On my site, testimonials rotate at the top of the home page and other pages.

- Books, columns, newsletters (lists, archives, and so on)
- Biographical sketch

This material, professionally created and aesthetically pleasing, will provide a continual credibility site for those who may never have spoken with you but have heard of you through word of mouth. This creates strong "marketing gravity," which leads to faster business and higher fees because of the power of your brand and your expertise, there for all to see.

## THE PUBLISHING PREROGATIVE

I watch aghast and with awe when someone plays the piano well, because I have tried, can't do it, and think it's a gift.

It turns out that people feel the same way about other people who can write well.

Fees flock to expertise. The dynamic is shown in Figure 11.1.

We tend to believe (as I used to) that fee follows value—in other words, the greater the value, the higher the fee. However, *the lines cross if you develop a powerful brand.* At that point, people believe they get what they pay for. There is a rewarding ego payback for buying the best, which other people recognize. No one needs a Bulgari watch to tell the time or a Mercedes SL for transportation. People purchase them for lifestyle reasons.

What has this to do with technology? The Internet is the ultimate repository of specific content. There are sites for left-handed fishing gear and

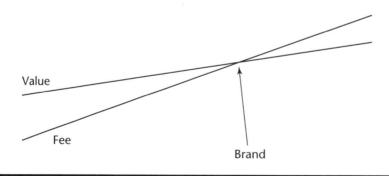

**Figure 11.1**  Fees Flock to Value.

nineteenth-century Tibetan history. Though buyers don't troll the Net to find consultants, everyone uses the Net to acquire information from experts.

Consequently, publishing on the Internet serves the following fee-enhancing purposes:

- You can rapidly gain credibility as an expert.
- You can create and disseminate unique intellectual property.
- You can obtain third-party endorsements for your expertise via columns (the publisher being the third party).
- You can respond easily to reporters' queries and appear in major media.
- You can send out press releases.
- You can send out newsletters.

You can create blogs (these are most effective after you have established a brand). Following are some examples that you can use tomorrow on the Web to enhance your fee strategies.

## Reporters' Queries

Through services such as PRleads.com (http://www.PRleads.com),[3] you can have tailored reporters' queries in your inbox each morning. I usually receive fifteen to twenty on subjects such as leadership, ethics, consulting, and teamwork. I try to respond to three a day, and as a result, I am usually interviewed three times a week. I have been featured on radio and TV, in *The New York Times* and *The Wall Street Journal,* and in scores of specialized newsletters and Internet columns. Virtually every Sunday, I find people in my mentor program quoted in the *Times.*

## Press Releases

Whenever you receive an award, accept a speaking assignment, launch a new service, travel to an exotic location, or pick up a new client, send out a press

---

[3]Contact Dan Janal. Note that I have no financial interest in any of my recommendations, and I use the services I recommend, so I have continuing experience. If you mention me as the source to Dan, he does make a charitable contribution, which is very nice of him.

release. I suggest that you keep a short list of local news and feature editors, as well as talk show producers. You can also reach national journalists, assignment editors, and their brethren through sources such as ExpertClick.com (http://www.expertclick.com),[4] membership in which not only lists you for reporters but also entitles you to send a free press release daily to a roster of ten thousand journalist subscribers.

## Columns

I write monthly for RainToday.com (http://raintoday.com), *Management Consulting News, Performance,* and other publications, even at this stage of my career. You may choose publications in finance or manufacturing or travel, depending on your focus. These offer the opportunity of strong brand building through constant appearances in your areas of value. Columns are far better than random articles in this regard.

## Newsletters

Many people tell me that the newsletter field is very crowded, and I tell them that Burger King builds its outlets across the street from McDonald's because they know people are going there to buy hamburgers. Competition doesn't restrict markets; it opens them. Focus on a high-content, low-promotion, pithy newsletter that you can also send out as a press release and can archive on your Web site. Do not charge for it. Your goal is to be seen as the go-to person in your field and to create "viral marketing," since people forward these readily to others. Make your subscription process automatic, using an electronic mailing list such as databack.com (http://www.databack.com).[5] Don't put arbitrary names on your list and always provide an "unsubscribe" so you cannot be accused of spamming.

There are other options that people use, such as LinkedIn (http://www.linkedin.com), a networking site that enables them to keep track of and inform people who may be able to recommend them or provide leads. I'm not as supportive of these more social networks, but you may want to investigate.

---

[4]Contact Mitch Davis.

[5]Contact Byron Lunz.

The key is to use the power of the Internet to increase your fees through a higher profile, greater marketing gravity, and decreased labor intensity. If you are not exploiting the Internet for publishing purposes, it's the equivalent of choosing not to use a cell phone for communication outside the office. You might as well put "Luddite" on your door.

## THE REMOTE CONSULTANT

Can you effectively serve clients from a distance? Yes, I've been doing it for years.

I had worked on projects for Hewlett-Packard for over a decade when a small one surfaced that my buyer and I quickly reached agreement on for $50,000, over the phone, with an electronic proposal. After we concluded the deal, we were chatting by phone about priorities when she asked, "When will you be here and for how long?"

"I don't plan on being there," I replied (HP is headquartered in Mountain View, California, and I live in Rhode Island).

"Never?" she practically yelled.

"Who is your boss and your boss's boss?" I asked.

"You know that. I report to Rob in Brussels, and he reports to Gloria in Hong Kong."

"And how often do you see each other?"

"We haven't seen each other in person for over two years."

"Well, I'm just trying to fit in."

I completed the project in six weeks from my home. It involved phone and e-mail interviews, analysis of documents I received as PDF files, debriefs with my buyer, and a final conference call with my recommendations to a committee she assembled to implement the next steps internally.

HP has been a leader in telecommuting, flexible hours, and remote workers. Why not be an equivalent leader with consultants?

I'm not talking about product sales and other passive income here (although I will in a few minutes as you read on) but rather honest-to-goodness consulting using technology to avoid travel and personal appearances. Note that this applies equally well to clients "down the road," because avoiding a two-hour commute twice a week for three months will gain you over a week of "found" time right there.

What can you provide in this way, when your august presence is not provided? Here are just some ideas:

- One-on-one coaching for managers
- Retainer availability on a fast-response basis
- Interviewing
- Participation in meetings via conference call
- Participation in meetings via a "virtual office"[6]
- Review of documents, analysis, recommendations
- "Shopping" the client via phone, Web, e-mail, and so on
- Providing newsletters, streaming video and audio, and special Web pages for clients

International advantages are huge. The ubiquitous objection that transporting a consultant from overseas doubles or triples the cost (or seriously erodes your margins) is gone. You can often make one trip, meet everyone you need to meet, and then continue on a remote basis thereafter. Or you may avoid the in-person meeting altogether.

> The remote potential of technology is by no means limited to marketing but also includes delivery. The more we are willing to believe and apply this, the higher our fees, often from new sources, can be.

I recall talking on my car phone to a client in London who needed my urgent attention and complaining to my wife that the connection wasn't perfect.

"You're talking to *London* from your car, instead of being there!" she reminded me.

"Oh, right," I agreed.

There are two keys to effective remote consulting: marketing and delivery.

---

[6]Better even than the cameras on many computers, this creates a panoramic view as if you are in the same room with others.

## Marketing: Find Clients Who Already Use Remote Services

As was the case with Hewlett-Packard, clients who employ remote communications themselves will be far more amenable to your being a remote consultant. The best prospects for this are the following:

- Multinational, global firms
- High-tech firms
- Firms that believe in and apply advanced technology
- Firms with small offices in remote locations
- Firms that employ remote workers and flexible hours
- Innovative buyers and executives

## Delivery: Reorient Your Approach for Remote Effectiveness

It is incumbent on the consultant to readjust approaches for maximum effectiveness without your physical presence. You should consider the following actions:

- Educate the client correctly from the outset.
- Use client resources for much of the implementation.
- Have materials in text, electronic, audio, and video form.
- Obtain equipment needed for your purposes.
- Be prepared to adjust your time frames for the client's locale and time zone.
- Have access to services such as virtual offices and teleconference bridge lines.
- Seek out local subcontractors to do classroom work, interviews, observations, and so forth[7]

With every month that passes, new and more sophisticated technology makes it easier for you to market and deliver from the comfort of your home office. There is nothing immoral, illegal, or unethical about doing so. Think of

---

[7]You can often trade services with an overseas consulting firm that would like to act remotely in your area of the country and is not a direct competitor.

it as an opportunity for clients to access your value on a more flexible basis, and do not lower or sacrifice your fees just because you don't have jet lag, aren't standing in the hallway, and aren't lonesome for home.

## PASSIVE INCOME

Technology allows for very diversified passive income. I once thought that passive income would become possible only *after* having built a strong brand, but I've since learned that a strong array of products and services *enhances* your ability to build a brand. (I'm continually surprised at how stupid I was two weeks ago.)

I define passive income more broadly than most people because I use two categories: traditional and local.

Traditional passive income is earned when people and organizations purchase products and services that do not require active participation from you. This is the stereotypical "make money while you sleep" situation. Someone buys a book, for example, from your Web site. You or someone else fulfills the order. You deposit the money in your bank account, or it's done automatically.

Local passive income derives from activities that take place in proximity to your office; even though they demand your interaction, they are easy to do, inexpensive to carry out, and require relatively little work (or pleasant work). For example, you might organize and conduct a one-day workshop ten minutes from your home to which people are attracted in significant numbers. You sleep in your own bed, commute a few minutes, and spend "a day at the office" earning money from every other person in the room. This income category also includes people visiting you, for a significant fee, for personalized one-on-one coaching. It also includes teleconferences that you conduct from your office with the dogs snoozing nearby and your feet up on the desk.

I'm not advocating that you engage in any or all of the foregoing. What I am saying is this: as your career progresses, you should be in a position to draw people to you, and it's completely up to you whether you want to provide products, services, or interactive experiences (or a combination of these) so that they can benefit from your value in various contexts. My advice is that it's almost silly *not* to do this, since $50,000 a year in passive income is $1 million over twenty years, assuming you never improve on it or raise fees!

Technology allows you to promote passive income alternatives in a variety of ways:

- As your career progresses, you should be developing a larger and larger list of contacts, and technology allows you to store, sort, and access these faster than ever before.
- Access to alternatives such as electronic mailing lists enable targeted, professional, regular promotions.
- Web site flexibility allows for new offers to be promoted effectively and attractively.
- Secure Web pages enable people to register or purchase using credit cards with confidence in real time, internationally.
- Credit card intermediaries (such as PayPal) or traditional merchant banks allow you to process credit cards online or through a terminal in your office. You can even process credit cards while traveling.
- Safeguards today (and your own precautions) virtually eliminate fraudulent transactions.
- With an electronic scale and a modern postage meter, you can ship all over the world. You can even buy postage online if you like, and meters can be refilled over the telephone. The U.S. Postal Service sells prepaid flat-rate boxes for priority delivery anywhere in the country and anywhere in the world, regardless of weight.

I suggest that you separate your marketing goals from your passive income goals. In other words, newsletters are popular when they are free but unpopular when there is a fee for subscription. Consequently, view your newsletter as a marketing device, and don't charge for it. The same applies to downloads of articles, lists, or guidelines. People tend not to want to pay for these, and they should serve as an inducement to visit the site. I offer about two hundred free downloads of all kinds on my site and add new ones periodically to keep people coming back.

Similarly, don't require an e-mail address or registration for visiting or downloads, because people (legitimately) fear that their names will be added to mailing lists or sold elsewhere. Use these marketing devices as an incentive to visit and to purchase legitimate passive income options.

People believe they get what they pay for, so try not to sell items cheaply (besides, your margins will be insignificant on low-priced items). If you're selling a product, always charge for shipping (some software will calculate this automatically), collect sales tax where appropriate, and provide options for expedited courier service. FedEx and UPS will pick up at your home office, and this saves you trips to the post office (though the U.S. Postal Service does provide home pickup in certain parts of the country).

If you produce books or booklets (or even CD or DVD albums), you can sell these through the Amazon.com Advantage program. You'll need an ISBN number and bar code on your package. Amazon will advertise your products, order them online from you to fulfill its orders, and electronically deposit your money into the account you designate. No hard copy correspondence is involved; it is all electronic. (It's interesting to notice your bank balance improving even when you've forgotten that Amazon is depositing money.)

My belief is that passive income derived through technology, which offers a low cost of acquisition, should be an area of aggressive fees. You can also offer options. If, for example, you offer a remote coaching program to generate local passive income, you can have "silver," "gold," and "platinum" levels, each successive level offering greater access, more frequent access, more diverse interaction, and so on. (The mentor program on my Web site offers three options.)

Passive income is greatly enhanced by technology. Think about whether you want to attract traditional or local passive income (or both), what value you want to provide, what form it should take, and how best to promote and administer it with current technology.

Oh, yeah—last year, my best year ever, more than 50 percent of my income came from services I wasn't providing four years earlier, and 75 percent of it was passive income.

## THE BOTTOM LINE

The beauty of revising a book is that you can include new insights with the existing foundation of value. No matter how prescient we believe we are, conditions change: economies, societies, technologies, infrastructure, regulations, competition, public perceptions, globalization, and so on. I know of no consultants or consulting firms, large or small, making a lot of money doing what they were doing ten years ago.

That figure used to be twenty or even twenty-five years, but no longer. There are several keys to utilizing technology—perhaps the most dramatic business change of our times thus far, at least in the industrialized nations—to maximize fees, enhance value-based premises for fees, and create long-term annuities for ourselves.

- It's really about the transfer of value. The greatest threat posed by technology—and thus far I've talked exclusively of opportunities—is that of mistaking it for value. It is merely a transfer mechanism. In using technology, you must accentuate the value provided—faster response time, individualized coaching, time-shifting learning, and so on—not the mechanism itself. The Web site is an unimportant conveyance; the value contained therein is always the key.
- Success, not perfection, is the polestar. We need excellent equipment and software, but not always the latest or largest or fastest. Updating your software every week or buying a new platform every year can be dysfunctional, as well as expensive and unnecessary. Why buy a four-line phone if you only need two lines? Focus on the technologies that most enhance your particular practice and client focus.[8]
- Some activity must be personal to make technology effective. John Nesbitt was one of the few prognosticators who was accurate when he forecast "high tech, high touch." Technology requires very intimate and personal relationships to make it effective with clients. Don't forget that I was able to conduct that Hewlett-Packard project without setting foot on HP soil precisely because I had established a long-standing and positive relationship with a key buyer. Counterintuitively, perhaps, using technology most efficaciously is a factor in creating and nurturing outstanding personal relationships so that you are trusted long-distance.
- Technology has to fit you just as your wardrobe does (assuming you dress well). My guarantee of a return call within ninety minutes can't be accomplished without technology,[9] but it also can't be accomplished if my attitude and organization aren't constructed to allow it. Your technology must

---

[8]I remember Merck executives explaining to me once that the company required world-class chemists but not world-class accountants.

[9]As a point of interest, I'm writing the conclusion of this chapter on my Mac in the Cancun airport and will transmit it back to my home computer using a Verizon USB device that works internationally.

be symbiotic with your discipline and talent. Using e-mail isn't wise if you tend to be sarcastic and spell poorly; using your cell phone is obnoxious if you're returning a call from the men's room (which I have witnessed repeatedly, amid the flushes).

- Diversity is vital. Finally, I believe that the more diverse your offerings of value are—consulting, coaching, speaking, writing, products, facilitation, teleconferences, and so forth—the more technology will enhance your efforts. Setting up a secure Web site to sell a single pamphlet is a waste of time. Keep in mind that wealth is about discretionary time, so using technology to create my version of passive income—people coming to you—is an important road to such well-being.

## CHAPTER ROI

- Enhance your service levels through appropriate technology, thereby increasing value and concomitant fees.
- Use the Web to publish and thereby create intensified perceived expertise, which in turn builds your brand, which is responsible for the value reflected in your fee. The buyer must always feel that he or she is getting what he or she is paying for.
- Move your practice to more and more remote interventions. Doing so decreases labor intensity, raises margins, and enhances the wealth of discretionary time.
- Passive income can represent the preponderance of your income if you embrace technology and use my somewhat wider definition of passive income. You should be planning to derive significant income from products, services, and sources that didn't exist five years earlier.
- Technology can be a catalytic tool or a slave driver. It's up to you whether you allow it to beat you into the ground or improve your wealth.

*Technology can kill you or make you a star. Use it wisely to both enhance the size of your fee and reduce your labor intensity, and you'll have found the royal road to great profit margins.*

# Appendix A

---

*Questions for Qualifying the Economic Buyer*

- Whose budget will support this initiative?
- Whose operation is most affected by the outcomes?
- Who should set the specific objectives for this project?
- Who will be evaluated for the results of this work?
- Who is the most important sponsor?
- Who has the most at stake in terms of investment and credibility?
- Who determined that you should be moving in this direction?
- Whose support is vital to success?
- Who will people look to in order to understand whether this is "real"?
- To whom do you turn for approval on options?
- Who, at the end of the day, will make the final decision?

# Appendix B

## *Questions for Establishing Business Objectives*

- Ideally, how would conditions improve as a result of this project?
- Ideally, what would you like to accomplish?
- What would be the difference in the organization if you were successful?
- How would the customer be better served?
- How would your boss recognize the improvement?
- How would employees notice the difference?
- What precise aspects are most troubling to you? (What keeps you up at night?)
- If you had to set priorities now, what three things must be accomplished?
- What is the impact you seek on return on investment/ equity/sales/assets?
- What is the impact you seek on shareholder value?
- What is the market share/profitability/productivity improvement expected?
- How will you be evaluated in terms of the results of this project?

# Appendix C

*Questions for Establishing Measures of Success*

- How will you know when this objective has been accomplished?
- Who will be accountable for determining progress, and how will this person be held accountable?
- What information would you need from customers? In what form?
- What information would you need from vendors? In what form?
- What information would you need from employees? In what form?
- How will your boss know that the objective has been accomplished?
- How will the environment/culture/structure be improved?
- What will the impact be on ROI, ROE, ROA, or ROS (return on investment, equity, assets, and sales)?

- How will you determine attrition/retention/improved morale/safety?
- How frequently do you need to assess progress? How would you assess it?
- What constitutes acceptable improvement? Ideal improvement?
- How would you be able to prove a level of improvement to others?

# Appendix D

## *Questions for Establishing Value*

- What if you did nothing? What would be the impact?
- What if this project failed?
- What does this project mean to you personally?
- What difference will this project make for the organization/its customers/its employees?
- How will this project affect performance?
- How will this project affect image/morale/safety/reputation?
- What effect will this project have on productivity/profitability/market share?
- What is this now costing you annually?
- What is the impact on ROI, ROA, ROE, and ROS (return on investment, equity, assets, and sales)?

# Appendix E

## *Questions for Assessing Personal Value Contribution*

- Why me? Can any speaker or trainer do this, or do I have special attributes?
- Why now? Is the timing particularly urgent or sensitive?
- Why is this being handled in this manner? Is there some aspect of the methodologies or relationships that is key at the moment?
- What's unique about our relationship? Does the buyer place special trust in me?
- What's my unique value added? To what extent can I "guarantee" success and exceed the buyer's expectations?

# Appendix F

## The Difference Between Inputs and Business Outputs

Here are some examples of inputs versus outputs.

| Inputs | Outputs |
| --- | --- |
| Run sales training sessions | Improve sales closing rates |
| Conduct focus groups on morale | Improve lateral communication |
| Interview former customers | Audit recruitment process |
| Redesign performance evaluation | Increase retention of new hires |
| Review expense procedures | Provide higher-quality, more frequent performance feedback |
| Improve senior officer teamwork | Decrease travel costs |
| Study technological needs of service personnel | Enable decision making at proper levels |
| | Improve service response time of personnel |

# *Index*

**A**

Abandoning business
    appropriate time for, 1, 100, 101–103
    being prepared to walk away, 157
    considering jettisoning bottom 15
      percent, 153
    ethical issues related to, 138–139
Access to you
    client understanding on meaning of,
      109–110
    offering service of "unlimited,"
      91–92, 110
    rapid responsiveness and, 123
    as retainer arrangement component,
      109, 112, 114
    *See also* Consultants; Services
Accountability, 73
Accounts payable, 159, 184
The Acquisition opportunity, 98
Advance payments, 130
Alan's fourth theorem of fee
    dynamics, 172
Albums
    CDs and, 193–194
    DVDs and, 194
American Institute of Architects, 33n.4
Andersen Consulting, 8, 215
Architects, 33–34

"Arkingson's Laws," 215
Attorneys, 35–36, 39, 74–75
Augustine, N., 215
"Augustine's Laws," 215
Authority/expertise, 73

**B**

Bartered services, 136
"Betting on the come," 35
"Big Four," 27
Billable hours. *See* Time-based fees
"Billboard on a highway" approach, 43
Blogs, 231
Boilerplate language, 159
Book products, 193
Bottom-line blindness, 21–22
Branding
    approaches, products, and method-
      ologies of, 214–215
    one's own name, 215–217
    publishing to enhance your, 96, 193,
      230–233
    vignettes on power of, 216, 217
Brands
    creating your own, 15, 158
    credibility and relationships
      accelerated by, 14
    fee progression transition to, 213–217

Brands (*continued*)
fees enhanced through, 12–15
power of your own, 14
"success trap" of, 213*fig*, 215
*See also* Consultants
Budgetary limits, 30–31
Budgets. *See* Client budgets
Burger King, 232
Bush, G.H.W., 187n.1
Business
appropriate time for abandoning, 1,
100, 101–103
avoid accepting same terms as
referring source for new, 152–153
considering jettisoning bottom
15 percent of, 153
don't accept troublesome or
unpleasant, 149
ethical issues related to abandoning,
138–139
paying for acquisition of new, 149
repeat and referral, 144
tips for collaborating on, 149
transition to a "going concern,"
209–211
transition to word of mouth, 211–213*fig*
walking away when appropriate, 157
*See also* Value-based proposals
Buyer commitment
compliance versus, 10
critical steps for, 11–12
importance of, 9–11
relationships between fees and, 10*fig*, 11
Buyer compliance, 10
Buyer resistance
common buyer's responses/
arguments, 174–175
educating prospect to overcome,
38, 180
filters to overcome, 164*fig*–165
four fundamental areas of, 165–170
ignoring your competition's lower
prices, 179–180
maintaining focus on value to
overcome, 170–172

major rebuttals to use to overcome,
171–172
management of, 222–223
offering discounts to overcome,
176–177
using "smack to the head"
comparisons to overcome, 177–179
understanding buyer's budget to
overcome, 30–31, 150, 173–175
Buyer resistance areas
1: I don't trust you, 166
2: I don't need you, 166–167
3: I don't feel any urgency, 168–169
4: I don't have the money to pay you,
169–170
Buyers
avoid the "go or no-go" position for, 77
combining multiple buyers under
single fee, 92
educating prospective, 38, 180
engaging them in diagnosing the
issues, 144–145*fig*
filters to overcome to reach buying
decision, 164*fig*–165
giving "choice of yeses" to, 75–79,
80, 189
higher fees create higher value
perception by, 152
impressing the, 13
locating new buyers within existing
clients, 94–97
power in ascertaining perceived value
of, 6
preventing and rebutting fee
objections by, 163–181
pursing late payments through the, 154
questions for establishing value with, 7
*See also* Clients

## C

Calgon, 123
Canceling projects, 131, 132
Capitalism
compared to state controlled
economies, 2n.1

ethical nature of, 2–5
ethical premises of, 2
Mercedes-Benz syndrome (MBS) of,
    5–9
Russian failures with, 3–4
CDs and albums, 193–194
Cell phones, 227–228
Change opportunities, 97
"Choice of yeses"
    advantages of providing buyer with,
        75–78
    professional speaking and, 189
    step-by-step, 80
    ten guidelines for, 78–79
Clancy, T., 15
Client budgets
    ascertaining buyer's budget
        expectations, 173–175
    focus discussion on investment aspect
        of, 175
    knowing the, 150
    preserving limits of, 30–31
Client improvement
    creating measurements for, 52–54
    focusing on, 156–157
    parameters for successful measures
        of, 52
    qualitative or subjective criteria of,
        51–52, 54
    quantitative or objective criteria of,
        49–51, 54
    two excellent indicators of
        contribution to, 72
Client objectives
    increasing value by broadening, 147
    QGTRIHF ("What Are Your
        Objectives"), 147
Client outcomes
    offering "value packages" to
        facilitate, 9
    transforming consultant past to,
        56–58, 57fig, 188fig
    value-based fee focus on, 42–45, 57–58
Clients
    ascertaining perceived value by, 6

avoid being influenced by past history
    with, 143
creating shared success with, 15–18
engaging them in diagnosing the
    issues, 144–145fig
establishing value by collaborating
    with, 143
establishing value with, 5, 7
fees based on what's important
    to, 44
financial trouble experienced with,
    132–133
knowing when to abandon a, 100,
    101–103
locating new buyers within existing,
    94–97
nonprofit, 133
providing pushback when needed
    to, 124
surveying past, 58
transforming consultant past to future
    of, 56–58, 188fig
value-based fee conversion of
    existing, 85–104, 221
value-based fee relationship to
    self-interest of, 54–56, 220
See also Buyers; Referrals
Coaching, 198–199
Collaboration tips, 149
Columns (publishing), 232
Commercially published books, 193
Comparison question, 153
Competition comparisons, 179–180
The Competition opportunity, 98
Conceptual agreement
    as consulting business acquisition
        component, 12fig
    as the foundation of value, 64–68
    "good deal" factors for establishing,
        72–75
    as linchpin, 221
    pushback when necessary, 156
    "rules of engagement" of, 120
    sample of retainer relationship,
        120e–121e

Confidentiality issues, 73
"Consultant hash," 57
Consultant-buyer partnerships
  consulting projects as, 11
  costs from expert versus partner
    investment, 16*fig*
  creating shared success through,
    15–18
  as first step in value-based project, 65
  gathering information on past, 58
  journey and progress of, 58–60
  retainer arrangements, 107–125
  role of trust in, 16
  time-based fee implications for, 23–39
  *See also* Relationships; Value
    proposition
Consultants
  avoiding the "vendor" category, 29–30
  becoming the Bentley of your field, 158
  caution against stereotyping
    yourself, 148
  client future transformed from past of,
    56–58, 188*fig*
  common mistakes made about fees
    by, 3–4
  creating shared success with clients,
    15–18
  establishing your unique value, 68–72
  impressing the buyers, 13
  providing pushback when needed, 124
  traits of a successful retainer, 123–124
  transition to ultimate, 217–219
  *See also* Access to you; Brands;
    Services
Consulting business acquisition
    sequence, 11–12*fig*
Consulting intervention
  goal of, 41
  keeping our aesthetic sense as part
    of, 60
  process flow of, 57*fig*
  remote, 197–202
  *See also* Services
Contingency fee, 107
Converting existing clients

  abandoning business if unsuccessful
    in, 101–103
  Alan's axioms on, 221
  deciding which clients to approach,
    86–89
  finding new buyers within existing,
    clients, 94–97
  finding new circumstances for, 97–99
  offering new value by revisiting ROI,
    90*fig*–94, 152
  overcoming resistance to, 99–100
  test to determining potential for, 87*e*
Copyrighting proposal, 134
CPAs, 36
Credibility, 14
Credit card payments, 137

### D

databack.com, 232
Davis, M., 232n.4
Decision making accountability, 73
"Deliverables"
  avoiding timed deadlines for, 48
  definition of, 45n.1
  fallacy and subversive nature of, 45–49
  key to avoiding talk on, 46–47
Deposits, 130
Discounts
  accepting cash in return for, 136–137
  "frequent flyer," 130
  offered to overcome buyer resistance,
    176–177
  for one-time full payments, 155
  phased approach rebates, 153
  *See also* Payments; Value-based fees
The Divestiture opportunity, 98
Documentation issues, 73
Drucker, P., 133, 215
"Duluth architect syndrome," 34
DVDs and albums, 194

### E

Emails, 228
Empathy, 123
Enron scandal, 215

Entry-level fees, 206–209
Ethical issues
  abandoning clients, 138–139
  accepting bartered fees, 135
  on canceling and rescheduling, 131
  charging different fees for same work,
    127–128
  clients with financial problems, 132–133
  copyrighting your proposal, 134
  credit card payments, 137
  deposits and advance payments, 130
  discounts, 130, 136–137
  eliminating temptations to behavior
    unethically, 28n.2-29n.2
  establishing coaching "client," 133–134
  exceeding high value and
    "gouging," 128
  lowering fees for nonprofits, 133
  overdue payments, 137–138
  padding expenses, 136
  quid pro quo for lowering fees, 135, 149
  related to increasing fees, 135
  related to retainer arrangements, 129
  related to subcontractors, 135
  related to time-based fees, 28–31,
    131–132
  RFP (request for proposal) and
    related, 134
  Robinson-Patman Act and equal
    services/fees, 129
  tax issues, 130, 135–136, 138
  underbidding competition, 134
Executive egos, 7–8
Expenses
  being clear on owed, 155
  having client absorb the billing of, 157
  reimbursement requests for, 155–156
  specified as being extra, 146
  travel, 989
  See also Payments

**F**

Farr Act, 134
Fee feng shui case, 225–226
Fee progression strategy

across categories, 211*t*
entry-level fees, 206–209
identifying where you are in the, 223
transition to "going concern," 209–211
transition to the brand phase, 213–217
transition to ultimate consultant,
  217–219
transition to word of mouth,
  211–213*fig*
Fee-setting
  by architects, 33–34
  by attorneys, 35–36
  bottom-line blindness case on, 21–22
  by CPAs, 36
  educating prospective clients on,
    38, 180
  for nonconsulting opportunities,
    185–204, 223
  by search firms, 36–37
  supply-and-demand illogic of, 25–28
  time-based, 23–34, 131–132
  See also Value-based fees
Fees
  bartered, 135
  common mistakes made regarding,
    3–4
  concept of, 1–2
  contingency, 107
  ethical exchange basis of, 3
  how brands create higher, 12–15
  perceived value basis of, 3, 6, 230*fig*
  relationships between buyer
    commitment and, 10*fig*, 11
  retainer, 107–125, 221–222
  See also Raising fees
Ferrari brand, 13
"First, do no harm" credo, 15
Fixed-fee formula, 79
"Frequent flyer" discounts, 130

**G**

Gerstner, L., 37
Girl Scouts, 133
Godek, G., 143n.1
"Going concern" business, 209–211

"Good deal"
   Alan's axioms for the, 219–223
   dynamics of, 72–75, 147
   equation of, 74*fig*
"Good deal" axioms
   1: you are entitled to be compensated
      for value, 219
   2: basing fees on time/material and
      not value is crazy, 219–220
   3: buyer self-interest is based on
      results, 220
   4: conceptual agreement is the
      linchpin, 221
   5: existing clients can be converted to
      value-based fees, 221
   6: retainer business is discrete and
      sound business, 221–222
   7: there are ways to raise fees and
      margins, 222
   8: you've heard all the objections
      already, 222–223
   9: nonconsulting activities are
      lucrative, 223
   10: identify where you are in fee
      progression strategy, 223
"Gouging," 128
*The Great Big Book of Process Visuals*
   (Weiss), 144n.2
The Great Year opportunity, 97
Guarantees, 73

**H**
Hawthorne studies, 74n.5
Hewlett-Packard, 49, 73n.4
The Horrible Year opportunity, 97
*How to Establish a Unique Brand in the
   Consulting Profession* (Weiss),
   212n.4, 215n.6
*How to Maximize Fees in Professional
   Service Firms* (Weiss), 142
*How to Write a Proposal That's Accepted
   Every Time* (Weiss), 17n.7, 79n.6
"HP frame of mind," 49
*The Hunt for Red October* (Clancy), 15

**I**
IBM, 37
Industry knowledge/experience, 73
Ingram Book Company, 193
Interludes
   annoying accountants case, 61–62
   bottom-line blindness case, 21–22
   fee feng shui case, 225–226
   loaded loading dock case, 105–106
   perverse purchasing agent case,
      183–184
   rebounding retainer case, 161–162
IPhone, 228
ISBN application, 195n.6

**J**
Janal, D., 231n.3

**K**
Keynote speaking
   developing options for, 189–190
   establishing your value for, 187–189
   overview of, 186–187
   using speakers' bureaus for, 190–192
   vignette on fee for, 206
Kinko's, 91

**L**
Laptops, 228
Late payments, 154
Leading edge factor, 74
Liability insurance, 73
LinkedIn, 232
Loaded loading dock case, 105–106
Lunz, B., 232n.5

**M**
Malpractice insurance, 73
Margin. *See* Profit margins
Marketing
   remote consulting, 235
   retainer relationships, 121–124
   seeking out new economic buyers
      during projects, 150

technological enhancement of, 229–230
  *See also* Referrals
"Marketing gravity," 191
Martin Marietta, 215
McDonald's, 232
McKinsey brand, 8, 13–14
"Membership" benefits, 93
Mentoring, 199–201
Mercedes-Benz North America, 47
Mercedes-Benz syndrome (MBS), 5–9
Merck, 96, 239n.8
Merrill, D., 165n.2
"Migratory range" fees, 76
Million Dollar Consulting Colleges and
  Graduate Schools, 4
*Million Dollar Consulting* (Weiss),
  88, 192
*Money Talks* (Weiss), 186, 197
"Motivational speakers," 188
Multiple invoicing, 159

**N**

Napoleon, 58
Needs assessments, 48n.2
New access points, 93
The New Buyer opportunity, 97
"New circumstances" approach, 97–99
The New Initiative opportunity, 98
New services, 92
*The New York Times*, 231
Newsletters, 232–233
Ney, Marshal, 58
Noncompete restrictions, 73
Nonconsulting fees
  coaching, 198–199
  keynote speaking, 186–190, 206
  lucrative opportunities of, 223
  mentoring, 199–201
  for products, 192–196
  remote consulting, 197–198
  situational consulting, 201–202
  some perspective on opportunities for,
    202–204
  for working with bureaus, 190–192

Nondisclosure restrictions, 73
Nonprofit clients, 133

**O**

On-site visits, 73
1Solution philosophy, 142
*1001 Ways to Be Romantic* (Godek),
  143n.1
Overdue payments, 137–138

**P**

Padding expenses, 136
Passive income
  technological facilitation of, 236–238
  traditional and local categories of, 236
Payments
  accepting local currency, 158–159
  avoiding subject to conditions
    requirements for, 156
  incentives for one-time full, 155
  late, 154
  in U.S. dollars, 157
  wire transfer, 159
  year-end early, 153–154
  *See also* Discounts; Expenses; Tax
    issues; Value-based fees
PDAs, 228
Perceived value
  fees based on, 3, 6
  power in ascertaining buyer's, 6
Perverse purchasing agent case, 183–184
Peters, T., 215
Phased approach rebates, 153
Powell, C., 45
Press releases, 231–232
*Principles of Scientific Management*
  (Taylor), 24n.1
PRleads.com, 231
Pro bono work, 122, 151, 202–203
Products
  profit margins as key to, 195
  selling your, 192
  types of, 193–194

Professional speaking. *See* Keynote speaking
Profit margins
  as key to product sales, 195
  multiple ways of increasing, 222
  quick tips for creating high retainer, 114–115
  setting value-based fees for excellent, 64, 66
  staying sensitive to margins, 151–152
  technology used to increase, 228–229
  time-based fees as limiting, 32–34
Projects. *See* Value-based projects
Proposals. *See* Value-based proposals
Proprietary material issues, 73
Prospect education checklist, 38
Published books, 193
Publishing
  business benefits of, 96
  columns, 232
  newsletters, 232–233
  selling products from your, 193
  technology facilitating your, 230–233
Push back, 124, 156

### Q

QGTRIHF ("What Are Your Objectives"), 147
Qualitative improvement criteria, 51–52, 54
Quantitative improvement criteria, 49–51, 54

### R

RainToday.com, 232
Raising fees
  fee progression strategy for, 206–219, 223
  1Solution philosophy on, 142
  seventy approaches and tips on, 143–159
  *See also* Fees; Value-based fee creation
Rapid responsiveness, 123
Referrals
  acquiring new business through, 144

asking current buyer for, 95
  avoid accepting same terms as referring source, 152–153
  "good deal" created through, 72, 147
  *See also* Clients; Marketing
Reimbursement requests, 155–156
Relationships
  brands as accelerating, 14
  as consulting business acquisition factor, 11, 12*fig*
  *See also* Consultant-buyer partnerships
Remote consulting
  marketing for, 235
  requests for, 197–198
  technological facilitation f, 233–236
Reporters' queries, 231
Rescheduling projects, 131
Responsiveness, 72
Retainer arrangements
  access to you component of, 109, 112, 114
  aggressively marketing relationships of, 121–124
  capitalizing on relationships of, 119–121
  case on perceived value of, 161–162
  caution against "SWAT team" mentality, 117
  choosing time frames/realistic expectations, 111, 112, 113–114
  ethical issues related to, 129
  optimal conditions for, 108–109
  organizing scope and management of, 112, 116–119
  prime directive of, 112–113
  sample letter of agreement for, 120*e*–121*e*
  as sound business, 221–222
  three key dimensions of, 112
Retainer consultants
  access to you issue, 109, 112, 114
  traits of successful, 123–124
Retainer fees
  definition of, 107

quick tips for high-value/high-profit, 114–115
ten criteria for lucrative, 109–111
RFP (request for proposal), 134
Robinson-Patman Act, 129
ROI (return on investment)
  of Alan's axioms for the "good deal," 219–223
  costs from expert versus partner investment and, 16*fig*
  establishing value through, 4–5
  ethical conflicts related to, 29
  as key criterion of setting value-based fees, 66
  offering new value by revisiting, 90*fig*, 94, 152
"Rules of engagement," 120

**S**

Safety issues, 73
*Saturday Night Live* pseudocommercial skit, 34n.5
Scope creep, 150–151
Search firms, 36–37
*The Second Great Big Book of Process Visuals* (Weiss), 144n.2
Self-interest motivation, 54–56, 220
Self-published books, 193
Services
  core value propositions regarding, 94
  ensuring client is aware of range of, 147–148
  fees for nonconsulting, 186–204, 223
  offering added value through new, 90*fig*, 154
  providing option that exceeds the budget, 146–147
  technology used to enhance, 227–230
  *See also* Access to you; Consultants; Consulting intervention
Shared success
  how to build, 15–18
  key factors in, 17

Shared values factor, 11, 12*fig*
Situational consulting, 201–202
Skills transfer, 73, 74
"Smack to the head" comparisons, 177–179
Speakers' bureaus, 190–192
Stereotyping, 148
Subconstractors, 135
Subcontracting fees, 208
"Success trap," 213*fig*, 215
Supply-and-demand illogic, 25–28, 151
"SWAT team" mentality, 117

**T**

Tax issues
  avoiding local tax deductions, 159
  out-of-state services, 130, 135–136
  setting up payments beneficial to taxes, 138
  *See also* Payments
Taylor, F. W., 24n.1
Technological compatibility, 73
Technology
  keys to utilizing, 238–240
  passive income facilitated through, 236–238
  publishing facilitated by, 230–233
  remote consulting using, 233–236
  service enhancement through, 227–230
Telephone systems, 227–228
Time-based fees
  ethical issues related to, 28–31, 131–132
  incorrect logic of, 23–25
  profitability limitations of, 32–34
Transfer of skills, 73, 74
Travel
  availability as "good deal" factor, 73
  including projected costs in your fee, 98
  technology facilitating communication during, 227–228
The Travel Need opportunity, 98

Trust
    buyer resistance due to lack of, 166
    consultant-buyer partnerships and
        role of, 16

## U

Ultimate consultant transition, 217–219
*The Ultimate Consultant* (Weiss), 58n.3,
    142, 166n.3
Underbidding competition, 134
United Way, 133
"Unlimited access," 91–92, 110

## V

Value
    of access to you, 109
    basing fees on, 143, 146, 230*fig*
    collaborating with client to
        establish, 143
    continuous journey of providing, 58–60
    differing fees for differing, 143
    establishing your keynote speaking,
        187–189
    establishing your unique, 68–72
    in the eye of the beholder, 64
    fallacy and subversive nature of
        "deliverables" as, 45–49
    fees as based on perceived, 3, 6
    as function of not being "yes person," 8
    higher fees create perception of
        higher, 152
    increased by broadening client
        objectives, 147
    increased through new services,
        90*fig*, 154
    measuring the unmeasurable quality
        of, 52–54
    Mercedes-Benz syndrome (MBS) and,
        5–9
    never use time as basis of your, 143–144
    overcoming buyer resistance by
        focusing on, 170–172
    qualitative or subjective criteria of,
        51–52

    quantitative or objective criteria of,
        49–51
    revisiting ROI in order to offer new,
        90*fig*–94, 152
    ROI (return on investment) to
        establish, 4–5
Value distance, 55–56*fig*
Value proposition
    avoiding "needs assessments" as part
        of, 48n.2
    "billboard on a highway" approach
        to, 43
    client initiation versus solicitation
        difference for, 71
    converting existing clients by offering
        new, 90*fig*–94
    examples of poorly done, 42–43
    examples of task/possible
        outcomes, 44
    focus on client's ability to
        improve, 43
    vignette on Mercedes-Benz, 47
    *See also* Consultant-buyer
        partnerships
Value-based fee creation
    "choice of yeses" approach to, 75–79,
        80, 189
    conceptual agreement foundation of,
        64–68
    establishing your unique value for,
        68–72
    "good deal" approach to, 72–75, 147
    key criterion of, 66
    precepts to keep in mind
        about, 64
    sequence in, 65*fig*
    *See also* Raising fees
Value-based fee formulas
    "choice of yeses," 80
    "good deal," 74
    strategic and conceptual, 82
    10 to 1 "halfway house," 81
Value-based fee tips
    adding premium when appropriate, 146

avoid getting cornered about fees, 148–149

avoid offering options for reducing fees, 145

avoiding boilerplate proposal language, 159

base fees on value, 143, 146

becoming the Bentley of your field, 158

citing time frame for proposal's acceptance, 153

clarifying client responsibility for expenses, 155

collaborating on business, 149

comparison question, 153

creating your own brand, 15, 158

do not consider past client history, 143

emphasizing year-end early payments, 153–154

expense reimbursement requests, 155–156

fee increases exceeding inflation rate, 158

focus on improvement, 156–157

higher fees create perception of higher value, 152

jettisoning bottom 15 percent of your business, 153

knowing client's budget, 150

knowing current range of market fees, 151

late payments, 154

on local currency payments, 158–159

managing accounts payable interactions, 159, 184

multiple invoicing, 159

never use time as basis of value, 143–144

new business acquisitions, 149

obtain firm agreement regarding fees, 145–146

offering incentive for one-time full payments, 155

offering new value by revisiting ROI, 90*fig*, 94, 152

payments subject to conditions, 156

phased approach rebates, 153

practice stating high, 144, 157, 159

pro bono work, 122, 151, 202–203

providing option that exceeds budget, 146–147

pushback on agreement fine print, 156

questions to ask validating your value, 69–72, 148

quid pro quo for lowering fees, 135, 149

for raising fees, 143–159

referred business, 152–153

remove fees from printed materials, 146

"scope creep" management, 150–151

sensitivity to the margins, 151–152

specify expenses as being extra, 146

"springboarding" to new buyers, 150

supply-and-demand illogic, 25–28, 151

U.S. dollar payments, 157

walking away when necessary, 157

wire transfers from clients, 159

Value-based fees

Alan's fourth theorem of dynamics of, 172

client's self-interest relationship to, 54–56, 220

comparisons on charge per hour versus, 27

converting existing clients to, 85–104

creating excellent profit margins using, 64, 66

definition of, 107

differing values mean different, 143

educating prospective clients on, 38–39

establishing, 63–82

ethical compromises removed through, 29

focus on client outcomes of, 42–45

"gouging" versus, 128

"migratory range" of, 76

multiple ways of raising, 222

Value-based fees (*continued*)
  for nonconsulting opportunities,
    185–204, 223
  phrasing on validity of, 42
  practice stating high, 144, 157, 159
  preventing and rebutting objections
    to, 163–181
  sequence of creating, 65*fig*
  strategies for progression of, 205–223
  testing potential for shifting client
    to, 87*e*
  on what's important to client, 44
  *See also* Discounts; Fee-setting;
    Payments
Value-based projects
  client budgetary limits for, 30–31
  client relationship as first step in, 65
  conceptual agreement as the
    foundation of, 64–68
  creating the "good deal" dynamic of,
    72–75
  establishing your unique value as part
    of, 68–72
Value-based proposals
  avoid boilerplate language, 159
  used as confirmations not
    explorations, 148
  establishing your unique value as part
    of, 68–72
  time frame for acceptance of, 153
  underlying rationale for successful,
    66–68
  value-based fees sequence in, 65*fig*
  *See also* Business
Vender identification, 29–30
Vignettes
  attorney's "good deal" equation
    approach, 74–75
  client budget as fee-setting factor, 150
  on inability to demand high fees, 158

Mercedes-Benz value-based fee, 47
  on power of brand name, 216, 217
  on professional speaking fees, 206
  remember to check your materials for
    constricted fees, 155
  on remote consulting, 197–198
  on situational consulting, 201–202
Volunteering activities, 96

**W**
*The Wall Street Journal*, 231
Websites
  applying for ISBN numbers, 195n.6
  audio and video samples on
    author's, 194
  databack.com, 232
  LinkedIn, 232
  marketing through your, 229–230
  offering "membership" benefits
    through, 93
  offering new access points through, 93
  PRleads.com, 231
  RainToday.com, 232
  on reporters' queries, 231
Why in this manner? question,
    70–72, 148
Why me? question, 69, 148
Why now? question, 69–70, 148
Wilder access, 92
Wilson, L., 165n.2
Wilson Learning, 165n.2
Wire transfer payments, 159
Word of mouth business
  "success trap" of, 213*fig*, 215
  transition to, 211–213
W.W. Bowker, 195n.6

**Y**
Year-end early payments, 153–154